"In my work with couples, I am very familiar with partners reporting connection and communication that seems outside the bounds of the normal transmission of information. ESP offers an explanation. *The Gift* is clearly written, with credible examples and solid research. Anyone interested in the subject will be well informed, and anyone skeptical of ESP will be challenged to disprove the phenomena."

—Harville Hendrix, PhD, author of the *New York Times* bestseller *Getting the Love You Want: A Guide for Couples*

"A wonderful book, filled with fascinating stories from the world's largest collection of ESP cases."

—Rupert Sheldrake, Ph.D., author of *Dogs That Know When Their Owners Are Coming Home and Other Unexplained Powers of Animals* and *The Sense of Being Stared At*

"A great read—suspense, drama, a sense of wonder, and any number of surprises. You'll find no better introduction to the world of ESP."

—Stanley Krippner, Ph.D, co-editor of *Varieties of Anomalous Experience: Examining the Scientific Evidence*

"*The Gift* is an extraordinary book that brings together many different kinds of ESP experiences with numerous case histories from ordinary people. . . . A great resource for those interested in paranormal experiences."

—The International Association for Near-Death Studies (IANDS)

THE
GIFT

*ESP, the Extraordinary Experiences
of Ordinary People*

• • •

DR. SALLY RHINE FEATHER
WITH MICHAEL SCHMICKER

ST. MARTIN'S PAPERBACKS

THE GIFT: ESP, THE EXTRAORDINARY EXPERIENCES OF ORDINARY PEOPLE

ISBN: 0-312-99776-0
EAN: 9780312-99776-2

Printed in the United States of America

St. Martin's Press hardcover edition / May 2005
St. Martin's Paperbacks edition / May 2006

St. Martin's Paperbacks are published by St. Martin's Press, 175 Fifth Avenue, New York, NY 10010.

10 9 8 7 6 5 4 3 2 1

CONTENTS

ACKNOWLEDGMENTS

First and foremost, I would like to thank those countless individuals who have sent accounts of their paranormal experiences to the Rhine Research Center over the years. And to my co-author, Mike, who first conceived the idea of this book and then worked so steadily to bring it to fruition. Last but not least, my husband, Bill Hendrickson, who cooked many a dinner while this book was under way.

—Dr. Sally Rhine Feather

I would like to thank two fellow writers with ink in their blood for their encouragement and support in seeing this book to completion: my wife, Patricia, and my son, Christopher. My gratitude also goes out to Nat Sobel, our bulldog agent, to Diane Reverand, our passionate editor, to Regina Scarpa, our communications lifeline, and most of all to my co-author, Dr. Sally, whose wonderful stories and psychological insights brighten these pages.

—Michael Schmicker

PREFACE

Can some people really see the future? Read other people's minds? Observe events unfold, as they happen, even when they take place hundreds or thousands of miles away from them?

Indeed they can.

This unusual, unpredictable but natural human ability is popularly called ESP, or extrasensory perception. ESP is the ability of the human mind to perceive or experience without the help of the five senses. The community of scientists studying ESP prefer the more neutral term "psi," which carries less historical and emotional baggage than "ESP." But both describe the same thing—a "sixth sense"—unlike our normal five senses of sight, hearing, smell, taste, and touch, that operates outside the limits of space and time.

A 2001 Gallup Poll found that half of all Americans believe ESP is real, and 65 million Americans have personally experienced ESP. Skeptics still try to dismiss ESP, but the scientific evidence is substantial and continually growing.

I know, because I am a director of the Rhine Research Center and a parapsychologist—someone professionally trained in the scientific study of ESP experiences. The Center is named after my father, the late Dr. J.B. Rhine, who, with my mother, Dr. Louisa Rhine, pioneered the scientific study of ESP in the United States starting in the 1930s at Duke University. My father took ESP into the laboratory and applied statistics, controlled experiments, and other scientific methods to establish the reality of ESP.

My father's work has since been duplicated and further developed by other scientists working at the Rhine Research Center and at other institutions in the United States and Europe. The list includes Princeton University and universities in Germany, Sweden, Holland, England, and Scotland. Psychic phenomena have been studied by the Parapsychological Association, the Parapsychology Foundation, and the American Society for Psychical Research, which counts among its founders the renowned Harvard psychologist and professor of philosophy, William James. Respected private think tanks like the Stanford Research Institute and Science Applications International Corporation have studied ESP, and the U.S. Department of Defense has conducted significant research on an ESP technique called "remote viewing."

Parapsychologists had to fight to gain the grudging respect of other scientists, most of whom were suspicious of paranormal claims. Not until 1969, more than thirty years after my parents began their research, did the Parapsychological Association become an affiliate of the American Association for the Advancement of Science, our nation's top science organization. Anthropologist Margaret Mead publicly supported us in our fight. Opponents attacked parapsychology as a "pathological science." Operating from the assumption that ESP did not exist, they concluded psychic phenomena could not be tested in a laboratory, and that any scientist conducting such research was a charlatan engaged in scientific misconduct. Dr. Mead noted in her rebuttal that the Parapsychological Association used accepted scientific methodologies. She argued that the history of scientific advance was based on the investigation of phenomena that the scientific establishment believed did not or could not exist.

Once considered outside the realm of possibility, X-rays, ball lightning, continental drift, heavier-than-air flight, and Lister's theory of infection by germs are now considered scientific realities or valid targets of scientific inquiry. The American Association for the Advancement of Science admitted us.

Our efforts today no longer focus on whether ESP exists; we have strong evidence that it does. Instead, we are studying how ESP works, by examining how personality, emotional relationships, mental and physical states, education, gender, and other variables may affect ESP experiences. We need to untangle the web of factors that affect this form of human communication. We continue to test new hypotheses in search of insights that might help us control ESP and put this special mode of perception to beneficial use in real life.

I grew up in the world of parapsychology. As a child, I participated in my parents' initial studies of ESP in children, and my first job as a teenager involved checking ESP records. After I completed my undergraduate degree in biology, I worked as a research associate with my father at the Duke Parapsychology Laboratory before I went on to earn my PhD in psychology at Duke. Since ESP deals with mind, consciousness, and reality, I eventually became a clinical psychologist, bringing these skills to the investigation of ESP. I have spent more than thirty years of my life working as a mental health counselor, at community mental health centers, at a psychiatric institute, and in private practice in New Jersey and North Carolina. I am a long-standing member of the American Psychological Association. I operate squarely within the accepted norms and standards of modern psychology, and I am familiar with its scientific studies, tools, diagnoses, and treatment methods. I know how good science works. I understand how people can fool themselves through tricks of memory, perception, belief systems, and psychological problems. Human testimony is unreliable. That is why only repeatable laboratory experiments can prove ESP exists. That is why my father brought ESP into the lab.

Laboratory experiments are required to prove ESP is real, but ESP usually happens outside the laboratory. Confining our study of ESP to the laboratory is like studying lions in a zoo instead of the wild. To see how lions act and behave, you have to observe them in their natural habitat. To understand ESP, we have to look at how it manifests itself spontaneously outside the laboratory in daily life. The extraordinary experiences of ordinary people included in this book are from the Rhine Research Center's collection of spontaneous ESP experiences—the largest such collection of ESP reports in the world.

In 1948, my mother, Dr. Louisa Rhine, began to collect letters describing interesting, sometimes bewildering, and occasionally unsettling ESP experiences. Unsolicited letters from persons of all ages, sexes, and socioeconomic backgrounds had been arriving at the parapsychology laboratory for several decades prior to that. Articles my parents had written about ESP, for popular magazines like *Good Housekeeping, McCall's,* and *Reader's Digest,* regularly drew a flood of stories. People seemed hesitant and even a bit apologetic to be admitting that such an inexplicable event could have happened to them. The most frequently expressed motive for writing was the hope that their stories would help the research effort.

My mother reviewed the letters and accepted any report that in her judgment was submitted in good faith, was made by an apparently sane individual, and which appeared to involve ESP. Her criterion for evaluating possible ESP experiences required that the event supply concrete, factual information not derived directly or indirectly from the five senses. She favored accounts with extensive detail. Less than half of the thirty thousand letters she received met those requirements and were accepted for inclusion in her database. She concluded that these stories collectively provided her with a glimpse into a reality difficult to explain away simply as a series of mistakes of testimony, overinterpretation, imagination, or coincidence.

Her work with spontaneous ESP experiences did not focus on scientific proof. By 1948, proof of ESP had already been established in the laboratory. She collected this anecdotal evidence for a different purpose, knowing that controlled laboratory experiments can impose artificial constraints on the reality they try to analyze. For her, the primary scientific value of such a collection of reports lay in the clues the raw reports provided about patterns of ESP experiences. These patterns could provide valuable new hypotheses to test in the laboratory as scientists worked to understand how ESP operates.

I still remember my father getting awakened in the middle of the night by telephone calls from people wanting to relate their extraordinary experiences—often seeking assurance that they were not crazy. Prior to his pioneering ESP experiments at Duke University, ESP was largely considered unscientific nonsense and persons who had such experiences often felt something was wrong with them, leaving them nervous or anxious. They had reason to be concerned, since psychologists of the day viewed claims of seeing the future or reading other people's thoughts as a sign of mental illness. My father's work produced a gradual change in public and professional attitudes toward ESP.

In 1934, five years after starting his research, he published a monograph entitled *Extra-Sensory Perception,* detailing his experimental methods and results. In it, he argued that ESP had not yet been explained, but it certainly existed, "puzzling as its explanation may be." ESP was a fact. What was left to do was to explain how it worked. *Extra-Sensory Perception* earned favorable reviews, including one by *New York Times* science editor Waldemar Kaempffert. Within the scientific community, psychologists showed the most interest in his research. Articles on my parents' research also began to appear with some frequency in the media, including *Time, Reader's Digest, Scientific American,* and *Harper's.*

In September 1937, Zenith Radio Corporation produced a series of weekly national broadcasts that allowed listeners to participate in ESP experiments using decks of cards Zenith provided with its logo on the back. A month later, my father came out with *New Frontiers of the Mind,* a book on ESP for the general public. Its impact was substantial. In that same year, ESP researchers established a scientific publication of their own, the *Journal of Parapsychology,* where they could present the results of their work to other researchers and academics.

In 1940, my father and his team produced *Extra-Sensory Perception After Sixty Years.* The book's title referred to the six decades of research on ESP by the parapsychological community since the founding of the Society for Psychical Research in England in 1882. His book became assigned reading for the 1940–1941 school year for students in the introductory psychology classes at Harvard University.

While my father focused on laboratory experiments, my mother began in 1948 to collect spontaneous ESP cases and eventually wrote four books of her own presenting the many and varied ESP experiences reported by ordinary people, further influencing public attitudes toward an open mind on the question of ESP.

Though my mother passed away in 1983, our collection of spontaneous ESP experiences continues to grow and now includes more than fourteen thousand cases. As my parents once did, I field an unending stream of calls, e-mails, and letters. Each new, reported experience adds something to our understanding of ESP, suggesting new hypotheses to test in the laboratory or intriguing questions to ponder. Do women have more ESP experiences than men? Why do ESP messages sometimes deal with trivial events—for example, the color of a dress your colleague will be wearing tomorrow—as well as important events like the death of a spouse? If someone foresees the future, can he avoid it? Why do we have more ESP about family and friends than strangers? Is emotional closeness involved? Why are very similar types of ESP experiences being reported in 2003 as were reported in 1883? We will consider these questions and more in this book.

Several years ago we established a Paranormal Experiences Group at the Rhine Research Center, which we call PEG.

Our monthly PEG meetings function as a support group, allowing people who have had spontaneous psychic experiences to meet and share those experiences without fear of ridicule or judgment. In our PEG meetings, I have heard hundreds of remarkable stories, told by sincere and honest people, describing unusual and often disconcerting psychic experiences. With their permission, I have included some of their stories in this book along with others who have sent me their stories. I have changed names and identifying details to preserve their privacy.

For a decade now, the *Diagnostic and Statistical Manual of Mental Disorders* used by the American Psychiatric Association has included a category titled "Religious or Spiritual Problem," which has proven to be a major step toward recognizing alternative models of psychotherapy and medicine when parapsychological experiences are involved. Unusual, reality-challenging human experiences like ESP can now be approached under this nonpathological diagnostic category rather than be treated automatically as mental disorders as they have in the past.

Despite this growing openness within the professional community, and greater awareness and general acceptance of ESP in our culture, spontaneous and unexpected ESP experiences can still prove unsettling.

I hope through this book to show you just how common ESP experiences are, to describe how they manifest themselves and operate, and to encourage everyone to accept ESP as a normal part of human consciousness.

Sally Rhine Feather
Rhine Research Center

THE
GIFT

1

THE FALLING CHANDELIER

All good science starts with observation, and humans throughout history have been recording observations about their psychic experiences. My father coined the generic term "extrasensory perception" (ESP) to cover the three basic types of these experiences: precognition, clairvoyance, and telepathy. In each instance, the mind receives information in an unusual way, without the help of the five known senses.

PRECOGNITION

The following mother's experience is an illustration of precognition—the ability to foresee an event before it happens; to break the barrier of time and peer into the future.

The Falling Chandelier

A young woman in Washington State, whom I will call Amanda, woke up at 2:30 A.M. so upset by a terrifying dream that she had to wake her husband and tell him about it. She had dreamed the large chandelier that hung over their baby's bed in the next room had fallen into the crib and crushed the baby. In the dream, Amanda could see herself and her husband standing amid the wreckage. The clock on the baby's dresser read 4:35 A.M. In the dream, she could hear the rain on the windowpane and the wind blowing outside. When she told her husband of the dream, he just laughed at her. He said it was a silly dream, and she should forget it and go back to sleep. In a matter of moments, he did just that himself, but Amanda could not sleep. The dream was too frightening. Finally, she got out of bed and went to the baby's room, picked her up, and brought her back to their bed. She looked out the window and saw a full moon. The weather was calm. Feeling foolish, she got back into their bed with the baby. About two hours later, they were wakened by a resounding crash. She jumped up, followed by her husband, and ran to the nursery. There, where the baby would have been lying, was the chandelier in the smashed crib. They looked at each other in amazement, then at the clock by the crib. It was 4:35 A.M. Stunned, they listened to the sound of rain on the windowpane and the wind howling outside.

The dream Amanda had several hours in advance of the accident had essentially come true. In her dream, she had foreseen the future in remarkable detail: the chandelier falling on her baby's crib, the time it would fall, and even the unexpected change in weather.

For most people, no type of ESP experience seems harder to believe than foreseeing the future. Prophecy, an older, more familiar term for precognition, dates back to the beginnings of human civilization. Many people, especially those coming from a religious perspective, accept the reality of prophecy, but they associate it with gifted individuals connected to the divine and living in ancient times—not with ordinary people. Parapsychologists have found that precognitive experiences are reported more frequently than any other type of ESP, making up more than half of all reported ESP experiences. Modern precognitive experiences, unlike prophecy, do not usually cover grand sweeps of time but typically involve only minutes, hours, or days. Modern precognitive experiences bring information involving everyday life, and they are predominantly realistic and often true to small details, as Amanda's chandelier experience was. Occasionally, precognitive information comes in symbolic form, similar to what people experience in their dreams.

CLAIRVOYANCE

Clairvoyance, a second type of ESP, is the ability to "see" an event as it occurs in a distant place, without the help of our five senses. The distant event can sometimes be seen in great detail with the clarity of actual sight at close range. Recently, I received the following clairvoyant experience from a woman in Michigan.

A Dog Named Brady

Betty and her son Chris had a dog named Brady that they loved very much. When he went missing for a week, they placed an ad in the newspaper with a fifty-dollar reward. According to Betty, "At about eleven o'clock one evening, I received a phone call from a man who was sure he had Brady. He gave me instructions to his house, which I quickly wrote down on paper, but in the rush of excitement to see if it was Brady, I forgot the paper on the kitchen table. I knew the general area and the name of the road that he lived on. Two of my sons jumped in the car with me.

"As I was driving, I said to my boys, 'I hope we can find this place, and I sure hope it's Brady.'

"My son Chris, who was about eleven at the time, said, 'Oh, it's Brady all right; I can see her.'

"When I asked him what he meant, he said he could see

her. I thought he was kidding, so I kidded back and asked him more.

"He went on to describe what he 'saw' in his mind: He said the house was long and white. There was no deck on it, just very long. The roof was black. He said there were two dogs outside, but neither of them was Brady. He said Brady was on the inside. He said when you walk in the house the TV set is very loud and to the left. He said a baby lived there. He said the man had a red shirt or jacket on. He said the lady had a shirt on that had a lot of green on the front. He thought it was a Green Bay Packers shirt. He said the living room was blue, all blue.

"When we pulled up the road, I did not know the exact house. We pulled into two driveways, neither one was like Chris had described. I told Chris I'd give him twenty dollars if he was right. I really didn't believe him, but he is a good kid, and he sounded so truthful and sincere.

"We pulled into the third driveway, and there was a white trailer home, no deck, black roof. Two dogs tied up outside. It was weird. When we got inside, down the hall comes Brady. We were so excited that I didn't think about what Chris had said. We paid the fellow and left. Chris said, 'I told you so.' The only thing I had noticed inside was the very loud TV, which was to the left. Riding home, we were all freaked out, so when I got back home, I called the lady to check out what we hadn't paid attention to because we were so excited to find our dog. Her husband had a red shirt on, she had a sweatshirt with a scene of a deer standing in the middle of pine trees. They had a two-year-old who was asleep in her crib. They had just remodeled their living room with new blue carpeting and a new blue living room set. The only thing that my son had wrong was the green pine trees, which he thought was a Green Bay Packers shirt. I would have never believed this story if it hadn't happened to me.

"The only other time Chris did this was when a friend of the boys had run away from home. He had stopped at our house and then left. Chris and his brother were walking down to the corner store and Chris said, 'There's big trouble coming over that hill.' A second later over the hill came two cop cars and the boy's parents. Chris really tried to do this again, but he only did it in small things that were questionable.

"My question is this: I believe that he was extraordinarily correct in his description of where our dog was. I am not exaggerating one bit. And I am wondering if he could somehow develop this, and is there any use for it? Is this what people do when they help people solve crimes? I also wondered if it only happens under stress as these situations involved a lost dog and a runaway kid."

Individuals with clairvoyant ability are being used by a number of police departments across the country to help solve crimes. *The Blue Sense: Psychic Detectives and Crime,* written by the late Dr. Marcello Truzzi, describes many such cases. Dr. Truzzi began collecting data and case histories on the "blue sense" in 1980. At last report, his Psychic Sleuths project files were the most comprehensive database in the U.S. on the use of ESP and clairvoyance in the service of criminal justice.

Recently there has been considerable public attention to a type of clairvoyance called "remote viewing," which will be discussed later in this book. Begun at the Stanford Research Institute in the early 1970s, the research effort quietly evolved into a classified program to employ psychics to use their ESP ability in the service of their country. The intelligence-gathering part of the research program wasn't publicly confirmed until 1995, when the government admitted that for more than twenty years the CIA and many other government agencies had used specially-trained clairvoyants in such operational missions as penetrating secret Soviet military installations, locating a downed Soviet Tupolev-22 bomber lost in the jungles of Zaire, looking for an American general kidnapped by Italian terrorists, and helping in other still classified missions.

TELEPATHY

Telepathy is what most people associate with the term "ESP." It is the paranormal ability to acquire information about the thoughts, feelings, or activity of another person— in short, the ability to read someone's mind. Experiences involving another person's thoughts are not necessarily the most striking of ESP experiences nor are they the most frequently reported. And yet, telepathy captured popular imagination early on. This ability was the easiest to accept—a seemingly natural consequence of close rapport between two people. Telepathy was the first type of ESP to get scientific and scholarly attention, because the earlier investigators believed it implied something about the human mind that went beyond the laws of matter and suggested a spiritual aspect.

What follows is a dramatic example of telepathy involving a woman in New Jersey who was contemplating suicide.

"Don't Do That, Marian!"

"I hadn't been able to sleep for several nights, and this happened in the middle of another sleepless night," she explained. "Due to a series of unhappy events concerning my family and myself, and to my rundown state of health, I just couldn't see any sense in my life going on. With my thoughts seething round and round in endless circles, I began to think of ways and means to end it all. Suddenly, as clearly as if she were in the room, I heard the voice of my close friend say, 'Don't do that, Marian!'

"I was so utterly dumbfounded that it jolted me right out of my senseless state of mind. My friend lived in Florida, and I was in New Jersey at the time. She was an older woman who had taken a great liking to me because she thought I resembled her only daughter who had died some time before.

"To hear her speak to me in the dead of night, when I knew she was more than a thousand miles away, was quite a disturbing experience. I thought it was all due to my over-wrought nerves, until the next day when she contacted me. She said she had been wakened in the middle of the night by an urgent sense that I needed help. She said she had arisen and prayed for me until dawn. It was one of the most beautiful and mysterious experiences I have ever had."

ESP IN THE LABORATORY

What can science make of these strange reports, however we label them? Are they mysterious experiences, or just distortions of memory, false reporting, or rare coincidences? Let's examine another ESP report.

I recently received an e-mail from a young woman in North Carolina named Lisa claiming some impressive ESP talents.

"All of my life," she writes, "I have sometimes been able to predict things before they happen. An example of this is successfully with 100 percent accuracy predicting the sex of the babies of friends and family. I grew to rely on my abilities so well I was buying pink or blue clothing for the baby even before the sex of the unborn child could be determined. Another example of this is knowing who is on the phone before I answer it. I've had this ability long before caller ID was even invented. I also sometimes know that I will have a visitor on a given day without them calling or telling me they are coming by."

Can she really?

How do we know Lisa's report is true? She offers no independent witnesses to confirm she made those predictions and got those results. She could be lying or just exaggerating the facts through selective memory, counting only her successes and conveniently forgetting her misses. Even if she is telling the truth, simple chance or coincidence might explain her performance, particularly when it comes to predicting the sex of babies—she starts off with a fifty-fifty chance of being right. We do not know how many times she was put to the test.

To be fair, Lisa's claims could basically be true. She could have real ESP ability, but her story would not be considered as scientifically established until she could demonstrate repeatable success under well-controlled test conditions. My father, Dr. J.B. Rhine, was a pioneer in applying this necessary scientific approach to a phenomenon previously considered mere superstition or folklore at best. He is credited with bringing the whole topic of the psychic or paranormal out of the séance room and into the research laboratory and to scientific respectability.

Both of my parents, J.B. and Louisa, had originally planned to be professional foresters or plant physiologists after earning doctorate degrees in botany from the University of Chicago. While there, they happened to attend a lecture on psychical research by the famous British author Sir Arthur Conan Doyle, the creator of Sherlock Holmes. Doyle believed firmly in the reality of an unseen world beyond death. The questions he raised eventually led them to abandon the pursuit of plant mysteries for the pursuit of paranormal mysteries.

My father then prepared himself for a career in psychical research by studying with leaders in that field along with other psychologists at Harvard University in 1926. At Harvard, J.B. and Louisa tried to find valid evidence for mediumistic communication, where mediums or channelers claim to possess the ability to talk with the presumed spirits of deceased individuals. But they either found fraud or no results at all. Before giving up on the paranormal, they decided to make one last effort by working with Dr. William McDougall, a highly respected British psychologist and psychical researcher, who had held the William James Chair of Psychology at Harvard University before leaving to set up the first psychology department at Duke University in Durham, North Carolina.

Duke University became the first academic setting for

parapsychology research when J.B. began his research there under McDougall's direction in 1928. The Duke Parapsychology Laboratory was established in the early 1930s and operated until J.B.'s academic retirement in 1965, when the work was moved to an independent setting now known as the Rhine Research Center.

In the beginning, J.B. focused on analyzing evidence for postmortem survival, but soon concluded it was not possible to produce a definitive answer to that question using the scientific methods of his day. He turned his attention to the question of whether evidence existed for paranormal ability in the living, a subject that could be studied by the scientific method, and a question he and Dr. McDougall thought could be answered.

In the three decades that followed, J.B. and his team conducted or directed hundreds of controlled scientific experiments on telepathy, clairvoyance, and precognition that collectively helped establish the reality of ESP. From the outset J.B. assumed that if ESP existed it would be a natural human ability—everyone could potentially demonstrate the ability if tested under the right conditions. With this assumption, J.B. didn't seek out the famous psychics of the day, but instead began testing the average man or woman on the street—or in his case, on the Duke campus.

In his early ESP experiments, my father typically had students in psychology classes attempt to guess a series of targets—numbers or letters—which he had in his mind to see if they could do better than could be accounted for by chance. Before long, the symbols on regular playing cards were used as targets, and this in turn led to the forming of a specially designed deck of twenty-five cards called a Zener deck. A Zener deck is made up of only twenty-five cards, five each of five different, visually strong symbols: circle, star, square, cross, and wavy lines. The Zener deck was easier to use than a standard deck, and the evaluation of the results was also simpler.

His first experiments focused on telepathy and clairvoyance, which J.B. considered to be sister phenomena. In terms of experiments, the major difference between them was that in telepathy a "sender" attempted to communicate mentally to a "receiver." In clairvoyance, the person tries to mentally see the target by himself, without the help of a sender. A pure telepathy test is hard to design experimentally. Even though the experimenter is mentally sending information to the receiver, how do we know the test subject isn't actually getting his information on his own, directly from the card itself, instead of from the mind of the sender? Given that clairvoyance would demonstrate ESP equally well, my father focused most of his efforts on clairvoyance experiments.

The card deck was shuffled and cut and placed face down on the table. The person being tested—the subject—was asked to identify the top card, and make his call, or prediction. This was recorded and the card removed. The next card was called following the same procedure until twenty-five predictions were made, and then the cards in the deck were checked against the call record to discover the number of successes or hits. Based on accepted laws of chance, the subject should be able to average five hits during each run of the twenty-five-card deck. If he correctly guessed six or more on the average, something other than chance was possible. Of course, in order to demonstrate psychic abilities, the subject would have to score above chance many times; a high score once or twice might have been just a fluke. Fortunately, the science of probability statistics was coming into its own just about the time J.B. began his experiments in the early 1930s. Statisticians could provide the necessary yardsticks to evaluate the experimental results and decide if they had produced evidence for ESP.

J.B. was not the first person to conduct card-guessing experiments of the paranormal. Psychical researchers had been using cards for studies of telepathy and clairvoyance as far back as the late 1800s, but J.B. was the first to develop standard procedures for conducting ESP research, to apply conventional statistical methods to analyze the results, and to publish those results in a scientific journal—all hallmarks of good science.

Eliminating chance as an explanation of ESP was only the first step. He also had to eliminate the possibility of fraud, cheating, or inadvertent sensory cues to explain the results. In the original experiments, the Duke lab staff had set up experimental controls to keep the experimenter and the subject being tested from accidentally or deliberately communicating with each other. They still worked in the same room. To further reduce any possibility of sensory communication, they soon decided to separate the experimenter and the subject in different rooms so they could not see or hear each other at all.

The first series of clairvoyance tests, conducted in 1931–1932, produced encouraging results. In eight hundred trials, twenty-four student subjects achieved a total of 207 hits (correct answers) as against an expected 160 hits. The probability of achieving this result by chance alone was less than one in a million. The scientific evidence for the reality of clairvoyance, and later pure telepathy, was gradually built up with many experiments like this, and subsequently repeated at other independent laboratories.

Many scientists, including J.B., considered the Pearce-Pratt series of clairvoyance tests to be the most convincing of all the early ESP experiments and one of the hallmarks of careful ESP research of its time, having operated under all sorts of safety precautions. In this series J. Gaither Pratt, J.B.'s assistant, sat at a table in the physics building on the Duke campus and dealt a card face down every minute, without looking at it, until he had gone down through the whole deck of twenty-five Zener cards. Hubert Pearce, a Duke divinity school student, sat in a room a hundred yards away and every minute recorded a guess. At the end of the session, Pearce's guesses were compared to the card order dealt by Pratt, then double-checked by another experimenter who compared the recorded order of hits and misses that had been delivered to him independently. Four series of tests were conducted this way with this duo separated first in one building a hundred yards away and then in one 250 yards away. Out of 1,850 total cards guessed in these trials, 370 would be expected by chance. Pearce and Pratt recorded 558 correct hits. The odds against this level of correct guesses is an astronomical twenty-two-billion-to-one.

Even more spectacular was one occasion when Pearce succeeded in getting twenty-five straight hits in a row in an individual test conducted informally by J.B in his office at Duke. The odds against such a feat? One in three-hundred quadrillion! I have often heard my hard-headed scientist father refer to this event with a kind of awe. In his book *New Frontiers of the Mind,* he describes Pearce's performance that day as "the most phenomenal thing that I have ever observed."

How far across space can ESP operate? The Pearce-Pratt results suggested that distance across the campus did not interfere with ESP, so tests of clairvoyance were then conducted over longer and longer distances, with the longest one spanning four thousand miles around the globe. Once again, ESP did not seem to diminish with distance. One of the most remarkable ESP experiments involving distance was conducted by the *Apollo 14* astronaut Dr. Edgar Mitchell in February 1971. Unknown to NASA, while en route to the moon, Mitchell conducted an ESP card-guessing experiment designed to transmit his thoughts across 150,000 miles of space to a group of targeted receivers back on Earth. The experiment was successful, with odds against chance of three-thousand-to-one, and the study is found in the *Journal of Parapsychology.* Two years after his historic moon trip, Mitchell retired from NASA and founded the Institute of Noetic Sciences, dedicated to studying the frontiers of consciousness.

Since distance did not seem to matter, what about time? As early as 1933, J.B. and his team began to ask this question, and then to initiate the very first experimental test of the precognition concept. The test was a simple one: It asked the tested subject to make his or her calls to match the order of the cards as they would be, following a future shuffling and cutting of the deck. When Pearce was tested for precognition this way, his scoring was quite comparable to that in his clairvoyance tests. In one series of 212 runs, he averaged 6.3 correct hits per run, while in another 223 runs his score was 7.1 per run. Both of these scores were statistically significant, and certainly indicated that ESP did not seem to be limited by time.

One of J.B's early precognition experiments involved a Duke University coed who had previously proven to be a good test subject. While studying in France as part of a year abroad program, she made a series of precognition calls and sent her guesses back to J.B. who kept them unopened. A year later, according to plan, her predictions were matched against the results of a target list generated according to the standard randomization method of that time. The results were statistically significant, even though she had made her guesses a whole year before the actual target list was even created.

A half century later, scientists aided by computerized random-event generators had finally accumulated enough studies to make a strong statement about the reality of precognition. Based on 309 experiments involving more than fifty thousand people and two million sessions conducted between 1935 and 1987, they conclusively eliminated the "chance hypothesis" as an explanation for precognition.

Eventually, all three different types of ability came to be considered different aspects of the same ESP phenomenon. In telepathy and clairvoyance, you see the target as it is in contemporary time—with the help of another person's thought in the case of telepathy, or with your own "sight" in the case of clairvoyance. In precognition, you see the target as it will be in the future.

In response to the increasing accumulation of statistical evidence for ESP, skeptics turned their attention from trying to explain ESP away by "the chance hypothesis" to focus their criticism on the design of the laboratory ESP experiments, sometimes suggesting that sloppy controls, inadvertent cueing, or even deliberate fraud might explain some of the results. Though these criticisms have occasionally been valid and helpful, the research methodology of parapsychology experiments in general has always been much better than most skeptics will admit. Further, the methodology has been consistently modified and improved since the early ESP tests in the Duke lab, thanks in large part to modern technology that makes randomizing and selecting targets, recording guesses, and checking results automatic. In the past, and certainly now, the methodology employed in a typical parapsychological experiment is superior in terms of design to that found in almost any other type of conventional research.

Parapsychologists sometimes even recruit professional magicians to assure that their test design is fraud-proof. That is how the field attracted Dr. Daryl Bem, a highly respected professor of social psychology from Cornell University, who also is a mentalist—a magician who specializes in faking ESP. Although initially dubious about ESP, he played a major role in one of the most famous ESP experiments. This series of experiments involved a procedure known as the Ganzfeld. The Ganzfeld ESP test was the brain-child of the late Charles Honorton, one of the most creative and innovative parapsychologists of all time.

The Ganzfeld is the most popular ESP testing procedure used today in parapsychology laboratories around the world, supplanting the card-guessing of earlier days. In J.B.'s day, the person tested made his or her card guesses while in a normal, everyday state of consciousness in a typical university laboratory without any special shielding for sounds from the outside or down the hall. Honorton theorized that ESP messages were subtle communications that were easily drowned out by the cacophony of internal and external sensations flooding our brains during normal waking consciousness. He knew that many mystics and psychics throughout the ages taught that the door to the infinite and the paranormal was an undistracted, inwardly focused, egoless state of mind. He reasoned that ESP experiments conducted in a relaxed, quiet state of mind would perhaps produce better results than those conducted under normal waking states of consciousness. If you try to empty your mind of thoughts with a lot of interruptions, random activity, and noise going on around you, it is hard to do so.

The Ganzfeld technique Honorton adopted for his telepathy tests basically reduces all distracting sounds and sights by seating the ESP test subject comfortably in a soundproof room in order to produce a mild state of sensory deprivation. During typical Ganzfeld ESP tests, split halves of Ping-Pong balls are taped over the receiver's eyes to eliminate visual distractions. All the subject sees is a diffuse, soft pink light. To eliminate unwanted sounds, earphones play white noise, a patternless, low-level background hiss, giving the subject nothing on which to focus aural attention. To reduce touch sensations, the test subject rests in a soft, reclining chair where he lies comfortably cradled and motionless during the experiment. Tight clothing is loosened, shoes and glasses are taken off. The room itself is acoustically isolated to keep out extraneous sounds. As the receiver lies there, he is given quiet relaxation suggestions through the earphones that can go on for ten or fifteen minutes. Finally, when the receiver's mind is relaxed, free of sensory distractions, and no longer thinking about the daily worries of life (Was that dinner tomorrow at 7:00 P.M. or 8:00 P.M.? I gotta remember to buy milk after this session is over.), the actual ESP test begins. Ganzfeld experiments also have a variety of special safeguards built into the testing protocol to guard against deception, fraud, or any inadvertent information leakage to the test subject.

The target for the test is normally a distinct, dramatic image—a photo, drawing, cartoon, video or film clip randomly selected from a large bank of targets with strong visual or emotional impact. For the next thirty minutes, one person will act as the sender and concentrate on the picture, trying to send the image to the now-relaxed receiver in another room. While this is going on, the receiver is being encouraged to say out loud whatever images pop into his mind, and this is recorded by another experimenter outside his room. The receiver is usually told not to work at seeking out images but simply to sit back and let them come naturally. After a half hour or so, the Ping-Pong balls are removed, the white noise stopped, and the test subject is "awoken." The subject then is asked to choose from a set of four pictures the one he feels is closest to the images that he experienced during the experiment. With a one-in-four chance of choosing the correct one by pure luck, the hit rate expected by chance is 25 percent.

In one typical Ganzfeld ESP experiment, the test subject received mental images of riding in a car on a pebbly road out in the country. The four pictures she ended up choosing from were a painting of a Chinese nobleman in exotic clothes; a still life with flowers; some cars in a parking lot buried in snow; and a *National Geographic* photo of a countryside with a rural road running through the scene and a lone pickup truck cruising down the road. This was obviously the closest to the ESP images she received during the experiment, and she chose it. She was correct.

In 1989, Honorton conducted eleven different Ganzfeld studies following strict guidelines specifically recommended by parapsychology's most famous critic, Dr. Ray Hyman, a retired psychologist from the University of Oregon. Since skeptics often argue that any good magician can produce amazing "psychic" results, Honorton enlisted the help of two mentalists, Dr. Daryl Bem mentioned earlier, and Ford Kross. Their task was to check out and sign off on the test procedures before Honorton conducted the tests. "The experimental protocols," wrote Kross, an officer in the Psychic Entertainers Association, "provide excellent security against deception by subjects."

The results? Ten of Honorton's eleven studies produced positive results. The overall success rate was 34 percent, as compared to an expected 25 percent if chance alone were at work. The odds against this positive result being due just to chance? Twenty-thousand-to-one.

These tests are highly regarded within the parapsychology world, because their design met the tight rules set by one of the top ESP skeptics, two magicians reviewed the test design to eliminate the possibility of fraud or trickery, and the results were definitely not explainable by chance.

These Ganzfeld tests for ESP are technical and complicated, but they are necessary if you want the scientific community or other careful, cautious individuals to consider the results as evidence of the paranormal. Tests like these allow us to continue to feel confident that ESP is a real phenomenon. We have the evidence.

Parapsychologists are very careful to avoid exaggerated claims. We speak like scientists, because we are part of the scientific community. The Parapsychological Association provides a very precise scientific definition of what they mean when they say "X" exists: "We mean that the presently available, cumulative, statistical database for experiments studying X provides strong, scientifically credible evidence for repeatable, anomalous, X-like effects." The Parapsychological Association then restates it in normal, human language: "With this in mind, ESP exists, precognition exists, telepathy exists . . ."

Will we ever convince diehard skeptics that ESP exists? Probably not. Unfortunately, even scientists, faced with evidence contrary to their belief system, can be reluctant to give up cherished ideas. The public regards scientists as paragons of rationality and objectivity, but studies have shown that scientists as a group can be just as dogmatic and authoritarian, foolish, and illogical as the general public, even when they are practicing science. British psychologist and parapsychology critic C.E.M. Hansel, for instance, once started his "scientific" evaluation of ESP by stating, "In view of the apriori arguments against it, we know in advance that telepathy cannot occur." Another skeptic was consulted by a journal editor reviewing a paper describing scientific ESP experiments submitted by Stanford Research Institute researchers Dr. Hal Puthoff and Russell Targ. Even though the paper, submitted to the *Proceedings of the IEEE* (Institute of Electrical and Electronics Engineers) met all requirements for a standard, professional journal submission, the skeptic's comment was simply "This is the kind of thing I would not believe even if it existed."

• • •

Parapsychologists no longer conduct scientific tests to prove the reality of ESP. There is ample evidence that it exists. Their experiments today are process oriented. They focus on trying to understand how ESP works, on looking for ways to help humans gain some control of ESP, and on applying it for some practical use.

As the remarkable stories in this book demonstrate, anyone can potentially have spontaneous ESP happen to them. But can anyone produce ESP on demand? Or will ESP forever remain an unpredictable, uncontrollable phenomenon? Parapsychologists have found some answers, although many other answers still elude us.

When he began his ESP experiments in the 1930s, my father had hoped to demonstrate that ESP talent was a normal human ability, not a special gift limited to exceptional people like mystics, prophets, shamans, or saints. His research, and the experiments of others who followed him, did in fact demonstrate that average people could demonstrate ESP in many cases, but laboratory research suggests that ESP talent is not spread equally among humans. Some people are clearly more psychic than others; some are almost psychic superstars. But even superstars have their bad days. Fifty years of experiments have failed to find anyone, even the most gifted psychic, who can repeatedly produce 100 percent accurate ESP under controlled test conditions.

Early on, J.B. confirmed what common sense would lead you to expect in ESP experiments in which subjects had to repeat the same type of card guesses over and over again—they got bored, lost interest, and their scores dropped. He dubbed this the "decline effect," and it actually gave him some assurance that he was dealing with a real psychological phenomena and not a statistical artifact. Physical scientists can heat fresh water at sea level and it will boil at 212° Fahrenheit a million experiments in a row, never showing a decline effect. Water does not get bored, tired, or lose interest in the experiment, but human beings are different. The novelty of predicting cards soon wears off. And novelty, enthusiasm, interest—from childhood to old age—appears to be a necessary psychological condition for strong, positive scoring in laboratory ESP tests.

Boring or not, some people clearly perform better than others under the same test conditions. This caused parapsychologists to wonder if their exceptional ESP performance was due to "nature" or "nurture" or some combination of the two? In other words, are psychically gifted people born with the gift (nature) or can it be taught (nurture)? Is ESP performance linked to heredity? A certain type of personality? IQ? Gender or age? Can we improve our ESP abilities with study and training or by entering an altered state of consciousness like meditation or hypnosis? Does our physical state when we do the testing affect our performance? How about our mental state? Do believers perform better than skeptics?

Let me share with you a snapshot of what we've learned to date. Please remember that what we have learned in the lab may be a far cry from how ESP occurs outside the lab. What follows is a general summary of what we have learned over all these years of laboratory research. I will skip the details, the statistical analyses, and all the cautions that accompany any good research findings. Readers interested in the caveats and shades of gray incorporated in the original studies will find them in the *Journal of Parapsychology* or in some of the references listed in the Appendix.

IQ AND ESP PERFORMANCE

A positive correlation has been found between intelligence and ESP in some studies, but a high score on an intelligence test doesn't guarantee a high score on an ESP test. Brighter children have been found to score somewhat better in classroom studies of ESP, possibly because they feel more comfortable in test-taking situations or learn more quickly how to adapt to the test setup. In other studies, conducted by experimenters familiar with their subjects' special needs, mentally retarded children have actually shown high levels of

ESP comparable to those found with brighter children. Historically, a number of high ESP scorers have had a variety of significant learning disabilities, some which definitely limited their intelligence.

GENDER, AGE, AND ESP PERFORMANCE

Outside the laboratory, women voluntarily report more ESP experiences, as you will see in the rest of this book. When men are polled directly in sampling studies, it appears that they experience ESP as often as women, the same types of ESP, and in the same forms—namely dreams, intuitions, and hallucinations. But biology significantly favors neither men nor women when it comes to ESP demonstrated in laboratory experiments. Inside the laboratory, small gender differences do emerge depending on what form of ESP is being tested, the type of target chosen to be sent or received, or the gender of the experimenter running the test.

Age has frequently been studied in an attempt to check on the common belief that ESP drops off with age, with school, or with adulthood. Once again, it does not appear that age itself is the variable, but rather the conditions of the test situation or who is conducting the study.

PERSONALITY AND ESP PERFORMANCE

After years of research using standard psychological measures of personality as well as specially devised measures, psychologists working in the parapsychology field have found very few personality characteristics that reliably identify good scorers in ESP tests. One of the most consistent findings relates to the trait of extroversion, the tendency to be outgoing and gregarious. In over sixty studies conducted by seventeen different experimenters, extroverts were found to have a clear edge over introverts, the latter often showing below-chance scoring (psi-missing) by way of contrast.

Along somewhat the same lines, there is a weak but generally consistent tendency for subjects who score high on social adjustment measures also to score well on ESP tests. Spontaneity is another factor that has been less studied, but has been found to be positively related to ESP test success.

In their Ganzfeld telepathy studies, Honorton and others have found that certain people typically do better than others: people who are artistic and creative; people who have personally experienced psi in their lives; people who believe in ESP; people who regularly practice some form of meditation or relaxation; extroverts and intuitive personalities; and people who have earlier participated in other psi experiments. Ganzfeld researchers have also learned that dynamic visual images, like video clips with motion and sound, seem more likely to be received than static images, such as still photos or drawings. Friends seem to make better "senders" than strangers.

One of the most interesting findings from later Ganzfeld studies suggests that ESP works better when the subject and receiver are related, whether they are parent and child or siblings. If this last finding holds up, it would coincide with the large number of spontaneous psi cases that are reported involving family members, as well as with the very high percentage of reports about ESP "running in the family." This could obviously have a bearing on the question of where psi may fit in terms of the evolutionary history of man.

MENTAL AND PHYSICAL CONDITION AND ESP PERFORMANCE

Parapsychologists determined in the early 1930s that sleepy, ill, and physically or mentally fatigued test subjects perform poorly on ESP tests—just as such people do in most other tests. Caffeine helped raise scores, and alcohol produced mixed results. No one was surprised by these findings, but confirmation was important. At the time these findings helped assure my father and his colleagues that they were working with a real ability and not just some quirk of statistics.

What about unusual states of consciousness—self-induced or drug-induced—would they enhance ESP? Outside the lab, most spontaneous ESP experiences occur in the dream or daydream state, and even mediums often feel they get their best messages when they are in a trance state. Early experiments were conducted on the effect of various drugs or chemicals that produce feelings of detachment or dissociation from the environment and the self, but little encouragement was found. Taking doses of the depressant drug sodium amytal produced a big drop-off in performance. Later, when the hippie culture exploded on the American scene in the 1960s, users of LSD and "magic mushrooms" (psilocybin) sometimes reported increased "psychic powers." Would these drugs unlock ESP performance? A few studies were done with hallucinogens. Though the subject's confidence tended to become higher, his ESP scores did not. In summary, it seems that ingesting drugs and chemicals does not improve ESP performance.

How about self-induced states of consciousness such as meditative and hypnotic trances? Research into these conditions have turned out to be much more promising. The Ganzfeld technique with its mild sensory deprivation has proven to be a very effective method in facilitating ESP, with average higher results than in the old forced-choice card tests conducted under normal, daily life conditions. A history of practicing meditation has proven to be a definite advantage to subjects performing in a Ganzfeld test.

Hypnosis has had an off and on linkage with ESP ever since its discovery by Franz Mesmer in the eighteenth century. My father abandoned the use of hypnosis early on as too time-consuming for his card test conditions. In later years, other studies have found hypnosis to be fairly promising. A summary of twenty-five studies concluded that the hypnotic state allowed better ESP results than ordinary states of consciousness, although not with just any experimenter/hypnotist. We can speculate that hypnosis helps by increasing one's testing confidence but also encourages relaxation and withdrawal of attention from the external world.

BELIEF AND ESP PERFORMANCE

Charles Honorton was not the first to discover that believers in ESP tend to score higher on ESP tests than nonbelievers. In a series of well-known experiments early in the history of parapsychology, Dr. Gertrude Schmeidler of the City College of New York found that those who believed in the reality of ESP got higher scores on average than those who did not. Believing is not guaranteed to make you psychic, but if you are trying to produce ESP an open mind will help. A recent meta-analysis of seventy-three published ESP studies indicated that believers performed better than disbelievers with odds greater than a trillion-to-one.

OTHER FACTORS AFFECTING ESP PERFORMANCE

Contrary to what scientists conducting physical experiments usually have to contend with in their physical experiments, it turns out that the personality, attitude or behavior, and even the ESP ability of the person conducting an ESP experiment can significantly affect the results. In some ways, this should be expected. If you are taking an ESP test—or almost any mental or physical test for that matter—it usually helps if you are performing in front of supportive, encouraging people. In ESP studies, it has been found that visibly hostile or skeptical scientists can have a negative effect on the subject's performance. A warm, friendly laboratory ambiance is more conducive to ESP than a cold, clinical laboratory setting. The psychological atmosphere surrounding the tests seems to affect the outcome.

My father became convinced of the critical importance of the motivation of the subject in achieving ESP success. A highly motivated subject has a better chance of producing ESP than someone who doesn't care about the results produced. Skepticism, doubt, and disinterest on the part of the test subject seem to reduce psychic performance, at least in a laboratory test setting.

Adding it all up, we have made solid progress. Science has established the reality of ESP, and parapsychologists have discovered some of the factors that encourage or inhibit psychic performance. We have a long way yet to go before parapsychologists understand ESP well enough to put it to practical use. Meanwhile, outside the laboratory, ESP continues to manifest itself spontaneously in people's lives, in consistent, familiar ways that suggest a universal, human phenomenon.

2

A FIRE AT THE PENTAGON

Shortly after the shocking September 11, 2001, terrorist strike on the United States, I received a call from a well-educated, forty-year-old woman named Marie living in North Carolina. A few weeks before the attack, she and her husband had been vacationing in Washington, D.C. Their planned sightseeing itinerary had included all the usual stops, including the Pentagon, but the weather had been very hot and humid, the traffic heavy, so they skipped the Pentagon.

A Fire At The Pentagon (2001)

"When we exited the city, my husband was driving," she wrote to me. "I was sitting next to him in the front. I was just trying to close my eyes to relax for a minute. Then he told me, 'Well, when we come around the bend up ahead, you should get a good view of the Pentagon because our road goes right by it.' It was one of the things we had said we wanted to do when we visited Washington. So I opened my eyes to look, and when I looked to the right, there it was. But it had huge billows of thick, black smoke pouring out of it, just huge clouds of smoke. I didn't see fire, I saw smoke, like a bomb had gone off, billows and billows of black smoke going up in the sky.

"I yelled out and slammed my hands on the dashboard. My poor husband didn't know what was happening. I mean, I really screamed out loud. His first thought was that we were going to be in an accident, and I was warning him he was going to hit someone. But it was pretty open on the highway, and nobody was cutting in front of us or anything at that moment."

When Marie saw the black smoke, it created such an intense, emotional feeling that she lost her breath. She was almost hyperventilating. Then suddenly, she felt like she was literally falling into the Pentagon itself—which was why, she explained to me, she slammed her hands against the dashboard. She described the feeling as being on a roller coaster when you crest the top and plunge forward and down. The combination of her vision and falling forward overwhelmed her. When she talked with me, she described it as sensory overload.

"I truly felt like we were in danger, even though we were actually on the highway and a couple of miles away from the Pentagon. I thought it was on fire. My husband said the Pentagon was not on fire, and then I finally realized that in fact it wasn't. And as fast as it had started, it stopped. It had all happened in a few seconds."

Marie was understandably confused and shaken by the experience. A pretty woman with dark, curly hair, Marie holds a business degree. She has had psychic experiences most of her life, but this one was different. Seeing something that was not there had never happened to her before.

Two weeks later, Marie's frightening precognitive visual hallucination came true. At 9:45 A.M. on September 11, 2001, just one hour after American Airlines Flight 11 slammed into the North Tower of New York's World Trade Center, American Airlines Flight 77 smashed into the Pentagon, killing 184 people and setting off fires that generated billows and billows of thick, black smoke.

Parapsychologists are still searching for a better term for what Marie experienced than an ESP "hallucination." "Hallucination" is a negatively loaded term, connoting abnormal psychology. Both ordinary hallucinations and ESP hallucinations are characterized by the mistaken impression that the object or person perceived by one of the five senses is actually present there in physical reality. But the two types of hallucinations differ in several important ways. The ordinary hallucination produces fantasy, nonsense, and verifiably false claims and usually occurs in people who are mentally or physically ill or in a drugged state. The ESP hallucination delivers accurate, factual information that can be subsequently checked out and verified and is experienced by sane, healthy, normal people like Marie.

I received dozens of calls and e-mails in the following weeks and months from people describing similar spontaneous precognitive experiences that seemed to foreshadow the terrible events of that day. Many came in vivid and dramatic dreams. Others reported during waking hours of getting strange intuitions or bodily feelings of something being terribly wrong, suggesting that they had some psychic awareness on an unconscious level of the approaching events. In a few cases, the experiences seemed so realistic that the people felt they were actually living through the events themselves. We'll have more to say on them later.

Now let's move backward sixty years to 1941. Two of the most dramatic events in the history of the United States are the 2001 terrorist attacks on New York and Washington, D.C., and the 1941 Japanese attack on Pearl Harbor in Hawaii that launched World War II. Sixty years separate Marie's ESP experience from the following one, but the two precognitive experiences share some striking similarities. The story was sent to my mother from a woman living in California in December 1941.

Attack On Pearl Harbor (1941)

"It happened when I was in high school. I wasn't feeling well, and I came home early. It was about two or three in the afternoon. I lay down on a couch in the living room and took a nap. This is what I dreamed:

"I was standing on a hill in the predawn darkness, shivering in the wind. I was looking at a large building below and ahead of me. An American flag was flying over it, and I knew it was a barracks. I knew there were men inside asleep. I even knew how many men there were, four hundred and something. For some reason, I had a terrible premonition, and I shook more with fear than with cold. I didn't know what was going to happen, but I knew something awful was, and I wanted to cry out a warning, but I couldn't.

"Then I heard a groaning sound, at first far off and then closer. I looked up, and there were squadrons of planes overhead. In a few seconds I knew why I had been afraid, because when they were directly over the building, they started dropping bombs, hundreds of them it seemed. The noise was deafening, and the flames leapt up at the dark sky. I could feel the ground shake under me but, most frightening of all, I could see inside that building. I could see the men caught in their beds, caught and ripped and burned and killed, and yet horrible as that was, that was not what caused the great feeling of panic that swept over me. The thing that was racing through my mind at that moment was a single thought, 'But why? We are not at war!' With that phrase playing in my brain over and over, I awoke, gasping with fear.

"I had never had a dream so vivid. I went into the kitchen where my mother was preparing dinner and told her about it. I wasn't in the habit of telling my dreams to people, because they were always obviously silly things not worth telling, but for some reason this was different, and that night I told my dad, too.

"Well, you can probably guess what comes next. That was on Thursday. On Sunday morning, December 7, I was listening to the radio when suddenly they interrupted with a special news bulletin. The Japanese had struck Pearl Harbor before dawn, the men were caught in their barracks, and we were at war.

"As is the case of those first bulletins, they are rather short and incomplete, and they tell you to keep listening for further reports that will come later. In this bulletin, they didn't have an account of all the damage done, but they said that as far as they knew at the moment, the greatest loss of life had occurred when one of the barracks suffered a direct hit. They told how the men were caught there before they were even fully awake, and he gave the number as four hundred and something, which was the number I had dreamed. The description followed everything exactly as I had seen it. The only thing I had not known was the identity of the enemy."

A UNIVERSAL HUMAN ABILITY

Reports like these suggest that ESP is remarkably stable and consistent in terms of form and content. As my mother declared shortly after she started the Rhine ESP collection, "Before I had read perhaps fifty of the letters, I began to realize that, whether they came from Portland, Maine, or Portland, Oregon, some of the experiences were basically identical."

Consider this case sent to my mother.

"Something Has Happened To My Mother!" (I)

"One Sunday afternoon, several members of our family were eating dinner at my paternal grandmother's house. Suddenly, and for no apparent reason in the midst of pleasant family dinner chatter, my mother stood up and screamed 'My mother! My mother! Something has happened to my mother!' We were all shocked. . . . About fifteen minutes after her experience, the phone rang, and she received the information from her father that her mother had indeed died fifteen minutes previously. My mother was not aware that her mother was ill, or even that she was in a hospital, where she expired."

Now consider the almost identical experience of the woman in the following case, also sent to my mother.

Something Has Happened To
My Mother!(II)

On Thanksgiving Day, a woman was at a dinner and was surrounded by happy people. Nevertheless, around 11:30 in the morning, when conversation consisted of nothing more serious than chitchat about the Thanksgiving dinner, she suddenly knew without a doubt that her mother, who lived far away in California, was in great distress. She tried not to disturb the party of fourteen people and managed to finish dinner. But her thoughts were perfectly clear. She knew her mother had passed away. She excused herself and went home. When she got there, a message awaited her. Her mother had died at about 9:30 in the morning, making the time of the mother's death and the daughter's reaction about the same. The mother was aged, but she had not been ill, and the daughter had no reason to expect her death.

Both women, in the middle of their pleasant dinners, had sudden intuitions that something terrible had happened to their mothers at that very moment. Both women were absolutely convinced that the information they received from their sixth sense was correct. And shortly afterward, both women received messages confirming their ESP.

Even more interesting to parapsychologists, spontaneous

ESP experiences basically identical to those being reported in 2003 can be found in ESP case collections stretching back to the 1880s.

Two major collections of spontaneous ESP experiences have been assembled during the last century and a half. The Society for Psychical Research (SPR) in England published the first in 1886. Entitled *Phantasms of the Living,* this monumental, two-volume work featured 702 reported ESP experiences that were each carefully investigated, verified, and authenticated in an effort to provide evidence for the existence of telepathy. With this proof-oriented approach, the investigators for the Society for Psychical Research preferred ESP experiences that had been written down soon after they happened, or at least told to someone else, while memories were fresh. They also sought out references who could vouch for the experiencer's character and honesty. That telepathy could occur between normal people who were not asleep or in a hypnotic trance was a novel idea at that time. The ESP reports came primarily from people in England, and the authors also included some ESP cases from France and Italy.

Studying spontaneous cases of telepathy and clairvoyance for evidence of ESP took a backseat to experimental work once that took hold in the early 1930s. By 1948, it was becoming clear to my father and his team that it was time for laboratory researchers to renew their familiarity with the basic phenomena on which the field was based. They needed to look for fresh ideas and clues to help them understand ESP better and perhaps to translate into better experiments.

My mother had been an experimentalist at heart, ever since her graduate training as a plant physiologist at the University of Chicago. When no one else volunteered to collect and study the anecdotal reports of ESP from the public, she stepped up. My mother's case collection was not proof-oriented, since she reasoned that experiments had already established the reality of ESP. Her objective was to acquire as nearly representative a sample as possible of all the ways in which ESP was reported to occur in daily life. With this inclusive criterion, the Rhine Center collection eventually dwarfed the SPR collection, adding thousands of extra reports for parapsychologists to analyze.

These cases are not meant to constitute scientific proof for the existence of ESP, but they do support the scientific evidence produced in the laboratory. The sheer number of these reports should make any reasonable, open-minded person consider the possibility that ESP exists. Can each and every one of the reports be the result of a hoax, mental illness, delusion, poor memory, wishful thinking, or simple coincidence? This would seem to be more of a miracle than ESP itself. A single ESP experience of any kind is likely to be unconvincing; a hundred or a thousand like it are not brushed off so easily.

In the early 1980s, Dutch psychologist Sybo Schouten used a computer program to analyze random samples of ESP experiences reported in the Society for Psychical Research and Rhine collections as well as a smaller German collection put together by the University of Freiburg. He identified a range of different variables, from the age and sex of the ESP experiencers to the form and content of the ESP experience itself, and then ran a comparative analysis. Even though the ESP experiences came from three different countries—England, the United States, and Germany—and spanned almost a century from 1886 to 1971, Schouten found a remarkable degree of consistency between the reports, with many of the characteristics of the ESP experiences in the Society for Psychical Research collection mirrored in the Rhine collection. This suggests that spontaneous ESP experiences are not the product of a specific time or culture but rather are real, genuine, universal human experiences.

Compare the two cases of "Something Has Happened to My Mother!" you have just read, taken from the Rhine Research Center's ESP collection, with the following ESP experience taken from the Society for Psychical Research collection published a hundred years earlier.

Something Has Happened
To Mr. C!

"A very old gentleman, living at Hurworth, with whom I was slightly acquainted, had been ill many months. My sister-in-law, who resides also at H., often mentioned him in her letters, saying he was better or worse as the case might be. Late last autumn, my husband and I were staying at the Tynedale Hydropathic Establishment. One evening, I suddenly laid down the book I was reading, with this thought so strong upon me I could scarcely refrain from putting it into words: 'I believe that Mr. C is at this moment dying.' So strangely I was imbued with this belief, although there had been nothing whatever said to lead to it, that I asked my husband to note the time particularly, and to remember it for a reason I would rather not state just then. 'It is exactly seven o'clock,' he said, and that being our dinner hour, we went downstairs to dine. The entire evening, however, I was haunted by the same strange feeling, and looked for a letter from my sister-in-law next morning. None came. But the following day there was one sent to my sister-in-law's brother. It said, 'Poor old Mr. C died last night at seven o'clock. It was past post time so I could not let you know before.'"

This 1883 English ESP experience reads surprisingly like the two mid-twentieth century American ESP experiences. In the middle of a pleasant time, without any conversation on the topic to spark the thought, the ESP experiencer has a sudden intuition that something terrible has happened to someone at that very moment. She is absolutely convinced that the information she receives from her sixth sense is correct. Shortly afterward, she receives a message confirming that it was. The only difference in this case is that the person who died was known to be ill.

One of the most commonly reported ESP experiences involves a mother who suddenly senses danger to her child. Even though she had no logical reason to worry, she panics, rushes out to find the child, and discovers her child is indeed in a dangerous situation.

My mother received dozens of letters describing such ESP experiences that stretch back to the 1920s. Here is one from the 1950s. In this case, the danger was drowning.

My Baby's In Danger! (1950s)

"Early last spring, in the late afternoon, my two older children were in the backyard playing. We had a fence around the yard, and they rarely left it as there was a street in the front and a marshy swamp, which hadn't been filled in, behind the houses in our new development.

"I was feeding the baby when suddenly the greatest feeling of danger and urgency filled me. I had just given the children crackers out the back door, but still I felt they were in danger. I raced out, leaving the baby in her high chair (something I would never ordinarily do) and ran out, calling for them. I was so agitated that several of my neighbors began to call them and search, too. We found them behind a house two doors down, wet to their knees in the swamp. An older child had lured them down there, and I knew that if I had wasted five more minutes they would have been bogged down and probably drowned in the water. They were only two and a half and three and a half years old at the time, and were weighted with heavy clothing and boots."

Now we move ahead to the year 2001. Here is a letter sent to me by a Latino woman in New Jersey named Linda. It is easy to spot the similarities between the two ESP experiences, despite their being separated by a half century.

My Baby's In Danger! (2001)

"I am a mother of three. Two boys and one girl. The two boys are the oldest and my girl the youngest. They are now grown-up and attending college. When my boys were about eleven and seven or perhaps a bit younger, I had taken them to my mom's house for the weekend. I am divorced and have raised my kids on my own with the help of my parents. I usually served a meal to my kids first, and they could go to play while the adults were having dinner. This Sunday was no different. My mom and I served the kids and made sure they ate their food, and then they were out to play while we were having dinner. This is a Latino custom. Children will sit with adults at the dinner table when they are old enough to behave properly and have impeccable table manners. As we were having dinner, the boys, as usual, took their bicycles out and went to ride on the sidewalk that runs in front of my mom's house.

"We were having a nice time while we were eating and chatting and talking about trivialities. As I was talking to my dad, who was sitting in front of me, I suddenly felt this incredible feeling of panic, and I stopped talking to him. I sat up, and screamed, 'Something happened to the kids!' I ran out, and as I reached the sidewalk, I could see my oldest kid walking uphill with my youngest son in his arms, with blood all over him. They had tied a rope to one of the bikes and my oldest son had made a sudden turn, and the little one kept on going. He flew all the way up in the air and landed on top of a lot of stones and debris. He almost killed himself. I had to take him to the hospital. There was no way for me or for anyone else in my family to know what was going on, I just felt it. These things happened mostly with my youngest son."

Linda ended her letter with a second child-in-danger ESP experience involving her youngest son.

"I had left the boys and my daughter at my mom's house, because I had to go to New York for a class. I kissed them good-bye, and off I went. I drove perhaps for about twenty minutes when I suddenly felt the same panic I felt with the experience I related above. I immediately turned back and drove as fast as I could to my mom's house. I knew something had happened to one of my kids.

"As I arrived, my mom was crying and my youngest son again had had a terrible accident where he had gone up one of the trees and had fallen on top of a small branch that had punctured his neck all the way into his throat. Again, I had to take him to the hospital."

Linda experienced in 2001 the exact same, sudden intuition of danger—and urgency to act immediately—as the mother in the 1950s. The experiences are almost identical.

Anyone who takes the time to look carefully through sample cases from both the twentieth-century Rhine Center ESP collection and the nineteenth-century Society for Psychical Research collection will find in both of them the same three types of ESP experiences—precognition, clairvoyance, and telepathy—manifested in the same three ways—through intuitions, dreams, and ESP hallucinations. We can thus reasonably conclude that we are tapping into a fundamental and universal human ability, the meaning and extent of which we are only now beginning to understand.

3

WHAT'S LOVE GOT TO DO WITH IT?

F.W.H. Myers, one of the pioneers of parapsychology research a century ago, was among the first to notice how often emotional bonds are involved in ESP communication between two people. Myers saw love as a kind of "exalted but unspecialized telepathy—the simplest and most universal expression of that mutual gravitation or kinship of spirits." Most of us instinctively feel this to be true. We describe people in love as being on the "same wavelength" or "in tune with each other."

It turns out Myers was correct. Parapsychologists collecting and studying spontaneous ESP experiences quickly noticed that most seemed to deal with events happening to people emotionally linked to the experiencer. In an attempt to confirm or disprove this impression, researchers at the Rhine Center selected from our files 2,878 "realistic" ESP experiences, all rich in detailed information that later turned out to be true. These realistic experiences involved no symbolic information needing interpretation, just detailed imagery matching the actual event as it happened. These cases were chosen for analysis because they are the hardest to explain away as simple coincidence, making them most likely cases of real ESP.

They found that 40 percent of these ESP experiences involved the lives of people in the experiencer's "immediate circle"—parents, children, siblings, spouses, and friends. The second largest number of experiences, 33 percent, dealt with events in the experiencer's own life. Just 14 percent involved "remote relationships," defined as in-laws, fiancés, boyfriends or girlfriends, neighbors, employers, and coworkers. And ESP about strangers represented the least number of experiences, comprising only 13 percent of the total.

The conclusion is that we tend to have ESP experiences predominantly about people with whom we share a personal or emotional interest. Emotionally close people, whether biologically related or not, are interested in each other's health and happiness. They worry about each other. They want to know how the other is doing, or if something could be wrong. This deep caring appears to activate or allow a special channel of communication to occur, unhindered by distance or even time.

The dreaming state seems to be the most common avenue for this ESP awareness to appear: 57 percent of all reported ESP experiences come in the form of dreams. Sudden intuitions received while we are awake rank second, making up 30 percent of reported experiences. Hallucinations, like Marie's experience in "A Fire at the Pentagon," are the least frequently reported form of ESP. Only 13 percent of ESP experiences shared with the Rhine Research Center involve seeing or hearing something that delivered accurate information unknown and inaccessible at that time to the experiencer through normal sensory channels. Whatever the chosen channel, the messages make it through.

ESP ABOUT FAMILY AND FRIENDS

The possibility of family members or close friends suffering death, serious illness, or an accident probably tops the worry list for most people. It is not surprising to find that when we have ESP experiences bringing information about our inner circle, these threats are the ones reported most frequently. Three out of ten psychic messages we get about family and friends concern death, and four out of ten deliver news of accidents. So seven out of ten ESP experiences involving loved ones convey negative news.

A mother's worse nightmare has to be the death of her child. It is hard to imagine anyone wanting this mother's sudden, psychic intuition, but ESP does not wait for permission to deliver bad news.

Death Of A Son

One morning, a woman in Florida was snatching a few moments of freedom in her neglected flowerbed while her new baby slept and her toddler Stephen was off for an hour with his father, who was making a sales call to a farm few miles away. Suddenly, with a stab of pain, she just knew. "Stephen is dead. I'm glad I didn't make him take the medicine he hates so much before he left this morning." To help her get rid of the awful thought, she went next door to talk to her father. He wondered why she was so pale—was she overworking with the arrival of the new baby? She admitted that perhaps she was, making her a prey to morbid thoughts. But, too soon, she learned her psychic intuition had been true. While his father's back was turned, Stephen had wandered off, fallen into an irrigation ditch on the farm, and drowned. All attempts to revive him after he was found had failed.

When any two members of a family are emotionally close, the death of one can generate a psychic shock wave capable of immediately reaching the other.

"Somebody Shot Uncle John!"

"Years ago, when I was ten, an incident occurred that stands out as one of the most vivid and terrifying experiences of

my life. My mother and father slept in a downstairs bedroom
and my sister, age twelve, and I slept in separate bedrooms
upstairs. One early morning, between two and three o'clock,
my father sprang out of bed with what at first looked like a
nightmare. He shouted so loudly my sister and I were awakened and ran downstairs. My father was gripped with terror
and stood there sobbing and trembling. My mother put her
arms around him and tried to quiet him. Finally he was able
to say, 'I just saw somebody shoot Uncle John!' Uncle John
and my father were very close, and nothing my mother said
could change my father's conviction." A little before six
o'clock the same morning, they received news that Uncle
John had been murdered by a man who shot him in the back
with a rifle sometime between two and three A.M. at a place
many miles away.

Mike Spradley is a fifty-eight year-old Texas executive,
employed by a major international oil company. It is somewhat rare to receive ESP reports from busy executives of
companies, so I was particularly pleased to receive Mike's
detailed accounts of his many ESP experiences. Most of his
ESP deals with his immediate circle of family and close
friends, including a buddy who had shared many adventures
with him. The close emotional bond between them probably
explains his psychic dream of the man's death.

Death Of A Buddy

"In August 1979, I was working on a seismic research ship
offshore from Cook Inlet, Alaska, which is west of Anchorage. Via radio, at around 10 P.M., I arranged for two of my
teams to be flown by small plane from our camp on the
Susitna River back to Anchorage, which was a twenty-two
minute flight. After the first two flights were successful, my
subordinate relieved me and told me to go to bed. He would
organize the third and last flight. One of the men on the
flight would be our client, an old friend of mine named Bob.

I had worked with him in the Sinai Desert, the Peruvian jungles, and now Alaska. Extremely tired, I fell into my bunk at the rear of the ship's wheelhouse at 11:30 that night. At 11:55 I had a dream in which I could see Bob in the backseat on the right side of this Cessna 206 plane. He was trying to keep his head above water while futilely attempting to open the back door. It would not open. It woke me up. I knew it was one of my 'dreams.'

"I immediately got out of bed and called Dick, our on-shore manager in Anchorage, waking him up. He had met the first two flights, then had returned to his hotel to go to bed so he was not at the airport to meet the third flight. I told him I thought the third flight had crashed, and I wanted him to go back to the airport to check. Twenty minutes later, he called to tell me that the plane was parked on the flight line and the guys were gone. So he went back to bed and so did I.

"At 6:00 A.M. we got a radio call from the aircraft owner telling us the flight had not arrived. Everyone on board was missing. It turned out that he had two identical airplanes, and Dick had seen the second one on the flight line—not the one that crashed. I later learned they had crashed not long after takeoff. The guy who placed them in the plane told me Bob was the last guy to board, which placed him in the right backseat. With the flaps down during takeoff, the back door will not open on a Cessna 206. We never found the airplane, though we did find two of the four bodies over the next two years."

Realistic dreams like the one Mike had are the most commonly reported form of ESP, although this dream about Bob provides greater detail than usual. Realistic dreams impress people who have them, because the similarity of the experience to the actual event is so striking. The amount and quality of detail make it extremely hard for the dreamer—or any skeptic—to explain his dream away as sheer coincidence or guesswork.

As we all know, twins can grow up very close emotionally. They're often raised in the same way by parents, burdened with the same academic expectations by teachers, and treated as clones by classmates. Their lives are forcibly intertwined. Do they communicate telepathically with each other more frequently and more easily than normal siblings? We simply do not know. We have some anecdotal reports but few well-controlled studies. My friend Joe McMoneagle, a member of the Advisory Board of the Rhine Research Center, is a decorated retired army officer and author of several books based on his extensive experience as a remote viewer (clairvoyant) for the U.S. government. Joe was one of the best remote viewers in the top secret Star Gate "psychic spy" program, declassified in 1995. Millions of Americans have seen him on ABC-TV or read about his exploits in *Time* and *Newsweek*, but few know that Joe had a twin sister Margaret to whom he was very close emotionally and who also had a history of psychic ability.

The day Joe's twin sister Margaret suffered the heart attack that later proved fatal, he was hundreds of miles away, working as a contractor on a house.

Death Of A Twin

"It was a beautiful day, cool, perfect for work, and about 10:00 A.M. in the middle of the week—all the reasons not to quit working," he told me. "But I suddenly had this overwhelming feeling that my twin sister was trying to contact me. I put away all my tools, paid all the help for a full day, and left the job. I got home three minutes before the call from the hospital in Florida telling me that my sister was in bad shape from a massive coronary. My wife and I drove down to Florida right away, and I got to see her about a week before she died. I'm absolutely certain she called out to me."

Margaret's early psychic gifts came at a high price. Joe remembers his twin sister Margaret admitting to him when she was twelve or thirteen that she could tell what people were thinking. He told her that he, too, sometimes had telepathy, but they made a pact not to talk about it. She eventually told their mother and an aunt, and they took her to a doctor who ended up medicating her, then later diagnosing her as schizophrenic. To this day, Joe believes that there was nothing wrong with Margaret, and that the doctor's mistaken diagnosis and treatment put her in an institution.

The number of ESP experiences that bring messages about accidents, illnesses, and injuries to family or close friends is almost as great as those bringing information about their death. Mike, the Texas oilman who had the psychic dream about his buddy Bob's Alaska plane crash, travels constantly all over the world, but his family is never far from his thoughts. He has had many psychic experiences during the last thirty years, and dangers to his family feature in many of them.

Injured Son

"In 1975, I landed in Amsterdam, Holland, after a six-hour flight from the U.S. I went to bed in my hotel and, within seconds, in a dream, I saw my twelve-year-old son flying through the air, then doing a handstand on his left arm. It woke me up, and I just knew he had broken his arm. I called home to Dallas to learn they were at the hospital. During a Little League ballgame, my son had run in from center field to make a diving catch. While landing on his left arm, he broke his wrist."

Wife In Danger

"In August 1986, while asleep in a hotel room in Beijing, China, I dreamed I could see the north side of my house in Houston—the kitchen end—on fire. It woke me up, and I recognized it was one of my 'dreams.' I called my wife in Houston and woke her up at seven A.M. She knows about my dreams so she went downstairs to check, but there was no fire. Later that day, at two P.M., she left a boiling pot on the stove and forgot about it while outside chatting with neighbors. It burned up our kitchen."

Mike's precognitive dreams are very realistic and detailed—events unfold like a movie on a screen—but they sometimes mix in unrealistic or symbolic details. "The strange thing was that, in my dream about my kitchen being on fire, my house wasn't sitting on my lot. It was sitting on my parents' lot in Dallas," he wrote. "So when my wife told me our house was not on fire, I called my parents to see if their house was on fire. It wasn't of course. It was my house—the fire just hadn't happened yet."

The following experience was sent to us by a forest ranger in New Mexico, impressed by his wife's psychic monitoring of an accident he suffered many miles from her, but still within range of her well-developed extrasensory perception.

A Husband Unhorsed

"I left my home that morning in a pickup truck with a crew of men to repair an earthen reservoir. The repair job progressed satisfactorily, so after eating lunch I left the crew and rode by horseback to another part of the range to look for a dam site. I looked at my watch at 4:20 P.M. I seldom paid much attention to quitting time, but this day I had the responsibility of taking my men home from work. So I turned my saddle horse in the direction of the guard station.

"Pat (my horse) liked to run and, since it wasn't fair to keep the men waiting, I let him. Pat stepped in a gopher hole and turned a somersault. I got clear of the saddle and hit the ground in a flat dive and played up the dust. Our momentum was so great that Pat turned a second somersault, and this time rolled over the top of me. It was a very hard spill and I was fortunate indeed to escape without serious injury. My crew saw Pat fall, although they were some distance away and remarked, 'We thought for sure you would be killed.' I had no bruises or scratches on my face. I brushed the dust off my clothes with my hat, took the men home, and then drove the pickup into the ranger station yard. My wife came running out to meet me. 'Pat fell on you, didn't he?' she said. I had to admit he had. 'I knew it. I knew it when it happened,' she replied. If I had not become more or less accustomed to this sort of thing, I would have been amazed."

Like many people who send us their ESP experiences, the ranger did not rush to conclude it was a psychic experience. He first tried to come up with a conventional explanation, but simply could not find one. You can hear the wheels turning in his mind: "My wife didn't know when I left the ranger station that morning that I was going to do any horseback riding. I didn't make this decision myself until before noon. My three horses were kept in a pasture six miles from the ranger station. There was no particular reason why I should have ridden Pat instead of one of the others. Further, neither my horses nor I were accident prone. I have ridden thousands of miles and a number of years without ever having a horse fall with me. And much of it was over dangerous terrain. This was a well-worn trail in an open valley. We had been over it that afternoon, and Pat and I both knew about the gopher hole. There was no excuse for taking such a spill."

It is not clear whether the following man got information about his family's brush with death in an auto accident through a daydream or through a vision, but the psychic message was extremely vivid and detailed.

Mom And Dad In Car Wreck

A young man in Washington, while "half asleep," reported that he "saw" his mother, father, and brother driving down a highway. He then saw a car trying to pass another car in front of his father, who was forced to swerve off the road, his two right wheels hanging over the edge of the ditch. The cars passed. His father continued to fight the wheel trying to get back on the road. Then the front wheel caught the ditch. The car made an 180-degree turn into the ditch on the other side, and rolled over onto the roof. He saw that his father got a bloody nose and a cracked ankle, and then he came out of it. Fifteen minutes later his parents arrived home, but he already knew what had happened and the injuries they had sustained. When he went with them back to the crash site, it was exactly as he had seen it.

Unfortunately, some ESP messages only bring a small amount of information, or lack critical details. In our worry, we may attempt to fill in the missing blanks—sometimes incorrectly, as this woman did when she received her psychic message regarding her mother's injury.

Mother Attacked

A couple in Pennsylvania had retired at about 11:30 P.M. and the woman had not yet fallen asleep when, as she reported to the Rhine Center, "Suddenly I saw my mother—no surroundings—just her. She was slightly bent over and holding her left hand and screaming, 'Help me! Help me! Somebody help me!' " Then the scene faded. It had been as clear as a movie projected on a screen in front of her, and it terrified her. She told her husband she feared that her mother might have burned herself. When she called her mother, she learned that at the time she had her clairvoyant vision, her mother had left the store where she worked and was unlocking the door to her car when she was attacked from behind by a man who held a knife to her throat. Her mother attempted to grab the knife, getting a bad slash along her left hand. She screamed, "Help me! Help me! Somebody help me!" The man hesitated then ran. He was later caught.

A different kind of hallucinatory experience involves feeling phantom, bodily sensations that match the actual, physical symptoms being experienced at the moment by someone emotionally close to the experiencer. Retired psychiatrist Dr. Berthold Schwarz coined the term "telesomatic" from the Greek words for "distant" and "body" to describe such psychic messages delivered to the body instead of the mind. The best cases are very difficult to explain as simple coincidence. This experience, emailed to me not long ago by a woman named Jody, involved the passing away of her husband.

A Blow To My Stomach

"My terminally ill husband was in intensive care at a hospital where he spent the last six weeks of his life. The day he died, I went to visit him before I went to work. When I left him, I couldn't go to the office but wandered aimlessly around the neighborhood stores with an intense feeling of anxiety. I finally went to the office, which I shared with another employee. At 12:50 P.M., I was standing at my computer station and experienced what I would describe as a blow to my stomach. I held on to my middle as though someone had hit me with a fist—it was like a strong contraction. I was immediately aware that my husband had passed away.

"A sense of extreme calm came over me. I knew that in five minutes the phone would ring, and it would be the hospital. I told my fellow employee that I might have to leave. I went to the restroom. When I came back, the phone rang and a nurse reported that my husband took a 'turn for the worse,' but I knew he was gone. When I arrived at the hospital, a nurse was waiting for me. I just looked at her and said, 'Is he gone?' I knew he was. After about six months, I visited his attending physician, with whom I had a lengthy discussion. He said he knew the questions I would have, but I don't think he was ready for what I asked him. I described my experience, and he became very sober and told me the same thing happened to him when his mother died, and that other patients had related similar stories."

I thanked Jody for sending the account of her remarkable

psychic experience, confirming that we had heard many similar accounts over the years.

Sympathetic pain experiences like this aren't only provoked by a death. Many involve a sympathetically-felt injury to a living person we love. Here is one sent to my mother.

I Feel Your Pain

A woman working in a Florida hotel as a housekeeping supervisor explained that her mother lived hundreds of miles away, in Pennsylvania. "At eleven o'clock in the morning," she wrote, "I was standing, supervising the room maids in my employment. Suddenly, without bending or moving in any way, a terrible pain shot through my right hip. It was almost unbearable, and I limped to my desk to sit down. Several girls witnessed this, and I knew of no reason for the pain. Standing, sitting, or lying down brought no relief. In the early evening, the hotel physician came in to see some patients and I consulted him. He advised me to come to his office for X-rays if I was no better by morning. As the pain was constant, I tried to divert my mind by going to the ballroom, where we have a movie once a week at nine P.M. but I was very restless, and the urge to get away from the ballroom was so great that I limped back to my office. Just as I entered the door, I was called to the phone. The news I received from the call was that my mother had fallen at eleven o'clock that morning and broken her hip. The fall resulted in three operations that left her a cripple. By morning, my own pain was gone, and I was perfectly well. I related my experience to the house physician, without too much comment on his part. He did say he was aware of similar events happening to others."

Fortunately, not all ESP messages about our immediate family involve death, accidents, illnesses, and injuries. Occasionally ESP brings positive or helpful information. For example, in the analysis done on the 2,878 ESP experiences, we found 95 cases dealing with locating missing articles.

One Ohio woman managed to retrieve her mother's stolen car with the help of accurate information received during a clairvoyant dream, surprising the police—and undoubtedly the car thief as well!

Mom's Stolen Oldsmobile

"About a year ago, my mother drove her Oldsmobile to church and parked in the church lot. After Mass, she discovered the car missing, so there was nothing else to do but ride home with friends and phone the police. After searching, the police told us to resign ourselves to the fact that the car must have been taken over the state line. At that time, there was quite a racket going on with stolen cars. They were taken to a different state, stripped, repainted, and resold.

"My mom's car was beautiful, and loaded with all the options imaginable. Because it was such a gem, the police doubted we would ever get it back. I was especially sick about the whole thing, because I used to drive it myself.

"Two nights later, I dreamed about the car, and in the dream I saw just what street in Cleveland it would be located on. At the time, I was living in a suburb about fifteen miles outside of Cleveland. After telling my husband and phoning my parents about the dream, I drove to this certain street in the center of Cleveland and found the car there. Cleveland is a very large city, with hundreds of streets, yet I knew exactly which street to drive to. The car had been driven over a hundred miles, and had been involved in an accident, but was still in very good shape."

Her clairvoyant dream of seeing the street where the stolen car was parked also included an element of precognition. As she explained: "The neighbors in the vicinity told me that the car had been parked there only five minutes before I arrived." Yet she somehow "knew" that it would be there when she arrived. The woman's report of the incident is in the Cleveland police files.

ESP ABOUT OURSELVES

ESP about ourselves—our own life, health, and well-being—ranks second in importance after ESP about our family and close friends, at least in terms of the total number of reported cases. Eight out of ten ESP experiences involving our own lives are precognitive. Unlike precognitive messages involving family and friends, we rarely report that we foresee our own death, but there are some cases that do involve predicting the subject's own death. It must be terrifying to receive such a psychic message as this man did. His wife shared the story with us.

Judgment Day At Butler's
Crossing

A seventy-eight-year-old man in North Carolina told his wife about a dream he had the night before. He dreamed he was standing at Butler's Crossing about three miles from their home when he saw a vehicle coming toward him at great speed. The light was so bright it blinded him. He screamed to his son, "Oh David! It's Judgment Day." At that moment the vehicle struck him, as he said, "hurling me into everlasting darkness."

His wife agreed it was a terrible dream, but she didn't know then that it was also precognitive. Her husband at the time was suffering from an allergy, for which twice a week he was taking treatments from a doctor in a nearby town. Three days later, he went to the town for his shots. On the way back, he caught a ride to Butler's Crossing where he got out of the car, stood a few minutes by the road lighting his pipe, and then started across the highway. He was at the center white line when a speeding car came around the curve.

He stepped back, the car swerved to the left, hit him, and threw him sixty feet. Fifteen minutes later he was dead.

The largest number of ESP experiences that people report concerning themselves involves warnings of accidents and injuries waiting for them around the bend. Jamie, a young teenager from California with a history of ESP experiences, e-mailed me this psychic premonition that saved her life as well as the lives of her two friends.

Buckle Up

"When I was sixteen, I used to get rides with some friends to and from school. There were four of us, and we rode in a pickup truck. Because there were four, we never wore seat belts. On one particular day, the fourth passenger went home early. The three of us remaining climbed into the truck after school. The moment I slammed the door shut, I had this horrible feeling. It was a warm day, and yet I broke out in chills. I just knew something bad was going to happen. I turned to my two friends and ordered them to put their seat belts on, and I buckled my own seat belt. The driver took one look at me and buckled his seat belt. His sister didn't want to. She repeatedly refused to wear it. I told her brother not to start the truck until she had her belt on. She still refused. Fed up, I reached over and put her belt on her myself. She refused to tighten it, but I didn't argue with her about it. Less than ten minutes later, our truck and a Volkswagen bug in front of us both tried to pass another vehicle on a rural road. We ended up rear-ending the VW. Both our truck and the VW flew off the road and crashed into a walnut orchard. Firefighters had to pry us out of the wreckage using Jaws of Life hydraulic cutters. My companions ended up being rushed by helicopter to the hospital. I was the only one to walk away unhurt. I overheard one officer telling another that if we hadn't been wearing seat belts, we would all have been killed instantly."

◆ ◆ ◆

Some futures foreseen for ourselves can be happy. Our analysis uncovered some fifty precognitive dreams dealing with winning bets, races, and contests. Why don't we see the headline PSYCHIC WINS LOTTERY more often? The answer is simple: Even though ESP exists, we don't know enough about how it operates to control it effectively. ESP may be a primitive ability that operates as an early warning system, better able to pick up on negative rather than the positive events in our lives.

An Alabama woman named Bambi e-mailed me a report of many accurate precognitive experiences she had, but concluded her e-mail with the rueful comment, "My brother kids me about lottery numbers, because one time when it was drawn on TV, I told him the numbers and they came up. Boy was he mad, and I was also! But it only happens unexpectedly. I never know when it will happen."

Occasionally we do have a psychic sense of the right moment. I recently received the following e-mail from a man I'll call Tom who has had ESP experiences all his life, starting at age two. Although he is back on his feet now, a few years earlier while down on his luck, he was making and selling necklaces to earn money. Every penny counted. One day a strong, psychic intuition overtook him.

Winner Take All

"I almost never buy lottery tickets," Tom explained. "But one day I had made about thirty necklaces and was able to sell them for a little cash to put away. I put all of it except two dollars into our bank account. When my wife asked me why I didn't save it all, I told her I was going to use the two bucks to get another two hundred dollars, that afternoon. She asked me how, and I told her that at exactly 3:45 P.M. I would be at the gas station and that I would purchase one lottery scratch ticket—an orange one—and that it would be a winner for two hundred dollars. At 3:40 P.M. I pulled into the station, went inside. There was only one game with orange tickets—the tickets had just been released by the state that morning. The game was called "Winner Take All." I bought one ticket, scratched it, and it had exactly two hundred dollars under the winning number on my ticket."

ESP ABOUT REMOTE RELATIONSHIPS

As emotional bonds lessen, so do the number of reported ESP experiences. Only one in seven cases in our study of realistic ESP experiences were about events in the lives of remote relationships—neighbors, employers, coworkers, and such. Psychically speaking, we appear far less concerned with them than we do with close family members or our own lives. But when we do have ESP experiences involving remote relationships, once again negative news dominates.

Marie, whose story "A Fire at the Pentagon" you will remember, exhibits the kind of wide-ranging psychic sensitivity that picks up on remote relationships, including fellow teachers and students at the school where she taught.

Teacher In Trouble

One night, she dreamed a certain teacher from school—a big six-foot tall man—literally fell on top of her. The very next day at school, the man had a stroke right in front of her. "I knew when it was happening what was going to happen. He was going to fall down on the floor so I had him sit down. It was just this strange feeling of déjà vu. I had just dreamed it all early that morning, and here it is 9:30 A.M., just a few hours later, and it's happening just like in the dream."

Marie worked as a resource special teacher at a public school for three years, teaching math and occasionally English to students who were either way behind or were gifted. She had left that job shortly before she called me for a consultation about her 9/11 Pentagon experience. She was not entirely unhappy about getting out of teaching. Her psychic sensitivity added to the normal stress of teaching adolescents. She didn't realize how much stress she was under until she finally left. The school had 160 to 180 students, from kindergarten to eighth grade, and Marie found herself continually picking up psi information about her students while walking down the halls, or in her dreams at night. According to Marie, what she picked up couldn't be explained as simply reading a situation from what she saw or heard. "It was mostly precognition. I knew when a kid was going to get beaten when he got home, or that his parents were going to get divorced. It was emotionally very difficult."

Mike, our Texas oilman, also occasionally picks up on dangers to persons outside his immediate circle.

Burned

"In 1994, while driving with my parents from Dallas back to Houston, I kept having a premonition that someone was going to burn his face very badly. Upon arriving in Houston, my wife told me she wanted me to barbecue, which worried me very much. As a precaution, I drove to the hardware store and bought a fire blanket, two fire extinguishers, and a large jar of Vaseline to keep next to the grill. My premonition definitely indicated it would be a severe burn to the face. While cooking, I allowed no one in the backyard with me. After eating, my mother fell and broke her hip. We rushed to the hospital. While we were there, a colleague of my wife rushed into the emergency room with her nephew. He had thrown gasoline onto their barbecue grill at a picnic and had burned his face off."

When we examine ESP involving remote relationships, we notice a special subset within this category—ESP between health providers, such as doctors and nurses, and their patients. Though most patients are not family or kin, an emotional bond often develops in these crisis situations that seems to spark ESP. Appropriately enough, the ESP message is sometimes delivered in the form of sympathetic pain, as in "A Blow to My Stomach." My friend Joanna works as a physician's assistant at a major university medical center in Virginia. Single and in her early thirties, she takes care of patients in the oncology department where the following psychic experience occurred.

Collapsed Lung

"In the month of June I experienced a phenomenon that was novel to me in terms of its degree of physical impact on myself," she explained in her e-mail to me. "I was seeing patients in the oncology clinic and came out of a patient room to look at some scans. Suddenly, I noted a sharp pain in the right upper quadrant of my chest. This occurred at two P.M. I continued to see my patients and finished the clinic. The pain in my chest continued until 5:30 P.M., when it suddenly abated, much to my relief. My boss and I then did the rounds on our patients. I came to find out that one of our patients had suffered a collapsed lung in the right upper quadrant at two P.M. A chest tube was subsequently placed in the patient to reinflate the lung at five P.M. Two days later I noted the same sudden onset of pain. I told myself over and over that this was not my pain. The chest pain lasted five minutes then disappeared. I found out later that my patient's lung had collapsed for a second time."

My mother once received a remarkable and touching precognitive dream report from a young student nurse assigned to a pediatrics ward. This time, a precognitive dream was involved. During her pediatric training, the student nurse I will call Jenny was assigned to a patient, a little boy six years of age. He was in for an exploratory operation for a stomach ailment. Upon opening him up, the surgeons found a rapidly-growing cancer, and he was sent back to the room with limited time to live. His parents were inconsolable and stayed with him day and night, filling the room with toys and food and anything that might make him happy. The student nurse could not help feeling for the child. One day while Jenny was off duty, his parents suddenly decided to take him to a hospital in New York where they felt he could be cured. The nurse trainees worked in teams of two, sharing a twelve-hour shift. Not long after the boy was removed from the hospital, Jenny was off duty and trying to catch a few hours of badly needed sleep. This is how she described her experience.

Please Carry Me

"That night, I dreamed that when I returned to duty the phone announced I was to get a room with a certain number ready since a very ill person was to be admitted. In my dream, I got everything ready and the phone rang again. I was told to go down and admit the patient. When I went to the front entrance, there was my six-year-old patient in a pitiful condition. He had on a pink-and-blue bathrobe and cap and insisted that I carry him to his room. He was so near death I didn't want to carry him, but I did so. Everyone was sad and emotional since his condition was so grave. In my dream I knew he would pass away before one P.M. the next day.

"The whole nightmare left me unnerved when I awoke; it was so vivid and frightening. I went back on the floor and told the entire dream to the head nurse. I described the color plaid in the boy's robe and cap, the style of headgear, the room number, everything in detail, even the hour of his death. But we both thought it farfetched, and we were sure the boy had passed away long before."

Other details of her dream seemed improbable to Jenny. Students never left the floor for that kind of assignment. All very ill patients were admitted by night emergency or ambulance orderlies. Also, seriously ill patients never came through the front door of the hospital. Further, Jenny had never been asked to carry any child of that age and had never seen a plaid cap like the one in the dream.

"A few minutes after the nurse left me, the phone rang. When I answered it, I knew what was going to happen. The night supervisor asked me to get the room ready for a very ill patient who would be admitted by ambulance any minute, though she didn't know who it was. I told her who it would be—and the whole story. Even when I described the robe and my meeting them myself at the front entrance, she did not believe it. She said the patient would be admitted as usual through the emergency entrance, by the usual nurse or herself, and that I was allowing an ordinary dream to run away with me.

"About ten minutes later, the telephone operator called and said I would have to leave the floor and come immediately, as a very ill patient had just arrived at the front door. It turned out the night emergency person and the supervisor were both involved in a sudden emergency operation and were unavailable at the time the child was brought in and that was the reason the operator called the floor for me to admit him. The boy's parents had arrived from New York, and an ambulance had been sent out for them, but relatives thought they could bring him to the hospital faster than an ambulance could.

"I went down, and there it was, just as in my dream. The parents and relatives crying, the child in a terribly pitiful condition. He was glad to see me and put out his arms for me to take him. I did and carried him up to his room. By that time, I was so unnerved I frightened myself. I couldn't understand it, nor could anyone else. They all looked at me as if I were weird. The supervisor could not explain it. When the day shift came on, I told them he would pass away before one P.M. the next day, even before he was examined by a doctor. That turned out to be true. He fell into a deep sleep when he got to our hospital. When the doctor arrived, the parents would not allow him to disturb the child. He passed away without having the doctor thoroughly examine him."

ESP ABOUT STRANGERS

Like a ripple from a pebble thrown in a pond, we have been traveling outward from our emotional immediate circle and self to remote relationships and finally we arrive at ESP dealing with strangers.

We report the fewest realistic ESP experiences involving strangers, people with whom we have minimal or no emotional bonds. They represent only 13 percent of the 2,878 realistic ESP experiences we analyzed. The natural question arises—why would we have ESP about strangers at all?

When we examined these reports more carefully, some possible explanations emerged. Some of these strangers were public figures and celebrities. Although we may not share a deep emotional bond with an entertainer or politician the way we do with our family or close friends, we do "know" them to some degree through TV and newspaper stories and often take an interest in their careers and lives. In other instances, the stranger featured in the ESP experience may not be famous, but the ESP experiencer has heard of the individual. In yet other cases, the stranger turned out to be a friend of a friend or was somehow connected through a colleague at work. It appears, then, that at least some of the "strangers" who intrude into our extrasensory perception are in fact not fully strangers.

In the following experience, the emotional connection between the ESP experiencer and the stranger was a bedside photograph. The case is unusual, because it is one of the few spontaneous ESP experiences in our files involving "retrocognition"—the ability to see the past, as opposed to precognition, which is the ability to see the future.

The Stranger In The Photograph

One summer, a young teacher took her class on an overnight outing to the seashore. She was assigned to stay in the home of a doctor and his wife. Both were strangers to her, and she had never been in the town before. As she recalled, "When I was preparing to go to bed, I noticed on the bedside table a small photograph of a beautiful young girl. I studied it for a moment, because I was impressed with an unusual spiritual quality in the face. I soon fell asleep, and it was early morning when I had this dream, or vision.

"In my dream, I saw a train bearing down straight toward me. I heard the grinding of the brakes as it came to a full stop before it reached me. People came running, and I stood beside the engine looking down at a young man whose lower body was pinned beneath the locomotive. I became very agitated, and tried to tell people that we had to hurry and get an ambulance. Then I became aware that there was someone else hurt on the other side of the train. I just seemed to 'know' it. I shook people's arms and tried to tell them, but no one noticed me. I was excitedly doing this when I was awakened from my dream by the doctor's wife knocking at my door."

Now wide awake, the woman feared that the dream concerned someone in her own family. Still agitated and thinking she needed to call home as soon as possible, she started to tell the doctor's wife about her upsetting dream, which she couldn't shake off. "I told her I had just seen a terrible accident, a young man killed, and how very real it seemed—not like an ordinary dream. She became very serious and said, 'You've just described the accident in which my daughter and her boyfriend were killed near here. That's her photograph next to your bed. They found him first and didn't know anyone else was killed until they found my daughter's body later on the other side of the tracks.' "

Even when absolutely no emotional connection at all can be identified, we still sometimes connect psychically. Perhaps the spiritual belief that we humans are all linked together at some fundamental level has a basis in reality.

Don't Put Out The Rose Bushes

A woman in Tennessee had a dream one night, which she remembered the next day because it "kept pressing in upon me so I could hardly go on with my work. It was about a definite person, but not anyone I knew. It bothered me until I finally went to the phone book and found there was such a person listed. As I remembered it, I thought the name was S.N. Byrd.

"So then I called the number. His wife answered. I took a few minutes explaining to her how silly I felt telling her about a dream I had just had the night before about her husband. She asked if I knew him, and I told her that I not only didn't know him but had never heard of him. Then I told her that, according to my dream, he had a very bad heart.

'Yes,' she replied, 'but how did you know about it?' I explained that I really didn't know. I just dreamed it. Then I told her I had dreamed about some rose bushes that he had bought and had been trying to get a fellow to come and plant for him, but the man kept putting him off and would not come and put the bushes in the ground for him. Also, before he left for work that morning, he had remarked that if the fellow didn't show up by that afternoon he was going to put the bushes out by himself.

"She said, 'Yes, he did say that just before he left to go to work this morning.' So I told her that she should keep him from doing it, because just as sure as he did, with his heart in the shape it was, that he would drop dead before he finished planting them. She had me describe her husband to her as I saw him in my dream, and I did, and she said, 'Well, that's him to a T, and you can rest assured that he will not put out those rose bushes when he comes home like he threatened to do just before he left.' Then she thanked me very profusely for the warning."

When the child in the next story passed from this world, more than parents and friends felt his leaving. A complete stranger took notice as well.

Death In The Pool

"I was giving my son a birthday party," she wrote to us. "The party was in full swing, so to speak, when my eyes were drawn to a clock on the wall. I noticed it was 2:20 P.M. Suddenly a perfect scene appeared before my eyes. A small child in a stroller was sinking to the bottom of a swimming pool. The stroller sank completely. Because of the clarity of the water, I could see the child, not moving, still in the stroller as if asleep. I was frightened, but since I didn't recognize the child or the pool, I eventually forgot it.

"Later that evening, my uncle, who is a fire chief, invited us to the fire station to see the new fire equipment and truck. When I arrived at the station, one of the firemen said they had already used the stretcher that afternoon. He said a child had drowned in a pool in a stroller. It rolled over the edge, just as I had seen it in my imagination. When I asked him what time this happened, he said the station was called at 2:30 P.M."

The sixteenth-century English poet John Donne, famous for his line "No man is an island, entire of itself," wrote that "any man's death diminishes me, because I am involved in mankind." ESP experiences such as this suggest that the bond may be more than mere poetry.

4

A MOTHER'S ESP

As a young woman, I was never very sentimental about the prospect of becoming a parent, so it was an incredible surprise when I held my firstborn in my arms many years ago. It was love at first sight. This experience is duplicated throughout the world and throughout all cultures. When it works right, there is nothing stronger than the mother-child emotional bond that begins with nine months of pregnancy and is often supplemented by the breast-feeding experience.

Scientists are now confirming some biological underpinning to this common feeling, finding that the brains of young mothers light up when they look at their babies in the same way as the brains of people who look at images of their lovers.

My friend Dr. Larry Dossey, MD, the father of mind-body medicine, suspects infancy is the cradle of telepathy. Psi-conducive states we experience as adults often involve the same dissolution of boundaries, the merging with the Other, mirrored in the deeply symbiotic relationship between a mother and her child.

During this early stage, it is as if no boundaries exist between mother and infant. As psychiatrist and parapsychologist Dr. Jan Ehrenwald, MD, once said, "The baby is the direct extension of the mother's body image." Communication between mother and infant seems truly extraordinary during these early months. This communication is not limited to normal sensory channels. Both research and anecdotal evidence suggest extrasensory channels open up as well. This telepathy between mother and child, far from being a mere psychological curiosity without apparent goal or purpose, is well suited to fill whatever communication gap exists between the two, says Ehrenwald.

We do hear from many mothers who report knowing when their infants are in distress, such as the following e-mail from a woman I will call Wendy.

Catch Me, Momma

Wendy wrote from Jacksonville, North Carolina, after seeing me interviewed on the local ABC-TV station there. She felt very connected to her children and believed she could often sense when something hurtful was going to happen to one of them. One such instance occurred in New Mexico in September 2002, while Wendy and her family were visiting her husband's parents. Wendy reports, "My husband, my three-year-old daughter, my six-month-old son, and I were in a hotel with two queen beds. My daughter was in one and my husband and I in the other. At about 2:45 in the morning, I awoke with an urgent sensation to go to my daughter's bed. Just as I got there, she rolled off the bed right into my arms, just missing hitting her head on the end table next to the bed. I have had many instances of mentally 'seeing' a dangerous occurrence with one of my children. I am not sure if this could be classified as ESP, but it is a curious connection I feel I have with my little ones."

Wendy certainly seemed tuned into her daughter's imminent danger, although some subliminal sensory clues could also be involved in this instance. I suggested that she keep a journal of these "curious connections." The evidence suggests such events are fairly frequent, possibly even everyday occurrences, for some mothers.

Our Rhine files contain many stories of mothers psychically sensing serious danger to their children and then taking action to avoid those foreseen threats. The following case is illustrative.

Choking Baby

A young mother had a new baby just a few weeks old, and was caring for her other little child as well. One morning, with the baby sleeping in the bedroom and the three-year-old playing in the living room, she was working in the kitchen. Suddenly, she "just knew" the infant was choking on something the older child had put into its mouth. There had been no sound, nothing to suggest it, but she rushed in to find the baby looking normal, though waving its hands a little. She snatched the infant up anyway, held her upside down and with her finger dislodged a round piece of candy from her throat. The older child had wanted to be good to her baby sister and had given her the candy.

Here is another case where the mother "just knew" and insisted on taking action at some risk of alienating her husband and causing public embarrassment.

Get Off The Boat

"My husband and I were on an excursion boat. We had saved and planned for the ride, and the gangplank was already up when I got 'butterflies.' Our two-month-old daughter was with us. I told my husband I was getting off the boat. He thought I was crazy. I said he could stay, but I had to get off, and I asked the men to put the gangplank down."

After they got off, the husband was so mad at his wife he refused to speak to her on the way home. The woman's intuition proved to be precognitive.

"The next news bulletin we heard said that there was a collision, and a freighter had hit the excursion boat we had been on. Within fifteen minutes the excursion boat sunk, though all aboard were rescued."

This mother was so sure that she was compelled to act. She herself had no explanation, no good sense reason, just an urgent need to act. Only later was she able to make sense of it.

Such sudden psychic intuitions or impressions make up about a third of the ESP experiences reported overall. They are very often accompanied by a strong feeling of certainty or conviction that it is a true message. There is more intense conviction associated with these sudden hunches, in fact, than for the other forms of ESP. This was true for the following mother, who absolutely knew something bad was happening at home but couldn't get back in time. Fortunately, someone else was there to stop the tragedy from occurring.

Little Sheriff

"One day, I took a trip to a city about fifty miles distant. I was about twenty miles from home on my return trip when I had a sudden premonition that something awful was happening at home to my small children. I started praying for their safety. When I arrived home, I was trembling. The babysitter met me at the door, ashen with fright. She said that about a half hour earlier she had heard one of the little boys say, 'No, I am the sheriff and I am going to shoot you. Stand still.' He had his father's gun and was trying to pull the trigger. It was fully loaded."

In the last decade, parapsychologists have begun to document in the laboratory a similar type of precognitive bodily reaction exhibited by research participants in advance of an unpleasant stimulus. But even the strongest measured reactions pale in comparison with the reactions and accompanying level of conviction felt by mothers' real-life ESP experiences.

"Where's Ruth!"

A woman had to make a quick trip into town one morning and decided to leave her six-year-old daughter Ruth with a babysitter. She started out, drove downtown, but just as she got to the store she suddenly knew she had to go back home immediately. She sensed her daughter was in great danger. "Where's Ruth?" she shouted to the babysitter as the car squealed into the driveway. "Oh, she's playing with Ann," the startled babysitter replied. Ann was Ruth's little six-year-old friend and neighbor. The mother rushed to Ann's house. Again, "Where's Ruth!" "I thought they were playing at your house," replied the stunned mother. Without thinking, almost as if she were on automatic pilot, Ruth's mom drove immediately down the street, over a railroad crossing, stopped, jumped out of her car, ran through a gate, up a little hill and down to an old brick quarry, now filled with water. There at the edge of the water sat both children, taking off their shoes to go wading. The water was much too deep, the sides of the quarry too steep for them to crawl out of once they were in. She was just in time. "I hate to think of what would have happened if I had arrived a few minutes later," the mother wrote.

Neither child had ever been to the pond before. Ruth's mother has no explanation of why she felt compelled to rush there instead of any number of other places in the neighborhood. Something more than reason was at work. "It was not so much a thought as an impelling message that drove me home and drove me to the pond immediately after." She never questioned it or asked herself how she could know. She simply believed it and acted on it. This is how psychic intuitions work. This certainty is what makes them different from ordinary hunches or run-of-the-mill intuitions. Psychic intuitions nearly always send us running, to the right place, leaving reason and doubt behind. Four out of five (83 percent) psychic intuitions are accompanied by a strong sense of conviction that something is wrong and must be addressed immediately. This is considerably higher than any other form of ESP awareness.

Occasionally, the mother is not instantly consumed by emotional panic. Instead, the mother takes action automatically, without really thinking about it. The psychic warning remains just below consciousness but still proves effective.

Gun Under The pillow

A young couple in Texas, visiting the home of an aunt, were playing cards one evening, their three-year-old son asleep in an adjoining bedroom. Or so they thought. The wife quite suddenly got up and left the card table.

"I didn't even know I was doing it," the puzzled wife explained. She went into the bedroom where she found her child sitting up in bed playing with a loaded handgun that her aunt had forgotten to remove from under her pillow.

Sudden psychic intuitions, while very common, are only one of the forms of ESP to deliver psychic warnings to attentive mothers. Mothers report precognitive dreams of danger involving their children as well.

Drowning In A Bathtub

"I had a dream in which I was bathing the children, and I left the bathroom a minute to go to the kitchen. While in the kitchen, I decided I might just as well do the breakfast dishes while the children played a few minutes in the tub. In my dream, when I got back to the bathroom I was horror-struck to find my son Brad lying underwater at the bottom of the tub. I grabbed him. He was unconscious and his fingertips and lips were blue. I put him across my lap with his head down and started working feverishly over him. At that point, the dream faded.

"The next day I awoke and had no recollection of the dream. I went about my chores. At lunchtime, I bathed the babies. Before taking them from the tub, I went into the kitchen for the towels and did a thing I had never done before—I started tidying up. As I did, a feeling came over me that I had lived this moment before. It was a strange feeling. As I tried to analyze it, the memory of the dream came back. I flew into the bathroom and found Brad exactly as I feared I might. He was lying absolutely still under the water. I had him out in a flash. Even though I was filled with terror, I noted the blueness of his lips and fingers. I followed the same procedure in the dream and brought him around. His cry that morning was one of the most thrilling sounds I ever heard."

Though it seems surprising that these frightening dreams can be forgotten, in fact we all forget most of our dreams including the bad ones on a daily basis. Think back and you realize that growing up you probably got lots of training or experience in learning to ignore bad dreams. Who has not heard from a parent in the middle of the night, "It was only a bad dream, now go back to sleep." The precognitive dream is rare among dreams even for the best psychics, so it is no wonder that they are often dismissed and forgotten, particularly when they have no special marker denoting them as an ESP dream. It is the fortunate person who remembers just in time, as this mother did.

Falling From A Windowsill

"In my dream," she wrote, "I heard a scream and turned around and saw my son, then two years old, falling through the window. I even heard the siren of the ambulances driving up in front of the house. When I awoke from my dream, I immediately checked the baby and then the windows. Everything was okay. A couple of days later, I put his mattress in the window for airing. The window was pulled tightly down on it. I was busy in the next room when suddenly I remembered my dream and ran into his room. He had somehow managed to push up the window and had climbed up on the windowsill. I grabbed him the moment he was going to fall. The mattress was already down on the street."

Again and again the same type of experience is repeated, to the point that they begin to all sound alike. The main difference lies in how the mother receives the psychic warning, with scary precognitive dreams and sudden, panic-inducing psychic intuitions most frequently reported. Foreseen events typically take place quite soon, within a few days. Less frequently, mothers report foreseeing danger to their children months or years in advance.

Four Years Into The Future

A woman in Iowa was in the hospital following the birth of her second child, a little girl who had been named Nancy. Her first child, Dennis, was a year older. One night the mother had a nightmare, and was awakened by the night nurse who heard her screaming. In the dream, she had seen Dennis with a knife accidentally hurt a little girl with long golden curls. She thought the little girl was her newborn baby Nancy. Although the injury was not entirely clear, she knew it was a facial cut of some sort. She could see the blood and the golden curls.

Nancy grew to have golden curls. One day when she was four, she ran out of the house and up behind her brother, who had been cutting grass with a small knife. He turned suddenly and accidentally struck her with it in the eye. Her mother saw again the blood and the golden curls of her nightmare four years before.

In one unusual case from our files, a mother in England also received her psychic warning several years before the foreseen event actually occurred.

Asphyxiation

The mother saw in her mind a vision of her ten-year-old son Herbert, dead in the bathtub. It haunted her so much that, for a while, she made a special point of quietly standing outside the door every time her son was in the bathroom, listening to make sure that nothing was wrong. She never shared her worry with Herbert, but did confide it to her other son, Peter. Two years later, Herbert went away to school and she forgot about her vision until he came home for the holidays. One evening during this visit, she heard him singing and whistling in the bathtub. The frightening vision suddenly came back to her. She was all dressed up to go out but just couldn't leave because of her worry. After a while, she heard the water running but no longer heard him singing. So she opened the door and there he lay, exactly as she had seen him two years before in her precognitive vision. English homes often have gas hot water heaters. The pilot light had blown out on the heater, and the bathroom window was closed. He had apparently been overcome by the fumes. She immediately opened the windows and called the doctor, who revived him. If she hadn't trusted her vision and stayed behind, her son would have undoubtedly died.

Precognitive warnings that extend far into the future have obvious advantages over sudden psychic intuitions that involve events already underway. In the previous case, the mother's precognitive awareness fortunately made a strong enough impression to embed the vision in her subconscious from which it rose to consciousness again when the scenario started playing out. The result was a life saved.

Parental ESP does not seem to diminish as the child grows up. As most parents have discovered, once a parent, always a parent. The mother-child psychic connection may remain strong throughout life as children head off to college or the army, then perhaps on to marriage and a family of their own. Children, particularly adult daughters, often tell me that their mothers seem to keep up with them telepathically, sometimes on a daily basis, monitoring even very trivial matters. Even when children do not call or e-mail, mothers sometimes "just know" when something is wrong.

Accident On The Stairs

"In May, I was attending college in Washington, D.C. One morning I slipped and fell down a small flight of marble stairs, dislocating a vertebrae in my spine. Not wanting to worry my parents back home in New York City, I didn't notify them. That same evening, as I was upstairs in my dormitory, I received a long-distance call from my mother. She wanted to know what was wrong, how badly I was hurt, and if she should come to D.C. to take care of me! I played dumb and asked her what made her think I was hurt. She told me she had a dream the night before in which I had fallen down a ladder and hurt my back."

Even though the mother's precognitive dream about her daughter substituted a ladder for a marble stairs, the psychic message still delivered the critical information—your daughter has been hurt in an accident.

An especially poignant letter from my mother's collection came from another college girl whose mother continued to receive psychic intuitions about her even after she had left home for school. One day, the daughter phoned her mother to tell her she would not be returning home that weekend as agreed, but instead planned to stay at school and finish a class assignment that Saturday afternoon.

Date Rape

"Saturday evening, on my way back to the dorm," she wrote, "a man I'll call Bill asked me if I would go on a picnic the fraternity he belonged to was having the next day. It was at a lake some fifty miles away. I had dated Bill occasionally before, and said I would go. I didn't think any more about it until about ten o'clock the next morning when Mom phoned me. She was upset, I could tell, and asked me not to leave the dorm that day but to stay in my own room, saying she would explain when I came home the following weekend. I comforted her by saying I would, and promptly after hanging up the phone began gathering things I would need for the picnic, including my swimsuit. But I was still a little worried over the phone call, since my mother is not an excitable woman and it was not like her to worry about me.

"Bill arrived in his car about then, and we drove to the lake. We were the only couple to go in swimming that day, and toward sunset we drove back. The drive back led through two stretches of forest where there were no picnickers, and it was there that it happened. To make a long story short, I was raped. I was too shocked and ashamed to mention it to anybody, and to this day no one knows.

"The following weekend I went home, and as soon as we were alone my mom asked me if I had stayed in the dorm Sunday. Recalling her phone call, I assured her that I had, not wanting to relive the memory of that day. I asked her why she had made that request, and she laughed and said she just wanted to be sure I had studied. But after some persuasion, she told me the truth. She had had a dream Saturday night in which she saw me at the lake with a boy who fit Bill's description very well, and she told me about the rest of the dream, which was practically word for word what happened on the way back from the bath house. Mom said she knew it was silly, but that the dream had been so vivid that it had upset her. I successfully concealed my shock, assuring her that no such thing had happened.

"I am a very happily married now and have a son of my own, so I want my name to remain secret. But I hope this experience may be of some use to your research, since it is not easy for me to remember this incident."

Most parents psychologically disengage from their children's lives in a significant way when their children get married. The spouse becomes the primary protector and comforter, but the mother-child psychic bond never seems to disappear.

My Daughter Needs Me

A woman from Fairbanks, Alaska, was vacationing in California one year when suddenly she "just knew" she had to telephone her married daughter back in Anchorage, Alaska. As she explained, "It simply came to me that I must call her, although I hadn't been thinking of her particularly. As soon as I got to Santa Rosa, I telephoned her. She asked me how on earth I had known she needed to reach me. It turns out her husband had been seriously injured and, since I had been traveling, she didn't know where to reach me. I told her I had just known, that's all I could say." The woman believed that her daughter's great need and troubled thoughts "had come straight to me and, since I was receptive, I got the message."

The above woman's belief is not unreasonable, based on the reported experiences we find in our case collection. We most often hear of a special connectedness between mothers and the child who is the most needy, the sickliest, or the most dependent upon the mother. It is hard to imagine a more needy child than one contemplating suicide. Shortly after my mother started collecting spontaneous ESP cases, she received a letter from an Englishwoman living in South Africa

whose life—and the life of her young child—were both
saved decades earlier by her mother's psychic intervention.

Murder Suicide Stopped

In January 1918, the Englishwoman living in South Africa
watched at the bedside of her only son, a little boy of five
and a half, suddenly stricken and paralyzed with polio. It
was only the second night of his illness; nurses had not yet
been procured. It had been determined that the child had
meningitis, too, and the mother had been warned that, even
if he recovered, his brain might be affected. As she sat there,
she decided she could not let him live to be a paralyzed,
mentally retarded person—a likely scenario back in those
days before modern medicine really understood or could
treat such illnesses. She fetched a loaded pistol, having decided that when he fell asleep she would put a bullet through
his brain, and then one through her own. At midnight he
slept but something stopped her hand. She could not do it.
She put the gun away and told no one about it. A few days
later she received a frantic letter from her mother in England. There was no cheap, convenient international telephone service in those days. The upset mother pleaded with
her daughter to write back immediately. As the mother explained to her astonished daughter, back in England at midnight the night of the aborted murder/suicide, she had
suddenly woken up from a deep sleep and "just knew" her
daughter was in desperate trouble of some kind. She fell on
her knees and prayed that God would help her daughter. The
child lived and, though physically handicapped, his intellect
was unimpaired. At the time my mother received the letter,
he was happily married and had three children of his own.

The six thousand miles between the mother and daughter
in this intuitive ESP experience were treated as if they didn't
exist. Surprisingly, parapsychologists have discovered that
ESP experiences involving longer distances are actually reported more than ESP involving shorter distances. Possibly

people living closer together, with more frequent contacts and normal communication opportunities, are less likely to develop the strong sense of separation and subsequent need or desire to keep in touch for reasons of affection or worry that long distances engender. On the other hand, it may simply be that long-distance experiences are more spectacular, and hence more likely to be reported.

Psychic awareness can persist even when a mother and daughter break off their relationship and become estranged. A mother from New Jersey with a history of ESP experiences did not want anything more to do with her daughter, but a psychic message alerting her to her daughter in distress made it through anyway. And once again, distance posed no problem to ESP. The daughter told us their remarkable story.

Watching A Strangulation

"Five years ago I was being strangled. I won't go into the painful details, but I nearly died. At the time, I was living 1,400 miles away from my mother, estranged from her, hadn't contacted her in many weeks. In fact, she had told me she never wanted to see or hear from me again. Four months later, I finally returned home and was welcomed back.

"One day, in a confiding mood, she told me that she'd had a terrifying experience one morning about four months before. She was working at the kitchen table when suddenly she saw my face before her and it was hideous—swollen and purple with my eyes popping out. She was very upset, but the family convinced her it was just another of her 'imaginings.' Her vision had shown what actually happened to me and at the same time. But I never let on to her, because I wanted to keep her from further upset and probing."

It is not only daughters who fall under the watchful psychic eye of mothers. Fortunately for this boy in college at the

University of Southern California, sons are also targeted by a mother's ESP.

Appendicitis Attack

A southern Californian woman and her husband were all packed and ready to head off for a vacation to Oregon. The night before they were to leave, she was disturbed by horrible dreams involving her son and a lot of crying. When she woke up the next morning, her pillow was soaked with tears. She looked so miserable that her husband kidded her about not looking at all like a person heading off for a vacation. She replied, "I don't think I am, not today at least. Sonny is in trouble." Sonny, an exceptionally talented child, was sixteen years old and attending USC in Los Angeles. Her husband, she wrote us, "wanted to know all the answers and I couldn't give them." They did not leave, however, and that morning a phone call came from the university and the doctor at the hospital. Their son had collapsed in class and was rushed to the hospital for an emergency appendicitis. Being a minor, they needed the parents' consent for the operation. Had they left town as they had planned, the boy's operation might have been dangerously delayed while they tried to find the parents.

Even when moms become grandmothers, the psychic bonds can remain. In the following case, grandmother's psychic antennae actually reached *beyond* her daughter to protect her daughter's child.

Baby Smothering

A grandmother in California awoke one night from a very vivid and frightening dream. In it, she saw her baby grandson fighting, struggling, and smothering in his blankets. His movements were getting weaker and weaker. It was almost the end. She awoke. It was 3:45 A.M. The young folks lived across town. Should she call them?

As she said in her letter to my mother, "After all, it was only a dream. I thought, 'If I call and wake them, they'll think I'm crazy. But if I don't, and anything happens . . .' " So she phoned and got a surprised son-in-law on the line. "What on earth are you calling for at this hour?" he asked. "Go to your baby at once," she said. "He's smothering!" The son-in-law answered, "Yes, he was. We're up. We heard him."

Some of our most interesting cases suggest that a mother's own body may at times detect important ESP information about her child, suggesting a psychic connection not only on a mental level but on a biological level as well. We saw two of these types of experiences in the previous chapter ("A Blow to My Stomach" and "I Feel Your Pain"). Here is one involving a mother and child, one of almost three hundred telesomatic cases found in the collection of my friend Dr. Berthold Schwarz.

Two Burning Hands

A mother was writing a letter to her daughter, who was away in college. Suddenly her right hand started to burn so severely she couldn't hold the pen. Less than an hour later, she received a phone call from the college telling her that her daughter's right hand had been severely burned by acid in a laboratory accident at the very same time the mother had felt the burn.

Our Rhine files include a number of cases in which a mother reports suffering pseudolabor pains mimicking childbirth, complete with muscular contractions, at the exact same time her daughter is going through childbirth in a hospital miles away.

Shared Labor (I)

"The experience I will never forget happened between 8:30 and 9:00 P.M. on the night of April 29. I had been anxious about my youngest daughter. She was expecting her first child and was a little overdue. Just after eight P.M. I was taken ill suddenly with terrible pains. Anyone would have thought I was in hard labor. My stomach swelled and contracted every few minutes. My children wanted me to go to the doctor, but I told them not to worry, that we would probably hear in the morning that their sister's baby had arrived. The next morning we got news that her son had been born between 8:30 and 9:00 P.M. the night before. My daughter had had very little pain, even though nothing was given her to ease it. It seems I had the pain for her."

How early in life can this special mother-child psychic bond manifest itself? Can it show up before the baby is even born, during pregnancy? Everyone is familiar with stories of expectant mothers who "just know" the sex of their baby, though being right once or twice is not that impressive since the odds are fifty-fifty. Occasionally, we do find some reports where a true sixth sense is strongly suggested. My friend child psychologist and fellow parapsychologist Dr. Athena Drewes had two such experiences.

It's A Boy

"I had dreams that foretold my pregnancy with both my sons, as well as the sex of my second son," she told me. "While pregnant with my second son, I kept dreaming of a gift being wrapped in pink paper. However, it kept getting covered over in blue paper. No matter how hard I tried to have the paper remain pink, it kept getting covered over in blue, until in the dream I remember finally saying, 'Okay, so it will be a boy.' Sure enough, two weeks later results of testing showed we were to have a son."

Another precognitive experience helped a mother in Oklahoma cope with a period of great anxiety that was to result from a subsequent premature birth. The baby was due in January, but three months before the baby arrived, the mother had a strange dream.

Healthy Preemie

"In my dream, I was standing outside a nursery window with my husband, parents, and some friends," she wrote us. "We were looking inside an incubator at a very tiny, three-pound premature baby girl. She was ours, and although so very tiny, she was very bright-eyed and active and perfectly formed. We were all of the opinion that such a lively baby would come through all right in spite of being premature and so tiny. In my dream, the baby had lots of long, black hair and perfect fingers and toenails. A baby perfectly formed in miniature. She was waving her arms and kicking her feet as any normal, active baby does, and even turned over.

"The next morning, I told my odd dream to my husband and parents and another relative who was visiting us at that time. It was such a vivid dream. I'll never forget watching that tiny baby and noticing all the small details about her that only a mother would notice. My family and friends dismissed it as just one of the many odd dreams that pregnant women are supposed to have.

"However, just sixteen days later, we were all standing at that nursery window looking into an incubator at my tiny, two-pound, fifteen-ounce baby girl. A baby girl perfectly formed in miniature, and in life the exact duplicate of my dream with only one slight exception. Although she was quite active, as in my dream, it was some time before she was strong enough to turn over.

"If I hadn't told anyone of my dream before the birth, I'm sure they would have found it difficult to believe after the baby's birth. Also, just like in my dream, I heard so many of them make the remark that such a normal-acting and lively baby would come through just fine. And she has. In a short time, she was a fat, roly-poly, normal baby. I'm sure my dream helped me over those first anxious days after her birth."

These helpful experiences suggest a utilitarian value to ESP ability. Both are examples of how psychic information can be very calming and helpful in preparing us for the future.

The following expectant mother from Texas desperately needed some calming and hope. What is unusual is the way the mother received the ESP message—through an auditory hallucination, "a voice" that came to her in her deep emotional distress. The fetus was placenta previa, an obstetric complication that occurs in the second and third trimesters of pregnancy that can cause mortality to both the fetus and mother.

Fear Not

The woman was pregnant with her first child, and her pregnancy was plagued by dangerous hemorrhaging and trips to the hospital. She and her husband had visited his parents, and her husband's father had told her she should "go ahead and lose the baby because it will never be normal." This sent her home in tears. She was alone there, crying hard, when a deep, resonant male voice told her she had nothing to fear, that she would have a lovely, healthy child. "This was a voice I heard with my ears, not imagined," she explained, "but I was home alone, and no one had come close to the room." From then on, she was relieved and experienced a great feeling of inner peace. The baby was eventually born prematurely, weighing only three and a half pounds, but he was perfectly normal. When she wrote the Rhine Center to share her ESP experience, the boy was nine years old, normal, and healthy.

• • •

In the next case, the mother-child link seems to have begun in pregnancy and continued despite an unusually sad circumstance of separation. The experience of this woman from Ohio, whom I will call Elizabeth, was reported to my mother several decades ago when it was the custom to raise severely retarded and handicapped children in an institutional setting without parental involvement.

Death Of A Handicapped Child

"I am twenty-five, happily married, and have two small children," her letter began. She described herself as someone of average intelligence, outgoing, but emotionally very sensitive. "Because of this, I am very perceptive to the feelings and moods of other people—often to the point of embarrassing my friends and confusing my husband," she admits. Elizabeth's first and most startling ESP experience took place a few years before she wrote the letter.

"My husband and I were living in Youngstown, Ohio. I was pregnant with our second child, while our first child was in a home for mentally retarded children in Dayton, Ohio. He was ten months old, and I had seen him only twice—both times at the hospital where he was born. From that time, neither my husband nor I saw or heard of him. Although I often longed to see him or know how he was doing, I knew the course we had taken was best in the long run. During my pregnancy with him, I knew I would never bring him home, although the pregnancy appeared normal. I often said this to my husband, but he would laugh at my worry. Common sense told me he was right, but it was a terrible, deep concern to me. When our son was born, his illness was not diagnosed immediately. Even when the doctor told me I had a healthy baby boy, I knew a mistake had been made. A day later, when the truth was found, it came as no shock to me. My attitude puzzled my family since I'm not a pessimistic person by nature."

Elizabeth and her husband quickly conceived a second child to help forget the child they had to abandon. A year later, when she was pregnant with her second child, "there was no doubt in my mind that the child I was carrying would be normal—and I continually told my husband this. My second pregnancy was a very happy one. I didn't have a blue day and was happy as a lark." Then one night in March, in her sixth month of pregnancy, a terrible, wholly unexpected gloom suddenly descended on her. "We had been out to dinner, arrived home early, and were getting ready for bed when this heavy, unhappy feeling began filling my heart. I tried analyzing myself, like I normally do when something is bothering me, but try as I might, I couldn't find the answer. My heart was so heavy I had to fight to keep myself from crying. I had no control whatsoever over my emotions. That night was a mixture of tears, tossing, and turning. When the morning finally came, the horrible, heavy feeling was still with me. My husband was reluctant to leave me alone and made me promise to get out of the house and be with someone. I didn't have any desire to be with anyone I knew, so finally at two o'clock in the afternoon I dragged myself out to the grocery story to buy food we didn't need."

Then it happened. "I remember vividly standing beside the meat counter when all of a sudden a glorious feeling as though a great weight had been lifted from my shoulders— no, that's the wrong word—lifted from my heart. A clock was directly across from me, and I purposely looked at the time, because I wanted to tell my husband everything that had happened, since it was such a strange experience. It was exactly three P.M. That evening, I told my husband everything, down to the detail of the time. We had just finished eating when we received a phone call. It was from the home our first baby was in, in Dayton. They told us that our baby had been very sick the night before, and had passed away that afternoon at three P.M."

Elizabeth concluded her letter by assuring us that "Every word is true. My spelling, grammar, etc. may be wrong, but

I feel I have described the events and my feelings exactly as they happened." She impresses me as a particularly sensitive person with a remarkable ability to tune into important matters in her life with her ESP, in this case with the child she had to give up. Perhaps the separation from her child actually deepened her feeling of connection and led her to be even more attuned to this other dimension. If so, it supports occasional reports we have of trauma subsequently leading to heightened extrasensory awareness.

Although ESP is reported more often between people who are emotionally and biologically close, we still do not know to what extent the biological connection is necessary. Is there any difference in the ESP ability of parents to tune into the needs of their adopted as compared to biological children? There are not yet enough case reports or laboratory research on which to draw a firm conclusion, but we do find a few relevant cases in our Rhine files.

Go To The Telephone

After fifteen years of a childless marriage, a Texas woman was desperate to have a baby. While she was ironing, a wave of despair swept over her, and she said, "God, I must have a baby!" Then, "just as clearly as a bell," came a masculine voice saying, "Well, go to the telephone." She looked around; no one was there. The clock just then struck eleven A.M. She went to the phone as the voice ordered and automatically dialed the number of a doctor whom she knew but had not seen for about three years. When he answered, she asked spontaneously, "When are you going to get me a baby?" "I was just thinking of you," he replied. "I have your baby here in the hospital right now." Then he explained that the baby was hers, but she and her husband had to be approved by the woman who was responsible for the baby's placement. The subsequent interview with the biological mother was brief but somewhat unusual. The woman asked her, "What were you doing at eleven o'clock?" After relating the experience with the voice at the ironing board, the natural mother told her that she had been praying about the whole decision to give her child up for adoption, and at eleven o'clock she suddenly "felt complete peace" and knew it was settled.

Discovering your baby is finally available and ready for adoption must be tremendously exhilarating after you have waited for what seemed an eternity. But what if you are not prepared for the child's arrival? This Oklahoma woman waiting for her adopted baby's arrival got an extrasensory warning that allowed her to prepare the room just in time. Though she had no rational reason for her actions, she trusted her psychic intuition and acted.

Get The Bassinet Now

She and her husband, a childless couple, had been promised a baby for adoption. It was expected to be born about February 15. All of the preliminary arrangements had been made, but the baby bassinet they would need had been loaned to a friend in Tulsa, many miles away. On January 13, a full month ahead of time, and even though a blizzard was raging, the woman suddenly decided to leave her job and go get the bassinet. Her husband objected. The baby was not due for a month yet, so what was the great hurry? She listened to all he said, but simply declared she was going anyway. The car trip was dangerous and slow, but she got back home with the bassinet late on the night of January 14. Early the next morning, they were awakened by a telephone call. The baby had been born at 3:30 that morning. Their child was snug in her bassinet that night.

In the following unusual case, the ESP of this mother from Washington State extended to her adopted child while the little girl was apparently still in the biological mother's womb.

Shared Labor (II)

"Seven years ago, we signed up to adopt a daughter," she wrote us. "The doctor had assured me that the baby was expected in September. I was especially anticipating this event, since we had several heartbreaking failures in our earlier attempts to acquire a child. The night our 'gift' baby was born to her natural mother was a night of torture for me. I was unaware that the natural mother was in labor, but I assuredly knew something physical was occurring to me. I had severe abdominal pains that caused me to pace the floor all night. When my physician called at 5:45 A.M. to tell me the baby had been born, my exact words were, 'You didn't have to tell me—I was in labor!' I will always feel that I wanted the baby so much I had to help her get born."

We see little difference in the few case reports we have between a birth mother and an adoptive mother in terms of ESP about their child. Indeed, an adoptive mother might even be more emotionally tied to an adopted baby, given how desperately she desires a child.

The mother-child psychic bond impresses us as a strong one, but we all know that fathers have deep love that can be as strong as any mother's. Is there any evidence in the Rhine files of a father-child psychic bond?

Careful readers have probably already noticed that the large majority of ESP experiences we have presented in this book are from women. More than 83 percent of ESP experiences in the Rhine Research Center collection are sent to us by women. Women are typically less embarrassed than men to recognize and share their feelings and intuitions with others, and reports that suggest the paranormal are no exception. Still, fathers as well as mothers seem to know intuitively when their children are in danger, judging from ESP experiences we have received over the years at the Rhine Research Center.

The following case deals with a father's psychic dream about a dangerous illness that was masquerading as an innocent fever. Diphtheria is a scary, life-threatening, contagious disease that once infected about 150,000 people each year in the U.S., 10 percent of whom died. Now there are only a few cases per year in America or other developed countries because of a combination vaccine called "DPT." Back in the days before diphtheria immunization was common, my mother received a letter from a "Crocodile Dundee" settler living in a remote, isolated area of Australia who wanted to share a scary ESP experience involving his son's near death from diphtheria.

More Than A Fever

"One night, I found my wife sitting up with one of the twins in her lap, rocking him. He had a slight fever. We agreed that it was a touch of malaria. Malaria is not uncommon here, and we were always prepared to treat it, usually without having to call a doctor (the nearest one was twenty miles away). I was satisfied with our diagnosis and went to bed and to sleep.

"About daybreak or a little before, I had a dream that our family physician came in, examined the boy, and said he had diphtheria. I awoke from the dream, startled, and tiptoed into the room where my son and wife were. She was still awake; he was sleeping peacefully, breathing naturally, and his temperature was normal.

"I went back to my room, but not to sleep. The memory of that dream kept nagging me. I reasoned with myself that isolated as we were with no contacts between my children and other children, with no case of diphtheria anywhere within many miles reported, it was foolish of me to be disturbed because of the dream.

"After a while, I could stand it no longer, but still I did not want to confess the reason for my concern to my wife. I went back to the room and asked my wife if the boy had indicated any pain in his throat, which is common with diphtheria. No, he said he didn't hurt anywhere. Still, I wanted to look at his throat. She took him up, and shining a light down his throat we made a thorough examination and found a tiny white spot about the size of a pinhead (one of the symptoms of diphtheria). I phoned the doctor and asked him if it was possible, in view of our isolation, that the boy might have diphtheria. He said it sometimes happened that way, and since it was a long drive and the spot on one side of the throat was grounds for suspicion, he would bring along enough antitoxin for all five of our children.

"It was about three hours after the spot was discovered before the doctor arrived. By that time, my son had a fever again and the white spot had become a white patch and had spread to both sides of his throat. The doctor said it was diphtheria and injected antitoxin into him. My son was critically ill for two or three days. The doctor told me that a few hours later would have been too late for the treatment to have saved his life."

Here is an interesting report from a father who received psychic information about his son's injury during World War II.

Seeing His Son's Wounds

As was fairly typical of the men writing to our research lab back in the 1950s, this man was careful to note that he was a "sane, conservative businessman. I am president of a bank, owner of a large real estate and insurance business, and a graduate economist of the University of Pennsylvania." My mother understood why the writer had gone to such pains to describe himself that way; in our culture, men are supposed to be hard-headed, skeptical, cynical, unemotional, no-nonsense. Although times are changing, today it is still psychologically and culturally more difficult for the average man to admit to an ESP experience than it is for a woman. At the time he was writing this sixty years ago, during World War II, such an admission from a man was even more suspect. His ESP experience had so amazed him that this father had felt compelled to share it with my mother.

"It was during the invasion of France and Germany. I had a son who had just gone over from the States, and I knew he was in there fighting since I had received one brief message from him when he left England.

"In September, I went up to Canada on a fishing trip and while I was there I became very depressed, and I couldn't help but feel my son Bill was the root of it. I came home, still feeling depressed, and I talked it over with my wife, since I could never conceal any mood from her. I said frankly I felt Bill was in trouble.

"A few nights later, we received a telegram saying Bill was critically wounded. We were frantic and tried every means to obtain information as to his condition with absolutely no results. I brooded over it for days, trying to imagine what his wounds might be. One night, possibly a week later, as I sat at my desk a feeling came over me. I could almost visualize a wound on his head, behind the right ear, and some other wound that had to do with his arm. The feeling was so strong that I wrote down my thoughts on a sheet of paper and placed it on my desk. I might add, though it may sound unbelievable in light of the end of my story, that I seemed to feel the head injury had somehow affected his eyesight.

"Three or four months later, we received word Bill was in a receiving hospital in New York. We rushed to see him, and here is the unexplainable: Bill had two shell wounds in his head, not right behind the ear, but more on the back of the skull, but still toward the right ear. The optic nerve had been all but severed, and he had been blind and partially paralyzed for weeks but was regaining both his eyesight and the use of his limbs when I saw him. He also had a shell sliver that had entered his shoulder, passed down his right arm and came out just above the elbow. On our way home, I told my wife of the memo on my desk, and when we reached home I had her get it and read it to her amazement."

• • •

As a new generation of fathers become increasingly involved in the birth and raising of their kids, it will be interesting to see whether the number and quality of reported ESP experiences between fathers and their children increases as well.

Women report many more ESP experiences involving birth and pregnancy, but we also get reports of men having ESP about these same events. Here is one e-mailed to me last year by Brad in Oklahoma. Brad reports having ESP experiences for as long has he can remember.

Father Knows Best (I)

"Some time in late September 1993 my wife casually mentioned she had a headache. I informed her she was pregnant with twins. She laughed it off. We'd only had unprotected sex once in quite a while, and she brushed it off.

"As the weeks passed, I continued my matter-of-fact assertion that she was pregnant. A home pregnancy test was negative, but I held firm. Somehow, I just knew.

"In late November, a blood test confirmed I was right. I then said we would have twin boys. I also told her that our next child after the twin boys would also be a boy.

"The doctors disagreed, saying my wife's blood workup indicated one fetus, and they patted me on the back for my optimism. I persisted.

"In January of 1994 during the first ultrasound, there were two children visible. Later it was confirmed they were boys. Mike and John were born in April 1994. In 1998, our third son, Tom, was born. Right again!"

The following father from Maryland psychically found out about his daughter becoming pregnant before even she and her husband knew!

Father Knows Best (II)

"My oldest daughter and son-in-law had been married for about eighteen months and had been trying to have children. This had been a concern of mine, too, and I had been thinking about it more and more, especially around Christmas 2003. Not long after New Year's 2004, I had a very vivid colorful dream where I saw my daughter in a pregnant state and then heard a voice say that my daughter would become pregnant in February and deliver in October. When I heard the voice say the word 'pregnant,' I also saw it spelled out, along with 'October' spelled out all in color. I told my wife about the dream.

"About two weeks later, my daughter, who is an X-ray technician, was training a new X-ray technician in sonogram work. She used herself as the example and something unusual was caught on the sonogram that at first was thought to be a mistake by the new technician. But upon further examination by the radiologist, the ovary area looked abnormal. Further testing and gynecologist consultation revealed a growth on my daughter's right ovary.

"Surgery was eventually performed in February and, during surgery to remove the growth, it was also discovered that my daughter had endometriosis. The doctor cauterized all effected areas—this condition can prevent women from getting pregnant due to abnormal bleeding outside the uterus—and then did a test to see if my daughter's fallopian tubes were clear. When he did, he found out she was pregnant. Her due date is November 4. Although this date is a little past what my dream told me, she could still have the baby in October."

One of the oddest cases in our files involves a man getting a possibly psychic premonition of a coming child through an unusual form of sympathetic pain for a male—morning sickness!

Male Morning Sickness

After five years of marriage with no pregnancy, a Wisconsin woman, whom I will call Carolyn, had just about given up hope that she and her husband would ever have a family. Then one morning, her husband woke up nauseated at the sight or smell of breakfast. He rushed to the bathroom to vomit. The next morning, the same thing happened. They wondered if he could have an ulcer. Then they discovered that Carolyn was pregnant! Carolyn had no morning sickness, but her husband's continued up to her fourth month. It persisted even when he was miles away from his wife, and even though he got teased mercilessly by his male friends.

You cannot help but appreciate the sensitivity of this father-to-be for having this experience—and his courage for allowing it to be reported.

Putting it all together, we find that fathers and mothers, birth parents and adoptive parents alike appear capable of tapping into telepathic and precognitive abilities to care for their children. This parental ESP ability manifests itself in ways ranging from the trivial to dramatic life-saving incidents and can sometimes persist for the parent or child's lifetime.

Over the years, I have come to believe that every parent is probably employing some level of telepathy or precognition in subtle ways in his or her child-raising. Responding to the cries or needs of an infant is undoubtedly instinctive and may in fact have been favored by natural selection over millions of years of human evolutionary history. If so, the ESP component of this evolutionary advantageous concern and care for our children has been obscured in modern life by the higher level cortical functioning. Paying attention to this possible ESP bond can help a parent strengthen the connection between himself and his child, resulting in added safety for the child and an increased emotional richness in the parent-child relationship.

5

THE ESP OF CHILDREN

The world of childhood is naturally conducive to ESP. Fantasy, imagination, and openness to different ways of knowing are acceptable, and ESP is less likely to be censored. If a child has an ESP experience, he tends to take it at face value until an adult tells him otherwise. Parapsychologists suspect that ESP occurs more clearly and strongly in the early years of life, before cognitive and social learning intervene to generate doubt, distrust, and fear.

Young children may demonstrate ESP by blurting out in a matter-of-fact way their parents' private, unspoken thoughts, or by telling a parent something about the world around them that they could not or should not have known. My psychiatrist friend Dr. Berthold Schwarz chronicled more than five hundred such telepathic episodes that he and his wife noted with their two children in their early years. He found it natural, normal, and ultimately helpful to be tuned into this usually unrecognized aspect of parent-child communication.

My mother, Louisa Rhine, also kept this type of record, though on a smaller scale. She kept a journal of the odd coincidences or puzzling incidents that she noticed in our early family life. You may be having similar incidents in your family, but only if you make a deliberate attempt to write them down do you become alerted to their presence. When it happens repeatedly, you begin to wonder about their meaning. As I look back over my mother's journal, I can see that most of the ESP occurred between her and my two younger sisters Betsy and Rosie, but especially with Betsy. They seemed to be in touch with each other on a different, deeper level. Betsy often seemed to be able to read my mother's mind. Here's an example from my mother's journal.

"Where's My Whistle?"

"After supper this evening, I urged Betsy to hurry up and get into her pajamas. No other subject and no toy of any kind had been mentioned all day, for I was very busy having my book club and did not talk much to the little ones. When Betsy was undressing, I opened my small dresser drawer looking for a safety pin and noticed the little whistle Robbie bought Betsy for Christmas. It was under some ties in the drawer. I covered it up again thinking, 'Oh, there's Betsy's whistle. But I won't mention it to her. I don't want it being blown in the house.' Betsy was standing about a yard and a half behind me, undressing. She said just after my thought, 'Mother, where is my whistle that Robbie bought me?' "

For a long time, my mother understandably brushed off such incidents as mere coincidence. But in time, as the incidents slowly filled her journal, she began to take them more seriously, looking for patterns and clues. One of the first things she noticed was the ease and effortlessness with which she and her child communicated. Here is another entry.

Momma, You're Fat!

"This morning after breakfast, while clearing the table, I glanced at a piece of bread to eat with the cup of coffee I was drinking. But I thought, 'No, I won't take it. I'm getting too fat,' though I said nothing. Betsy was playing contentedly on the floor. Just then, she looked up as if I had spoken aloud and said, in her true, unflattering child voice, 'Momma, you're fatter now than you've ever been before.' And then she was back to her own pursuits again—no follow-up, just as there had been no introduction to her comment. For several reasons, I was really stirred up, but she was entirely oblivious. The remark was evidently based on an impression received so easily and naturally that she was entirely unaware of its extraneous source, and also of the fact that it had no rational introduction or relation to anything that went before or after."

Little incidents like this—nothing dramatic, but cumulatively quite noticeable—continued between them for years. I always believed their special bond existed because Betsy tended to be less resilient than the rest of us. When she was in preschool, she was hospitalized for pneumonia and in fact almost died. Betsy never married, but lived with my folks all her life—she ran a dog business out of an adjacent barn— and died at the age of sixty. I tended her during her final months, and she used to confide to me when she was ill how much she missed my mother. We all did, but it seemed especially true for her.

Like my mother, a woman in Pennsylvania also noted the number of times her small daughter seemed to catch her thought.

Arno Kraus

One day, a mother was thinking about the workman who had started a job of excavating and then had been called away without finishing it. Weeks had gone by. She was annoyed by the delay. "At dinner one night," she explained in her letter to us, "I was going to suggest to my husband that he phone the man. Then I thought, no, I won't mention it since my husband had other problems and I'd only add to them by having him worry about one more. Just then my daughter, about three, said 'Arno Kraus,' the name of the workman I was thinking of phoning. I don't remember her ever saying it again."

In analyzing his own family's episodes, Dr. Schwarz noted that nearly all of them involve telepathy—children picking up the thoughts of the parents. The content of the telepathy changed as the children grew older, from incidents relating to food in the early years to birthday presents and such as they moved into school age. He also noted that the telepathy incidents increased during times of good parent-child rapport and decreased for them during busy hectic times like the holidays.

Although Schwarz noted his children's telepathy related only to benign or trivial issues, sometimes children do pick up on serious disasters, as the youngster did in the following report sent in to my mother.

"Daddies Are Hurting"

A two-and-a-half-year-old boy had a father who flew airplanes. As a result, for him every pilot was a "Daddy." One day he was playing outside in the yard when he suddenly began to cry and rushed into the house. "Mommy, Mommy, a big airplane fell down," he wailed. "Daddies are hurting." His mother tried to calm him down, but just then news came over the radio that an airplane had crashed in the Pacific Ocean.

This little boy seemed to have a clairvoyant knowledge of a disaster happening outside the family circle, although it might have felt like something happening to his own daddy.

Instances like this may tell us something about the nature of ESP in the early cognitive stage when a child has not yet learned to make category distinctions between the airman who is his daddy and airmen who are not. Unfortunately, such experiences may often be missed or misinterpreted by unaware adults. The typical psychically gifted child looks, acts, and plays like any other child; the only difference is the child's more frequent ESP experiences, which tend to surprise the people around him.

We also have reports of ESP between young children, such as this one involving two siblings.

"Chris Wants You, Mommy"

A mother in Illinois had two small boys, one-and-a-half-year-old Chris and three-and-a-half-year-old Vic. One day she left Chris asleep at his grandmother's house a block and a half away. In about forty-five minutes, she explained, "Vic began to run to the window, looking down the street and calling frantically to me that Chris was crying. I was busy, and it was only 2:10 P.M. I didn't expect them back until 3:00 P.M. I told Vic he was mistaken and went on with my work. He was very persistent and burst into tears, crying 'Chris wants you, Mommy.' About five minutes later, my mother arrived with a tearful Chris, saying he had awakened crying at 2:10 and then ran all over the house sobbing, 'Mommy, Mommy.'"

We have reports in which children seem to have a psychic awareness of things happening to members of the extended family, in this case a clairvoyant experience about an aunt and uncle.

Wreck At A Railroad Crossing

A Wisconsin family was returning home from a trip when their four-year-old in the backseat suddenly and unexpectedly asked, "Did Aunt Myrtle and Uncle Charles have a wreck with a train?" The father asked in a disgusted tone, "What are you talking about?" The child answered, "I see'd they did." The next day, the child's parents received word that the aunt and uncle had stalled their car on a railroad crossing. They had gotten out of it before the train hit and demolished the car. As far as could be estimated, it happened at the time of the child's remark.

Precognitive experiences reported by children before they reach adolescence typically concern members of their own family or close relatives. Here is a dramatic precognitive ESP experience involving another four-year-old.

Death On A Duck Hunt

In a New Jersey home, a little boy named Craig woke up screaming. His father went to him and with difficulty succeeded in soothing and quieting him. Then the boy told his dream. "I dreamed you were in the water, Daddy. There was tall grass all around, and you were in the water. I called and called to you and you kept trying to come out of the water to me."

Of course, the parents promptly forgot the episode. The father and his brother had a duck-hunting trip planned, and they set out two days after Craig's dream. The two men sat in the duck blind in the tall weeds for most of the day. Before they were ready to come home, they shot two ducks that fell out in the water. They got into the boat to retrieve the ducks. Before long, a terrific wind came up, and they were forced a long way out. The water was very rough and the boat capsized. The brother was drowned and Craig's father thought he would never make it to shore. He said the thought of Craig's dream was before him constantly.

Less often, we find reports of children picking up warnings related to people outside their circle of family and relatives.

In the following incident, the child apparently had a sudden intuition about a neighbor's relative.

An Ambulance For Jim

A nine-year-old child was visiting a neighbor, Mrs. D, and was completely absorbed in activities there when suddenly an ambulance siren was heard out on the highway. The little girl suddenly became afraid and started crying. Mrs. D tried to comfort her, asking why she was so afraid. The little girl blurted out, "Mrs. D, that ambulance is going after Jim. He's been hurt bad."

Jim was the husband of Mrs. D's sister. The couple owned a store several miles down the highway, but they had never experienced any trouble at the store. The shocked Mrs. D could only pray the little girl was wrong. Unfortunately, it turned out that the ambulance had in fact been racing to the store. Jim had been shot in the back by a drug addict trying to rob the store. Jim died a few days later.

Some of the saddest episodes reported are about children who seem to foresee their own death, as happened to a boy from Massachusetts with an eerie precognitive dream.

"I Saw Myself In A Coffin"

"My wife's brother—about eleven years old at the time— came into the kitchen one Saturday morning early in February and said to his mother, 'Mom, I had a very strange dream. I was skating on the pond when the ice gave in and I fell into the pond. The dog tried to save me, but he was only in my way.

"'I then saw myself in a coffin and there were all my school friends and you were crying. I tried to raise my hand, but I couldn't. I tried to speak to you to tell you that I wasn't suffering anymore.'

The next day, Sunday, late in the afternoon, his dog came to the back door, barking persistently until he caught the mother's attention. The first thing his mother did was look for his skates, which weren't there. As the dog ran toward the pond, there was nothing left for her to do but to follow the dog. From the shore, they could see a large hole in the middle of the pond. The body was recovered the next morning. The funeral unfolded exactly as the boy had dreamed it.

Our records suggest that children have a higher percentage of visual and auditory hallucinations than adults do. If this is a real difference, it raises questions about how ESP operates: Is the hallucinatory form a more primitive form of ESP that fades with age? Or is it simply that some folks learn with age not to report "visions" or "voices" as openly and honestly as they might in their childhood out of fear of what others will think?

This report of a visual hallucination by an eight-year-old girl is a particularly good case, because the child's upset was noted by an accompanying adult at the time the vision manifested itself, helping to substantiate the report. It is also interesting, because it involves a fairly rare experience, an "apparition of the living," about which we will say more later. Finally, it shows a close, sister-brother psychic bonding that seemed unaffected by the significant physical distance separating them.

Brother By The Sandbox

A single mom, a nurse with two young children to support, had enrolled her eight-year-old girl in a Catholic boarding school and, some twenty miles distant, the older child, a boy, in another boarding school. One morning the mother was called by a nun at her girl's school, who told her that the child was quite upset, because she claimed her brother had come and stood beside the sandbox where she was playing alone. She said he had been trying to tease her by beckoning with his finger, and that he would not go away.

Of course the nun knew it was all imaginary, but the little girl was quite disturbed. The nun, thinking it was strange, decided to tell the mother about it. The mother immediately called the boy's school and found that he had just been brought back to school after suffering from a serious accident on a field trip. He had waded into a fast-moving river and had fallen into a thirty-foot-deep channel. He had gone down several times before he was rescued by a diver and given artificial respiration. They were just getting ready to call her.

Many people saw the touching 1999 movie *The Sixth Sense*, starring Bruce Willis as a child psychologist trying to help nine-year-old Cole Sear (Haley Joel Osment) who "sees dead people." Of course, like all movies, this was overdone. But it is not entirely Hollywood make-believe. Children do report psychically "seeing" the dead with some frequency. Often, these hallucinations or apparitions match the physical descriptions of deceased relatives within the family, or within the family's extended circle of friends and neighbors.

The Real Sixth Sense

In New York City, a bright three-year-old girl had a playmate Anne, who was seven. Anne was diabetic and died. The little three-year-old was told that Anne had gone away on a trip. She did not see her or go to the funeral.

Several days after the funeral, the mother told us, "I sent my daughter to get a broom for me from the hall closet, and she returned without it. I asked her why. She said Anne would not let her. I asked what she meant, and she said Anne was standing in the hall closet and would not let her by.

"When I was convinced she was not joking or telling a story, I asked what Anne had on. She said a pretty white

dress and veil, and that they could not go out because Anne
had no coat. Anne had been buried in her communion dress.

"I tried not to become upset, but the following day while I
was sitting in the living room, I heard my daughter talking to
someone in the hall and called to her. She again told me the
same story, that she had seen Anne. I went to the hall and
asked where. She pointed but said Anne was going out the
door. I took her to play at the neighbor's, and I told the neighbor of the incident. Together we prayed and sprinkled holy
water in the apartment, but I had a very uneasy, sorrowful feeling. Two days later, my daughter became ill and two weeks
from the day Anne died, my daughter died of pneumonia."

Unlike adults, very young children who see these apparitions of the dead normally take it in stride. They have no real
understanding of death or dying, and so they bring a matter-
of-factness to their observations, as Danny did in the following case.

The Bleeding Lady On The Bike

Four-year-old Danny was sitting in the family van with his
mother during a trip to the store. The traffic was stopped for
a period of time, which indicated some type of problem existed up ahead. While they were waiting, he suddenly said to
his mother, "Why does that lady have blood on her?"

His surprised mother quickly looked outside the window
and all around but could not see anyone. When she inquired
further, Danny replied that she was standing outside the window next to him, bleeding, with a bike helmet on, and "she
looked sad."

Soon after, traffic began to move again and they discovered an accident had occurred, though they did not know
what had happened. The next day, the mother learned from a
newspaper that a woman riding a bicycle had been hit and
killed by a car on that road about a half hour before they encountered the traffic. Danny had not known the woman.

• • •

As might be expected, visual hallucinations involving the dying or the dead are very memorable, even to younger experiencers. Experiencers do not forget them even over a lifetime.

Daddy's Dead

A woman in Maine recalls an experience when she was ten that, if not a dream, was hallucinatory. She knew her father had had an operation and was in the hospital, but as she told us, "I didn't know about death, since I had never had anyone die who was close to me. I was sent next door to stay overnight with my girlfriend. I woke up and at the foot of the bed was the most beautiful light I had ever seen. There was my father with his arms open to me, and as I watched, he was rising up. I called to my girlfriend, telling her that my father was dead. We got up and turned on the light. It was just ten after four in the morning. Soon my uncle came from the hospital to tell us my father had passed away and that he had called to me as he was dying. He passed away at exactly ten after four. I was a child who knew nothing of death, yet I knew he was gone."

When the New York City mother first heard her daughter speak about her dead friend Anne, the mother did not believe her at that time, but neither did she make a big fuss nor scold the child. Unfortunately, not all parents are so understanding of such childhood ESP experiences. Parents with strong religious beliefs associate seeing apparitions with the work of the devil and they may get angry or scared. Even nonreligious parents might view stories of seeing dead people, or claiming to have had premonitions of death, accidents, or catastrophes as psychologically unhealthy behavior and intervene to keep the child from telling such stories. The end result of this kind of parental response may be painful memories and emotional scars that are carried over into later life.

The Spanking

A twenty-five year-old woman in New York had a series of unusual experiences as a child. One of them, at least, had the earmarks of ESP. When she was eleven, she had been sent off to camp for the summer, knowing that her mother was very ill and would have an operation. One day, she won the swimming contest and had gone to bed that night very happy. When falling asleep, she thought she saw her mother lying unconscious in the street with her aunt standing beside her and calling her. The impression was so real that she cried until she finally fell asleep on the counselor's shoulder. When the message came next day that she must go home, she took it calmly. She already knew that her mother was dead, before the circumstances were confirmed, just as she had seen. Perhaps if this had been the girl's only unusual experience, it would have been easier for her. But others, some evidently mixed with and confused by a vivid imagination, kept occurring. Finally, at thirteen, she told her father about it. He gave her a spanking—a doubtful cure either for imaginative fantasy or ESP. It convinced her that experiences like hers were not normal and raised questions all the more worrisome, because she dared not discuss them, questions only answered when as an adult she learned about ESP.

Children are very sensitive to parental disapproval of such claims, even if it does not involve a spanking. Many years ago, a young girl named Penny from Watertown, New York, wrote my mother after reading an article about my mother's ESP research in *Reader's Digest*.

"My Mom Thinks I'm Goofy"

"I read your article and decided to write you about my experiences with ESP," Penny began. "I am thirteen, so maybe you would not want to hear mine. One summer a couple of years ago, I dreamed that my grandfather was dead. When I woke up, my mother was leaning over me and told me my grandfather died late that night. Then this winter, before New Year's, my grandmother died, and I had dreamed it the night before."

She included in her letter an auditory hallucination that had caused her considerable guilt. "I was eating lunch, and suddenly I thought of my little sister. I thought I heard her screaming. The scream was in my head. Nobody else heard it. I did not think of her again until I finished lunch, then I went home. There she stood crying, holding her hand. I went over and it was almost cut in half. I went and got the doctor just in time. She could have died from loss of blood. I was all upset, because I hadn't gone in search of her when I heard her scream (she was one city block away). It has haunted me so."

The young writer ended her letter with an apology. "My mother thinks I should not write to you about this, because she thinks I am goofy anyway. Throw it away if you want."

My mother wrote back to the young girl with some wonderful advice I still use myself when answering such letters. "You are not goofy," my mother responded, "and I don't think your mother thinks you are. Maybe she is trying to keep you from taking all this too seriously. And I would agree that it would be better if you didn't. Nevertheless, these experiences of yours sound like ESP, and so I think you should understand that it is a normal and widespread human ability. When it happens to you, it is just as if you had better eyesight or better hearing than other people. In cases like the one involving your little sister, I will bet you are glad you have got it. But I say again, don't let it upset you any more than if you suddenly got new glasses or a hearing aid, and were able to see or hear things that you missed before."

My mother subsequently went on to write a book specifically for children and teens called *PSI: What Is It?* to help make psychic experiences more understandable and less threatening for them. She included some factual material from their laboratory experiments to back up her information and advice.

My friend Marie ("A Fire at the Pentagon") was raised the second youngest of four kids in a strong Catholic family and attended church every week. Though she later drifted away from religion, as a little girl she enjoyed sitting in the pews looking at the beautiful stained-glass windows and listening to the music. It mentally put her in "another place." As she explains, "I think I was meditating at a young age. I just didn't realize it. I continued doing it all through my childhood." She had a number of troubling ESP experiences as a child that she found impossible to share with her parents.

Dead Grandfather And
Dead Jogger

When Marie was six years old, her grandfather died. When the family gathered at the big wake, Marie sensed his presence so strongly in the room that she tried to convince her mother he was not dead. It didn't go over very well with her mother. Another time a plane crashed behind an elementary school, and her parents were sitting at the kitchen table talking about it. Marie walked in. "I told them, 'That didn't just happen. That happened days ago. I saw it happen.' They didn't believe me, but I really had. Even today in my mind I can see this little plane go down behind the school. But they kept saying, 'No you couldn't have seen it. It just happened.'"

The next big ESP experience happened to Marie in middle school. She was running track during physical education class and another student named Tom was running track, too. He was way behind her, perhaps a half-track length, when she picked up that there was something wrong with this boy. She was within the last few jogs of completing her mile when she felt this, so she looked back and watched him run about a tenth of a mile before he just suddenly collapsed.

He had had a heart attack. "He was maybe twelve or thirteen years old," she recalls. "He died instantly. Evidently, he had a heart condition that nobody knew about, a genetic defect, so he died right there. And you know, I didn't tell anybody, I didn't talk about it. I just kind of internalized it. I felt sick for about three days."

Marie was only in her teens and just did not know how to deal with knowing something before it happened. "I really didn't have anybody to bounce it off, or give me labels or terms to help me understand it. Nowadays, kids see all kinds of psychic stuff on TV and in movies that give them some ideas, that offer some explanations for these things. I was totally clueless. I had no idea." Later she met people her own age who somehow had heard about ESP and my father J.B. Rhine's parapsychology research when they were in grade school. "I felt ripped off," she told me. "How did they know about it and I didn't? If I knew then what I know now, I would've felt much better. If only I'd had someone tell me about all this. I would've been able to come to terms with all these psychic experiences a whole lot better if I had had some labels, or a support group."

When you do not have a label to help identify your experience as normal, it's natural to begin to worry that it's abnormal. For a young person, it can turn a natural phenomenon like ESP into something fearful, something to be repressed. My friend and fellow psychologist Dr. Athena Drewes had a distressing ESP experience when she was ten years old that left her feeling both crazy and lonely for years.

Don't Tell Anyone!

"I was reading in bed the last few pages of the book *Ben Hur,* which had been made into a movie, and which we were going to see in two weekends. My mother told me to go to sleep and turn off the light. I protested, saying I just had a few more pages to read. She then had my oldest brother come in and turn off the light. I was furious as I fell asleep.

"That evening I dreamed that my family and I were in a car accident. In my dream I heard the crash and then saw my brother Nick sitting in a wheelchair at the hospital. But I 'knew' he was not hurt. As the dream continued, I saw my mother being wheeled in on a flat, raised-up stretcher on wheels. I had never seen a hospital gurney before. I 'knew' my mother had been hurt.

"I woke up in the morning and the dream had left a strong impression on me. It felt somehow different from other dreams I had had in the past, so it continued to stick in my mind.

"Two weekends later my family and I went to see the movie. On the way home it was raining, and my father was driving with my mother in the front seat. My two brothers and I were in the backseat. We got into a car accident just like in my dream. While we were in the hospital, the scenes I dreamed involving my brother Nick and my mother also occurred exactly as in my dream. My mother wound up having a broken hip and remained in the hospital in almost a full body cast for three months. I told my father while we were in the hospital that I had dreamed the exact scenes just two weeks before. My father turned to me and said emphatically, 'Don't ever tell anyone about that!' "

Athena was consumed with guilt over this experience. In her child's mind, she wondered if the anger she had felt toward her mother for making her turn off the light and go to sleep that night had somehow caused the accident to happen. Consequently, as she grew up she avoided directing her anger at anyone, fearing it might harm them. She also avoided telling people about this experience or about any of her subsequent precognitive and telepathic experiences. "I was afraid they would be frightened of me, think I was a witch, or think I was crazy. It felt very lonely," she told me.

Athena's experience eventually led her on a healthy quest to learn more about dreams and psychic phenomena. When she was twenty years old, she heard about research on ESP dreams being conducted at the Dream Laboratory at Maimonides Medical Center in New York City. She became a research assistant there, helping conduct telepathic dream experiments, having worked through her own early worries about the normality of telepathy by that time. Athena went on to become a clinical child psychologist and now counsels children troubled by ESP experiences in her role as consultant to the Parapsychology Foundation in New York.

She helps other parents and children talk about and understand their ESP experiences, and advises parents on how to manage the situation and respond effectively to their children. One of her clients, a woman named Connie, commented on how as a child she had had various psychic experiences and now her daughter, age three, was showing similar signs. "My family thought I was strange and even a bit crazy," she told Athena by way of explanation. "They were not truly supportive and even laughed at me. I know I am not a freak. And my psychic experiences have often been helpful to me in many ways. But I don't want my daughter to suffer what I went through, or feel desperate and confused because adults or her peers do not believe her and tease her."

Preteens and teens are especially vulnerable to criticism and ridicule since they desperately want and need to be accepted by their peer group. In an attempt to understand this group better, Dr. Drewes recently analyzed 157 ESP experiences originally sent to the Rhine Research Center by young people ten to eighteen years old. The average age of the writers was fourteen years old, and females outnumbered males by two to one. Of the total group, 76 percent were precognitive experiences, 14 percent were clairvoyant experiences, and only 10 percent were telepathic types of experience. These results were basically similar to surveys of experiences reported with adults.

In terms of content, children's and adolescents' ESP experiences did show some differences from adults. The ESP messages were more concerned with what we as adults would call trivial matters (54 percent) compared to adult

ESP messages that more often deal with accidents or other disasters. Psychic experiences reported most by children and adolescents often centered around such items as grades, clothes, relationships, dating, and school. Almost one in ten of the psychic experiences were about family pets! Sometimes, ESP brings positive or helpful information. That's what happened to Betsy A. who found herself struggling with a difficult language class at her prep school.

Prepared For A Pop Quiz

"I am a high school senior. Like every other student, I've had problem subjects. The one that most upset me was Latin. I eventually fell into a funk and began to give up. I prayed to God for help. After about two hours, a calm fell over me, and I went to sleep.

"In my dream I saw, as clear as day, my Latin teacher making out a pop quiz for the next day. I saw every question and her answers. In my dream I took the test the next day, and saw the mistakes I would make.

"When I entered Latin class the next morning, I nearly fainted when the teacher said we were going to have a pop quiz. I was even more amazed when the questions were the same ones I'd dreamed of. I remembered the correct answers and made my first 100. Every night thereafter, I had dreams about Latin. My grades went up, and I passed."

Friendship with peers rather than family becomes a major focus of teenagers' lives, and we find a corresponding shift in the focus of their psychic attention from family to peers. Almost half (47 percent) of teenagers' ESP experiences involved a friend or acquaintance while only 13 percent involved anyone in the immediate family. This is in marked contrast to studies analyzing letters received from adults. This fact, uncovered by Athena, is fascinating because it argues for ESP being just part of our normal psychological makeup since it mirrors psychological concerns typical for that developmental phase. Teenagers are more appropriately connected to peers, spending the greatest amounts of time with them, and at this age they are experiencing age-appropriate separation and individuation from parents. It would be normal at this stage for peers to replace family as the center of a young child's social and leisure activities and interests, since they are spending almost a third of their waking time and emotional investment in the company of friends.

Teenagers do sometimes receive ESP messages about their family. In the previous chapter, we heard about a mother ("Two Burning Hands") who experienced a severe burning sensation in her right hand at the same moment her daughter's right hand had been severely burned by acid in a laboratory accident at school. Here, the situation is reversed. The teenager feels the parent's pain.

Pain In The Arm

A high school girl in Ohio was writing a paper for English class when her right arm began to hurt. The pain finally became so bad she couldn't finish the paper and had to stop writing. She couldn't find any reason for the sudden onset of the excruciating pain. That evening, her father was late coming home from work. At 6:30 they got a phone call. That afternoon, her father's right arm had been caught in the gears of a crane he was operating. The arm had to be amputated.

My father started testing children for ESP in the late 1920s, beginning with initial pilot testing of children at a summer camp, before he realized that working with college students was quicker and more expeditious. My mother, Louisa Rhine, conducted the first ever published study on the subject of ESP in children. It involved testing children around the kitchen table at our house in 1934—a feat that still earns my admiration, because of her ability to manage so much bedlam and noise while also being a careful and cautious experimenter. In those days, before sophisticated experimental design and setup, it was still possible to do credible home studies, and probably the only way my busy mother could continue her work as a scientist. This study involved testing to see if different sizes or types of ESP target cards made a difference—either very large symbols, very small ones, or ones with multiple similar targets on each card. While my mother found considerable ESP ability among individual subjects—my older brother Robbie and I were among the best scorers—the type of card used did not appear to make any difference. As she noted in her report, children are less analytical than adults about such things as the makeup of the target. The scoring was better when two children were competing against each other in a situation as much like normal play as possible. Of the seventeen children, including three in our family and fourteen neighbors, the scoring was the highest among those aged from three to seven years of age, the younger ones having trouble with attention and the older ones seemingly put off about being involved with much younger kids. Her pioneering study appeared in the very first volume of the *Journal of Parapsychology*.

A second study in the same journal reported on highly successful ESP tests on low-IQ children in a classroom setting in Florida. ESP tests with children comprise only a small percentage of the overall parapsychology research, probably because it takes special skills to work with children. The teacher who conducted the Florida tests was a warm, child-oriented person who later worked as a staff member in the early Duke lab, and I expect her patient approach made the difference in the success of those children.

Dr. Drewes and my good friend Dr. Sally Ann Drucker tested children using M&M's as rewards, but their biggest contribution was a bibliographic book summarizing all the ESP research conducted on children up to 1991. They note that neither age, intelligence, nor developmental level appear to be a critical factor in enhancing or limiting psychic abilities or experiences. What seems more important in affecting the ESP scoring of children are personality differences—just as with adults—and how the child adapts to the test situation. Withdrawn children score significantly lower than outgoing children, while children who are "believers" in ESP achieve higher scores than nonbelievers.

Often one child in the family seems to have many more spontaneous ESP experiences than the others. I noted earlier that my sister Betsy had many more telepathic experiences with my mother than the rest of us. Here is a more dramatic example reported by a concerned mother.

Lone Star

In a California household some years ago, Joan, the youngest of several children, began to stand out from her three siblings, because she seemed to know things in a way her mother could not explain. For instance, she "knew" what Christmas gifts had been bought for her ("my little blue purse"). Her mother was sure the secret had not been given away, and the gifts not the expected ones.

Joan also began to tell her mother when certain relatives were coming to call, even though her mother thought their coming impossible.

Then her parents separated. Her father had deserted the family and her mother later obtained a divorce. Joan began to tell things about her father, even though in reality she scarcely knew him. In fact, one of the unexpected visitors she had predicted had been her father.

Later, her father was very ill. He was taken unconscious to the hospital and put on the critical list, the doctors thinking he would not make it. At home, Joan kept insisting her father would get well and, in spite of the opinions of experts, he did so. She told her mother correctly when her father's blood transfusions stopped, when he was first given food, and when he first walked to the window.

By this time Joan was nearly five, and her mother wrote for advice to the Rhine Research Center. We suggested that she test Joan's ability with some simple ESP card guesses, conducted at home and done as much like a game as possible. In the ESP card test where five correct guesses is the average expected by chance alone, Joan first guessed fifteen correct, then eleven, then twelve, and finally only four correct out of the twenty-five card pack. These were very high ESP scores, except for the final score, and her total score could scarcely be explained as only "chance." When she got the twelve, her mother noted that Joan was "nonchalantly sucking a lollipop." When she got the eleven, she was drawing with a stick in the dirt. When she got the score of four, she had not wanted to do the tests anymore.

Understandably, with a five-year-old the novelty of guessing cards soon wore off. And novelty, enthusiasm, and interest—from childhood to old age—appear to be necessary psychological conditions for positive scoring in laboratory ESP tests. In real-life ESP this is not an issue, because ESP happens infrequently and spontaneously. That is the difference between life and lab. But even under the less interesting and more formal card-testing experiment, Joan demonstrated that she had ESP.

Joan was unusual in that she was among the first children we found who exhibited spontaneous ESP but who could also demonstrate ESP ability using the card-calling method informally at home.

Early in my career as a parapsychologist, I witnessed an even more impressive demonstration of ESP card guessing by a child. A Minnesota teacher wrote to my father claiming that several of her students in a one-room schoolhouse were producing remarkable results on the ESP card tests that were regularly being used at the Duke lab. Sent up to investigate, I sat in the back of the classroom and observed a feat that I have personally never seen before or since. A seven-year-old girl stood by the blackboard with her back to us and, as if in a trance, slowly pointed to which one of the five symbols marked on the blackboard that she thought was correct, and then repeated that twenty-five times, while I recorded her guesses. Her teacher to whom she was very devoted sat several feet away and looked at each card before the child made her guess. We had prerecorded the cards, so I could follow her success. She missed the first card and then, one after another, she correctly pointed to twenty-four cards in a row! I never published the results, because this was a preliminary, warm-up test for a tighter experimental test we had planned with the teacher at a further distance from her pupil, but I have no doubt in my mind that I had witnessed a stunning display of telepathy in action.

Over the years, we have conducted many telepathy and clairvoyance tests between teachers and students of varying age groups that have yielded significant results. The close bond that develops between many teachers and their young pupils, as in the case above, appears to be an important factor. Students score higher on ESP tests administered by teachers they like as compared to others.

Recently I received an e-mail under the humorous name "Wonderful Me!" from a serious young boy obviously impressed by his psychic skills. Wonderful Me believed he knew about future danger in the U.S., and sought my advice on what to do.

Attack On The Space Needle?

"Hi! I'm ten years old (I know I'm very young), and I have premonitions as well as ESP. On the ESP cards, I got all twenty-five right one time. My best friend's mom and dad are in the military, and most of my family is in the military. Well, I had a premonition of something happening at the Space Needle in Seattle, and I've never been there or seen it before this premonition. I have no idea when, what, or how it's gonna happen, I just know something is going to happen. It could be good or bad, I still don't know. Please reply to me ASAP."

I honored him with a serious answer. "Dear Wonderful Me," I replied. "I don't think that ten years old is too young to write a letter to the Rhine Research Center. My mother

Louisa E. Rhine collected many ESP experiences from people your age. I would like to hear more details about your report that you guessed twenty-five cards correctly, as that would be most unusual if you didn't have any sensory cues. Did anyone else witness this happening or help you with the testing? Also, if you would like to describe one of the premonitions that you actually know the ending to, then I could comment about that as well. About your dream about the Space Needle, unfortunately there is no way of knowing in advance if that is true or not. And of course, as you know, we often have vivid dreams that never come true. Knowing how to tell the difference in advance is still one of the biggest questions scientists like me are working on. Thanks for writing us."

How should you respond if your child or teen does show psychic ability? Dr. Drewes and I have developed a number of suggestions for parents looking for tips on how to handle ESP exhibited by their child in a positive way.

First and foremost, you should listen to your child without judgment. Create an accepting atmosphere of understanding and caring, without ridicule, so that your child will not be afraid to speak of the experiences. Allow your child to talk freely about the experience. Try not to display your disbelief, fear, worry, or embarrassment to your child. Otherwise, she may withdraw or avoid talking to you about her experiences. Casual comments such as, "Oh, you picked up what I was thinking," "Isn't that interesting?", or "Tell me more about your dream and why you think it will come true," are the types of reinforcement and encouragement you can subtly provide. Do not force a child to explore or consciously develop psychic abilities if the child does not wish to do so.

Make sure you normalize the experience. Let your child know that similar experiences have happened to other children and adults, and there has been research conducted on such occurrences. Be matter of fact about the child's experience to avoid frightening her. Let your child know there are places to get answers to her questions about her abilities and experiences, and you can help her if she wants.

Do not force the child to "perform" his psychic abilities. Children's ESP experiences will often be spontaneous, and the child will most likely not be able to control such events at will. ESP usually occurs when no efforts are made to force it to happen. Being pushed to produce psychic events "on demand" may diminish the very thing parents wish to encourage. ESP is a tool and not an end in itself. A child should not be pressured to produce psychic events, or perform as a "superpsychic." Such approaches may actually cause abilities to decline, result in feelings of exploitation or an inflated sense of ability, or push the child to fraudulent tactics to keep the attention and positive regard of the adult. Set apart because of these talents, the child may begin to feel something is wrong or may feel bad or unloved. The child will focus on using these talents to gain attention rather than using them as potential tools for personal growth and development. The pressure will force the child to live up to another's expectations and desires and inevitably inhibit development of his own natural abilities. Do not focus on using psychic abilities for personal gain. These abilities are there for the child to use, grow with, and share.

Keep your child's psychic abilities in perspective. Let your child be a child, not treated as a little adult. Let your child develop all sides of herself, including psychic abilities. Help your child to understand that these abilities are just like any other talents or skills people have like being a gifted pianist, artist, actor, or athlete. If a child seems to be getting too involved with ESP or seems to believe that she has too much ability, as Wonderful Me did, playing an ESP card game is one good way to show the child that he or she is not always right. It helps normalize the ability.

Keep a journal of ESP experiences occurring in the family. Encourage the child or teen to record such events or dreams. Write them down as soon as possible after the event to keep information fresh and get as many details as possible. Over time patterns can be seen, and the ability to distinguish a regular dream from one that might have precognitive components develops. Journal writing also helps the child and family discover if dreams or impressions were accurate and how long it takes for them to "come true." Try to add documentation when events occur, but also record the times when predicted events did not occur or significant details were missed. Often psychic impressions come through during sleep, during car rides, or when daydreaming, when there is minimal interference and the conscious mind is not distracted by other things.

Keep communication open. If a child tells you about a psychic experience, accept what has happened, whether you feel it is coincidence or otherwise. If a child's statements are received negatively, your child may not approach you again about another experience. As a consequence, the child may try to suppress her psychic abilities, lose creativity, and possibly develop feelings of distrust and anger toward a parent.

Just remember that ESP is real, it is often exhibited by children, and it is something natural, not abnormal nor supernatural. By doing so, you'll be prepared as a parent to experience a new level of communication if your child manifests such a gift.

6

ESP AND ROMANCE

Remember when you were first in love? Wouldn't you have liked to know what was going on in your loved one's mind or heart? Or when your spouse is away on a trip, wouldn't you love to have an extrasensory connection to check on her well-being? We know from life and lab that ESP occurs most often between emotionally close people, so it is not surprising that we frequently find ESP bringing information about this intimate area of our lives.

We have reports of ESP happening at every stage of emotional attachments—during initial infatuation and dating; through the normal doubts, misunderstandings, quarrels, breakups, and makeups of courtship; and ultimately marriage and perhaps divorce. As the dramas unfold, there's a powerful need to know what's going on in the loved one's mind and heart, and both our sensory and extrasensory antennae can become unusually active.

A common characteristic of young girls is to fantasize about who their future husband will be, but it is less common to get a psychic preview. The following precognitive dream reported by an Indiana woman brought a realistic picture of her future husband, a man she did not yet know.

Future Husband

"When I was nineteen, I had a dream so real I related it to my mother the next morning. In my dream, I saw a specific young man—tall, fair, blue-eyed, with curly black hair. I told my mom he was the man I would marry, although I didn't know who he was or even where he lived."

Six months later, the girl was working in a furniture factory at a table next to a doorway that saw a lot of foot traffic in and out, though she never paid much attention to it. "As I worked, I faced the wall so I never saw who was coming down the hall in back of me. That morning, however, I had the strangest feeling of a force drawing me to something. I looked up just in time to see two men walking past me through the doorway. I could only see their backs vanishing into the other room. One was my boss, but I didn't know the other one.

"That evening, while setting the table for supper, I said, 'Mom, I saw my man today.' She asked if he had blue eyes and black curly hair. I told her I didn't know, since I only saw his back. But a few days later I saw his face. He looked just like the young man in my dream, except he had a cap on, and I couldn't see his hair. It later turned out to be black and curly." Three months later, she married the man of her dreams.

My friend Natalie, a single professional woman in her midfifties, has experienced a number of ESP incidents in her life, almost all involving folks to whom she has been emotionally close. I knew Natalie as a fellow clinical psychologist but was not aware of her interest in psychic phenomena, or that she had personally experienced ESP, until she appeared at the Rhine Research Center to attend some lectures. She later joined our Paranormal Experiences Group where I heard more of her psychic experiences. I was pleased with her intelligent and grounded insight about them. A bond of love is almost always present in Natalie's ESP experiences. "When I look back over my lifetime, I do absolutely feel that love helps make ESP possible," she says.

Happy Birthday

For some years, Natalie was very fond of a clinical psychologist friend. She feels her emotional attachment to him primed her to be psychically receptive to him. One night shortly after they met, Natalie awoke with a start, the thought in her head that it was his birthday that day. She had actually seen him on that very day, but there had been no mention of birthdays, and neither she nor anyone in his office knew what day his birthday was. Still, she says, "I woke up absolutely convinced of it." The next day, she went to the library to look up his biography and discovered the psychic information she received while asleep was true.

Psychic incidents continued to happen between them, although Natalie was usually the one who experienced them. This is not unusual. Women are more likely than men to report psychic awareness of troubles in the relationship or of danger to their spouse or partner. Most of Natalie's ESP occurred during the period when she felt most attached to him, but they continued even when the relationship began to cool.

I Missed You

One day, Natalie was upset with her friend and drove over to his office. His car was not there, and he was not at his office on a day and a time he ordinarily would have been. It made Natalie feel very little, and caused her to flash back to a traumatic childhood experience. Her family had moved to North Carolina when she was four, leaving behind in Ohio a black woman named Shaila whom Natalie loved very much and who took care of her as a child. Natalie apparently had not understood that Shaila was not coming with them to North Carolina. In the first few days at her new home, she rode her tricycle all over the neighborhood desperately trying to find Shaila until her brother finally explained the situation to her.

"As I was preparing to leave my psychologist friend a note at his office, the thought that went through my mind was, I will just get on my tricycle and try to go find him as I did for Shaila. Back in my car, the only way I can describe it is that I saw a map in my mind and followed it. I drove my 'tricycle-car' to a place I had never been before, a gym where he was working out. I did not know he went there—in fact, I didn't even know a gym existed there—and right there was his car. I put the note on the windshield and left.

"All the time this was happening, I felt I was in a dissociated state psychologically. My mind was intensely focused on the need to find him, in the same emotional, urgent way I had desperately wanted to find Shaila, a mother figure to me I had lost as a child. So I do absolutely feel that ESP is about love."

Natalie's ESP experience seems to have been triggered by her own personal dynamics, a fear of abandonment by someone she loved. This illustrates how ESP experiences often manifest themselves in ways and forms that reflect our own personal psychological makeup, reminding us that ESP is a normal part of human consciousness.

In one of the oddest love triangle experiences found in our ESP collection, two women vying for the affection of the same man met in a psychic dream.

"All Is Fair In Love And War"

Joy worked in a photo store. One day a young man named Gil came in, and they started talking. They had a cup of coffee together after work. He walked her home.

That night, she had a particularly vivid dream. In the

dream, she saw an old rundown, vine-covered house on a hill with a gate in front. A girl standing in front of the house told Joy to leave Gil alone. She said Gil was "her property." In the dream, Joy replied in a childlike, singsong, 'All is fair in love and war. If you can keep him, you can have him. I don't care.' She awoke covered with perspiration, convinced it was not just an ordinary dream. She decided it meant Gil was married, and that she'd better stay out of trouble and skip seeing him again.

The next time he phoned to go out, she turned him down. "No, you're married," she said. He said she was crazy, but she hung up on him. He kept phoning, with the same results. Finally she agreed to see him, and told him about her unusual dream. He looked stunned. Joy was not surprised that he didn't respond.

In the end, they got married. While on their honeymoon, three hundred miles from Joy's home, he said he wanted to show her something. He drove along a winding road and up a hill—and there was the vine-covered house she had seen in her dream. He then admitted that for six years he had been engaged to the girl who lived there, but the very night after he met Joy he called the other girl to break their engagement.

He knocked on the door of the house, and the parents of his former fiancée opened it. There on the wall was a picture of the same girl Joy had seen and fought with in her psychic dream. Their daughter had gone away to work after the engagement was broken.

Gil later explained to Joy that he did not want to tell her at the time how accurate her dream had been. He was afraid she would have cut him off if she knew of his earlier engagement. He had waited until they were married to tell her.

A woman named Megan e-mailed me to say that she had had many experiences that were "out of the ordinary," beginning when she was very young. She appeared to be sensitive to other people's emotions and thoughts. One of the most intense psychic experiences she recalled involved a boyfriend who was similarly gifted.

Spy In The Bedroom

"He was a veteran who had been in combat situations. He believed that he had developed his sensitivity as a means of defense. Anyway, he was able to pull me into his dreams and I drew him into mine. I would see him before he was actually in my presence, and when he did show up physically, he would be wearing what I had seen and was standing in the way I had seen him. I couldn't play card games with him because I knew what his cards were, and he mine. One of the weirdest experiences happened during a period of time when we hadn't seen each other for a few weeks. I was asleep. As I was dreaming, I saw the woman with whom he was having sex, but through his eyes. I knew I was seeing through his eyes even though I only saw her. It really was quite disconcerting. I didn't know this woman, had never met her, and yet there she was in the most vulnerable of situations in my dream. Several weeks later, I asked him an offhanded, casual question, using her name. He gasped in disbelief. He pulled me off to the side of the room and began drilling me about how I knew her name. He was suspicious and shaken. I told him to calm down. I then described the scene in my dream, what they were doing, what she looked like, the night that it happened, etc. He confirmed, rather reluctantly, all the details of my dream as having happened to him, exactly as I had seen them."

The next account describes a psychic warning of possible danger in a dating situation. It was sent in by an uncle in Mystic, Connecticut, who wanted to share the following experience about his niece. This story illustrates the powerful but nonspecific "gut feeling" that so often accompanies an ESP intuition. In this case, it may have saved a young girl's life.

Date From Hell

"A number of years ago when my niece Cynthia was living with her parents as a fifteen-year-old teenager, she hitchhiked a car ride home from a young man in his twenties. During the ride, they exchanged pleasantries and the man, named Michael, revealed that he was in the insurance business. Michael asked Cynthia for a dinner date and she accepted.

"When she told her parents an insurance man had asked her for a date, even though they didn't want her to go out with boys until age sixteen, they were delighted. Her mom had been anxious about the caliber of people that Cynthia chose to associate with. It was a typical concern that moms often have for teenage daughters, especially those that are as attractive and well-developed as Cynthia was at this age. Her mom had seen Cynthia dropped off before by long-haired, tough guys on motorcycles, known for late nights and drinking. Getting a date with a guy who wore a suit and tie was a very welcome sign.

"When Michael arrived for the date, he was met by Cynthia's mother and father and was escorted into the living room to wait for Cynthia to finish getting ready. The parents were very impressed with Michael and were trying their best to make a good impression on him.

"When Cynthia finally joined everyone, before she could utter a word, her eye caught Michael's eye. She immediately retreated to her bedroom. Her confused parents tried to smooth over the social infraction, writing it off to the immature behavior of a teenager.

"After an uncomfortable ten minutes, her dad went to find Cynthia in her bedroom and encourage her to speed it up, as it was starting to get embarrassing. Cynthia said she was not going anywhere with Michael. She told her father there was something wrong with Michael, and she would not be alone with him. Her father pleaded with her, pressuring her to fulfill her commitment to the date. He finally demanded that she come out and tell her date directly.

"Cynthia composed herself and approached Michael with extended hand. She told him frankly that, while he was probably a very nice guy, she was sorry but there was something about him that made her very uncomfortable, and she didn't want to go with him. Michael left and never returned.

"Cynthia, who never locked or even closed her bedroom door before, locked the door and windows that night. Several years later Michael was on the front page of all the Connecticut papers. He was Michael Ross, the serial killer who murdered four young women in eastern Connecticut before he was caught."

Though many relationships do not end in marriage, even when two people move on, there may remain enough emotional interest to serve as a conduit for an ESP message.

Old Flame

One Sunday morning in a small, Southern town, a young woman was smiling to herself while fixing breakfast. Her husband came in. "You look happy this morning," he noted.

"Yes," she replied, "I was thinking of a dream I had last night. I dreamed that an old boyfriend of mine came back. I haven't seen him in years and years. In the dream, it was about five o'clock and I was in the kitchen getting supper. You had just come home, and as you came in the doorbell rang. I asked you to go to the door. You opened it, and there he was."

You can probably guess what happened. That evening at five o'clock she was in the kitchen getting dinner ready. He husband had just come home, and as he came in the room, the doorbell rang. She asked him to answer it. He came back a few minutes later and announced, "Your old boyfriend is in the living room."

She didn't believe him. "You're just teasing me because of the dream," she laughed.

"Go see for yourself," he replied.

• • •

Concerns about infidelity are not uncommon among married couples. Perhaps because it is such an emotionally charged event, our files contain quite a few reports of women using their ESP to zone in on cheating husbands or check up on boyfriends. A young Ohio woman named Cheryl sent me an interesting e-mail.

The Other Woman

"When I was pregnant with my son," she wrote, "my then-husband traveled out of town. I had repeated dreams that he was with another woman. In the dreams, I followed him around with the baby in my arms and asked how he could do that to us. I did confront him about the dreams, but he accused me of being paranoid. However, a few years later I found proof of his adultery and divorced him."

This story was sent in by an unfaithful but chastened husband who confessed to a strange ESP experience he had when he was young.

"You're Awfully Quiet, Ed"

Ed was married and living in Rhode Island. During the winter his wife had the opportunity to go to Florida with her married girlfriends, and he encouraged her to go. While she was gone, one of the husbands called him up, they got together for a weekend, and wound up in New York City.

Ed met a woman at the hotel bar and fell very hard for her. He introduced himself to her under the fake name of "Ed Tucker." He did not tell her he was married. Nothing happened that weekend, but he thought about her a lot, and a few days later he phoned the woman, Phyllis, at her home in Bridgeport, Connecticut. "She sounded quite pleased to hear from me," he says. But his wife came home from her trip, and things returned to normal for a while.

Ed ran a gas station. A single friend, a customer named Bill, came into the station one Friday and told Ed he was going to New York. He was dating a New York model whom he later married. "I secretly called Phyllis and told her I would be in New York over the weekend, and she agreed to meet me. Then I called my wife and told her I had to be in New York over the weekend on business."

Ed and Bill headed to New York to meet their dates. "The four of us had a nice evening with a lot of drinks, dancing, etc. Phyllis and I spent the night together in her room, and Sunday morning we awoke somewhat hungover. She said, 'Good morning, Ed. I had the funniest dream! I dreamed that I was at your home in Rhode Island, and you were married and lived on the waterfront. Your house had a concrete wall in front of it with a dock and boats tied to it, and you had three children. Your oldest girl kept running after me saying, "Oh, you go out with my father." Your wife was very slim, had dark hair that she wore behind her ears and a bun on her neck; she was very young, and had a black tooth in the front of her mouth.' "

Phyllis's psychically received description of Ed's wife and house was almost perfect. "The only thing that she missed on was the children," says Ed. "I lived on the waterfront, there was a concrete retaining wall with a dock and boats, my wife at age twenty-two was ten years my junior, she was tall and slim, had dark hair that she wore behind her ears with a bun on her neck, and she had a front tooth that had darkened due to a dead nerve. I was stunned, not knowing what to say, and in a few minutes she said, 'Ed, What's the matter? You're awfully quiet.' I certainly was."

A woman in Florida, alerted by a psychic dream, stopped her husband's indiscretion before it could develop into a full-blown affair. She had never had any cause to be jealous of him, but one morning she was awakened by a troubling dream.

Fooling Around

"In it, I saw him standing against a wall with a woman in front of him, he had his two arms around her, and they were talking and laughing. I forgot about the dream during the day, but when he came home, suddenly it came to my mind again. I started laughing and said, 'Honey, if you were standing against a wall last night with a woman in front of you and you had your arms around her like this, just who would that woman be?'

"He started to laugh and said, 'Oh honey, I didn't do anything wrong. That was just Lois, the night-shift waitress. She always comes over and says, "How's my sweetie?" Why, were you down there?'

"I started off thinking I would joke about my dream with him, but when he verified it, I didn't want him to know how I learned about it. So I said a girlfriend and I had gone down for a cup of coffee, and that I saw him with the girl and wouldn't go in. I'm still angry about it."

Cheryl, the Ohio woman we met earlier, had a second interesting psychic dream involving a failed romance.

Two Cheryls

"When I was twenty-three, I had been living with a man for two years. We were in a very stable relationship and were discussing marriage. One night I awoke from a dream with an incredible feeling of anxiety and dread. I was crying. I had dreamed that my boyfriend was with another woman who had my same name and birthday, but she wasn't me. He and I broke up suddenly about six months later, by his choice. Immediately afterward, he began dating another woman named Cheryl. I eventually learned that her birthday was March 30. Mine is March 31, though I had been due the day before, which is my father's birthday."

• • •

The psychic warning delivered in the following dream may have prevented a gullible waitress from being tricked and a pregnant woman from losing her husband.

Two-Timer

In North Carolina, a waitress in a café met a good-looking young customer who began to pay attention to her. He claimed he was a regional sales manager based in Boston, and was single. He invited her out. After several dates, she began to fall for him and they even started talking marriage.

One evening, he said he had to make a quick business trip back to Boston but would return in a week, and they would set a date for the wedding. The night after he left, the waitress had an upsetting dream. A sad, frail woman with dark brown hair and who was in the last stages of pregnancy, appeared to her and said she was the man's wife. The next day the waitress learned from someone who had overheard the man's telephone conversation that it was not a business trip that had sent him back to Boston but rather a phone call from his wife, who was about to have a baby. The man returned a week later, and when the waitress confronted him with her dream and the overheard telephone conversation, the stunned man admitted his unfaithfulness, while also confirming that the description of the woman in her dream fitted his wife.

Some spouses seem to have their psychic antennae on all the time, leaving their partner baffled and nervous about straying too far. Kathleen wrote to us explaining that she had a "lifetime of weird things to tell. I know there is something different about me. My family will attest to it, and since we come from a very 'white bread' bunch, they are as perplexed as I am on occasion. I would love to be your lab rat just to find out about myself." Kathleen offered the following example:

"I'm at work on a beautiful, sunny day, managing a computer operation at a hospital. I'm very busy focusing and getting mounds of work complete. I'm in the 'groove.' The phone rings. It's my husband calling from his cell phone.

"He says, 'You'll never believe what just happened.' All of a sudden I was looking through his eyes. 'You are on Beaver Brook Road and you just saw a power transformer explode.' He is stunned, because there is no way I could have known that."

In her staccato writing style, Kathleen also shared two psychic experiences involving her relationship with her husband Ray.

Girlfriends And Porno Mags

"One day at home I'm vacuuming, happy as a clam, no worries, life is good. All of a sudden, smack, the thought—*Ray's been in touch with his old girlfriend from high school* (we are now forty-five years old). I've never suspected him, life's been all great, never looked through his computer.

"I go upstairs. Takes me two tries before I've got his password and am logged in. And there it was. Several e-mails back and forth to the old girlfriend, whom I didn't even know about, complaining about his marriage.

"Another time, middle of the night, 2:30 A.M., I'm fast asleep. Smack, the thought—*My husband is hiding porno magazines under the newspaper pile on the floor of his bathroom closet.* I have never ever had such a thought. I am not a suspicious person. I was in REM sleep when it woke me up cold.

"I get up, go to his bathroom and into his newspaper pile (which I've never done) and there it was—hidden porno. You should have seen the look on his face when I woke him up! He was as surprised as I was. I thought it was so cool that I nailed him. Twice! The guy is scared to lie about anything these days. It's really kinda funny."

◆ ◆ ◆

You almost feel sorry for Kathleen's husband. Psychic gifts can also be used to help a spouse. A remarkable example of this was reported to me by a friend, retired judge Stanley Peele.

And The Answer Is

"When I was in law school we read many court cases. When we were asked to cite a case, we generally responded by giving the last names of the cases, followed by the date of the decision, in this fashion: Smith *vs.* Jones, 1944. My wife, Carolyn, had already completed her undergraduate degree and was working full time. One day, I was given a problem and asked to cite a court case which gave the answer. Around ten P.M. that night, I began to study the problem. I racked my brains trying to figure out which case would provide the answer. The question was how long a 'squatter' would have to live on land to establish title, and then how to establish the boundaries of the squatter's land. I scanned some likely cases, but none of them was correct.

"Our house was small, so I used our bed to spread out my papers. At eleven o'clock, my wife came to bed. I cleared the bed off, put my papers on the floor, sat on a corner of the bed, and continued to try to find the answer to the problem. Carolyn went to sleep. At 11:30 P.M., I still hadn't found the case. Frustrated and mumbling, I whispered to myself, very quietly, 'What is the name of the case that controls a boundary dispute with a squatter?'

"Suddenly, Carolyn sat up in bed. In a very clear and assured voice, she said, 'Housten *vs.* Gallagher, 1927.'

'What?' I asked. 'How did you know?' My question was answered by a gentle snore. Carolyn was sound asleep. I was astonished.

"I stood up, gathered my papers, and went to our little study, turned on a light, and looked up the case. She was right on target.

"The next morning I said, 'Carolyn, do you realize you gave me the correct name and correct date of a case I was looking for last night?'

"'You're kidding,' she responded. I told her what had happened. She knew nothing about that aspect of the law. She had no memory whatsoever about what had happened, nor did she have the slightest inkling about the case. I learned that day that Carolyn is smarter than me, even when I'm awake and she's asleep!"

Carolyn has had a history of intuitive experiences, and one of the first involved her future husband Stanley. One day, when Carolyn was a teenager, a boy she had never seen before, and about whom she knew nothing, rode by on a bicycle. She surprised her girlfriends—and herself—by announcing, "I'm going to marry that boy someday." Sometime later they met at school, but it was not until years later they became engaged. They now have been married over thirty years.

An ESP connection can sometimes continue even if the partners divorce. In the following case, an ex-spouse's remarriage seems to have been the emotionally painful stimulus for this woman's sudden psychic intuition.

Remarriage

While chatting with her daughter, a divorced woman suddenly changed her expression to astonishment without warning in the middle of the conversation. When her daughter asked what had happened, she told her that somehow she just knew that her ex-husband, the girl's father, was getting married again. Her daughter, who was close to her father and had spoken to him regularly, laughed at the idea. She had just received a letter from her father and he hadn't mentioned anything about a marriage. But the mother insisted, and a short time later the daughter received a letter from her father. He had indeed remarried on the same evening that the mother had received this sudden extrasensory knowledge.

• • •

The divorce rate in the United States climbed during the twentieth century until it peaked in the late 1970s. It is still four times higher today than it was in the 1950s. If there is a silver lining in this cloud, it is that some divorcing couples continue to maintain cordial relations with their ex-spouses. I first heard of this very unusual ESP experience from a woman I will call Penny, who related it at one of our Paranormal Experiences Group meetings. Penny had maintained a close and friendly relationship with her ex-husband, and their continued emotional bond suggests a possible basis for the scary psychic message Penny received involving his new life.

Dream Of An Ex

"On this particular night, I dozed off in quite a normal fashion, feeling no anxieties or apprehensions. As my dream begins, I am being pursued by my ex-husband Paul and my daughter. The intent of their pursuit was to kill me. I should add at this point that I continue to have a very caring relationship with my ex, and a very loving relationship with my daughter.

"In my dream, I was in a house that was unfamiliar to me, and the dream took place in the kitchen area. I can't begin to tell you the horrifying fear that was pulsing through my body. I could feel their presence in the kitchen where I was lying on the floor, trying to hide in a very small area behind a counter bar that divided the kitchen from another room. I was trapped at this point, because I could see that the only door to escape was at the opposite side of the kitchen, where I sensed them to be.

"I managed somehow to access a telephone while in this position. Again and again I dialed 911 trying to seek help, but to no avail. I would begin to talk to someone on the line, and then be cut off for some unknown reason. By this time, my frustration and fear had grown to such an enormous level, and my fate was so apparent, that I could hardly breathe.

"It was at this point I awoke from the dream. As I stared into the darkness, my heart was beating at a tremendous rate. I was, of course, so relieved to have escaped this nightmare, but couldn't let go of the 'reality' of what I had just experienced. As I calmed down, I drifted back to sleep, and slept until morning without any reoccurrences of the dream.

"Upon waking, I remember sitting on the side of my bed recalling every detail, and questioning out loud to myself, 'Why would my daughter and ex-husband be involved in this horrendous ordeal?' Persuading myself that this was only a nightmare, I tucked it away in my subconscious and went on with life.

"That afternoon, I received a message from my ex-husband that something had happened to a good friend of his and that he would call me in a few days to tell me about it. My first assumption was that it was obviously not someone we knew in common, or he would have told me a name. So, once again, I just dismissed the message content and waited until I heard from him three days later.

"When Paul called he was distraught and began to tell me what had happened to his friend. The 'friend,' as it happens, was someone with whom he had fallen in love. Her ex-husband, who had been very abusive to her during their marriage, was not dealing well with their separation. He had made many threats and consequently she was quite afraid of him and what he might attempt to do.

"On this particular day, her ex-husband obviously had a plan in mind. He had an extra set of keys to her car.

"He had their daughter, who also was hoping that they would be able to get back together, take him to the office where his ex-wife was working. He took her car, and then called to tell her that he had the car. He said that if she would just take him to their former home, where he resided, so he could have the opportunity to talk to her, she could have the car back.

"She was apprehensive about this arrangement. She

called Paul, who lived in another city, and told him what the plan was. She would not go into the house with her ex-husband, and would call him as soon as she left with the car. She was never heard from again.

"For reasons unknown, she did go into the house where ultimately he killed her and then himself. Paul told me that she tried several times to reach 911, but when she began to talk she was cut off.

"My response at this point was just to the grief that I knew Paul was feeling. Later that day, as I was sitting quietly, I remembered the 911 calls that I tried to make in my dream, and the vivid recollection came flooding back. Did I experience this through her point of view? Was it her extreme fear and frustration that I was feeling? Did I see her husband and daughter as my own so that I had a way to relate to the meaning of what was happening?

"I didn't feel it was an appropriate time to discuss my dream with Paul. However, about three weeks later, I went to visit him and decided to tell him about it. I knew that he had never been inside her former home, but I described to him, in great detail, what the kitchen looked like in my dream. I knew that the floor was basically blue, with specks of white. I described where I was lying on the floor, and that the room was very narrow at this point, and was only about the width of my body length. There was a counter bar dividing the kitchen from another room. The door and sink, with a window above, were on the opposite side of the room from where I was lying.

"A week after I returned home, Paul called me to say that he was drawn to go to her house. It was still cordoned off with the police tape. He said he was able to peer through the window that was over the sink to get a view of the kitchen. It was pretty much as I had described it to him. The floor covering was blue with white running through it. The narrowness of the room and the counter bar dividing the kitchen from the dining room were as I had related. The only access out of the kitchen was the door located beside the sink. He also noted that the telephone was located in a place that I would have been able to reach from my position in the room.

"There is no longer a doubt in my mind that I actually shared her experience. My only question is, why? Perhaps, it was to open my mind even wider to learning, accepting, and experiencing the higher consciousness of our universe."

Penny seems to have psychically tapped into the terror that Paul's new girlfriend probably experienced, the only link being Penny's continuing friendship and concern for her ex-husband. This is very unusual among the realistic type of dreams in our ESP collection, because the dreamer finds herself dreaming from the perspective of someone whom she did not know nor even knew existed at the time of her dream. Penny's dream occurred after the actual murder, but before she knew of her ex-husband's distress or talked to him.

Despite the frequently failed romances, high divorce rate, and sharp emotional arguments that accompany many relationships, millions of men and women each year do fall deeply in love and make it work, often for a lifetime. And they can sometimes find themselves literally sharing their dreams.

Lovers

A woman in California awoke one night and recalled a dream that had been so vivid and beautiful that she wanted to share it with her husband. In her dream, she was standing outside a building admiring the beautiful, shimmering, dark blue sky with the moon bright, round, and silver. Then as she watched, six other smaller moons of varying sizes rose, one by one, in different arcs and at different speeds. Some were more golden than the actual moon, some paler; their light turned the sky almost to daylight. In the dream, she watched, entranced. Not wanting her husband to miss such a wonderful sight, she called him out of the building, and they stood there happily watching the moons and commenting on their beauty. When she finished describing her wonderful dream, he laughed, "You can't have dreamed that—*I* did!" His dream was identical to hers, except he had called *her* out to see the moons.

Many marriage ceremonies still include the words "and the two shall become one." ESP experiences such as this one suggest that more than the flesh is united if we are lucky enough to share love with someone. Our minds may also become one.

7

PREMONITIONS OF DEATH
AND DISASTERS

The majority of ESP reports concern the lives of our family, our close friends, and ourselves. Although many trivial ESP experiences probably go unreported, the majority of those reported deal with negative news.

Some parapsychologists have proposed an "anxiety hypothesis" to explain this ESP bias towards negative news. We do not want anything or anybody to hurt people we love, so we are always psychically scanning the horizon looking for trouble. Death is the absolute last thing we want to catch them unaware and unprepared. If we can foresee it coming, we might be able to prevent it. And if we can't avoid it, at least we might be able to prepare ourselves for the inevitable, thereby minimizing the shock and pain.

Premonitions of death make up a significant number of the ESP reports in our Rhine ESP case collection, and they come in every form—intuitions, dreams, and hallucinatory experiences. A Missouri man's terrible, intuitive premonition involved his favorite sister, Betty. His wife sent us the account of his ESP experience.

"I Think She's Dying"

"On the morning of July 5, my husband came to the breakfast table without his usual calm and cheery disposition. He showed signs of extreme nervousness and the results of a sleepless night. Finally, he said, 'Something is wrong with my sister Betty. I think she's dying.'

"The day before, we had been with Betty and her husband. She was apparently in excellent health and, though she and her husband had not yet told the family, they thought she was pregnant. Knowing my husband wasn't a 'flighty' person, I was alarmed at his condition and said nothing when he went to the telephone to call his sister's home to see if she was all right.

"Before my husband could make the call, his brother-in-law opened our front door, came in hurriedly, and said, 'Herbert, come with me! Your sister is in the hospital and we think she's dying.' Needless to say, he was surprised at Herbert's simple answer, 'Yes, I know.'

"Betty had been ill all night long. She had a tubular pregnancy and lingered at death's door for many days thereafter, but somehow my husband knew of her danger before he was told of it by her husband. This particular sister and my husband had been unusually close to each other from early childhood."

In another intuitive premonition of death, a woman from Oregon became suddenly worried one afternoon about her mother who lived in Minnesota.

Something's Terribly Wrong

"I became filled with a deep feeling of urgency and foreboding that something was wrong with my mother. I tried to put the idea aside, but by evening I was pacing the floor.

"My husband said, 'I don't think there's anything wrong or they would call you—but call them if it will help relieve your mind.' I called, and my sister who was living with my mother picked up the phone. She said Mom was a little frailer but had had a checkup and the doctor had declared her in very good condition for her age.

"The conversation should have been reassuring for me, but it failed to cheer me up. In fact, my feeling of foreboding increased, if anything. By two P.M. the next afternoon, I ran upstairs and threw myself on the bed, giving way to uncontrollable sobbing. It went on for an hour before I could throw the feeling off and join my family downstairs. Just as I reached the bottom of the stairs, the phone rang. And as I expected, it was my sister saying that Mom had passed away. Automatically, I said, 'It happened at three o'clock our time, five o'clock there.'

"'Yes,' she answered, adding apologetically, 'If I'd had the least inkling of this when you called yesterday, I'd have told you to come.' What puzzles me is how I—living eighteen hundred miles away—could pick up on what my sister, who lived right there, could not."

Intuitive premonitions of death rarely bring details, just a direct gut feeling of impending tragedy, unmediated by reason or logic. Women are commonly believed to be more in touch with their emotions than men. In the case just described, the husband, typical of many men, uses logic to dismiss his wife's worry about her mother. If she were really in danger of dying, wouldn't somebody have noticed it and called his wife? Our Rhine ESP files also contain cases in which a man is the one with the intuitive precognition of death and the woman remains clueless. This report is from a young man in California who psychically picked up on a danger his mother completely missed.

Deadly Collision

"One night we had just finished supper, and my brother-in-law Bob was getting ready to go to a meeting in San Jose, which is twenty-five miles from our house. Suddenly, for no reason, I started crying—me, crying, twenty-five years old! I begged him not to go.

"Well, there was quite a fuss, and I got everyone upset. My mom kept saying, 'He'll be all right.' You know, the usual soft soap you give an upset person. This went on for about fifteen minutes. Then the feeling left me, and I announced, 'It's all right for Bob to go now.'

"By this time, the guy Bob was supposed to ride with had gotten tired of waiting at their meeting place and had already left, so Bob had to drive his own car to San Jose. He got as far as Bayshore and Charter Streets when the traffic began to back up. It was a car wreck, which is nothing unusual here.

"When Bob got to the corner, he said he almost passed out. There, spread out on the highway, was the man he was supposed to have ridden to the meeting with. His head was half gone. The car was a total loss. They found later that his brakes had locked on one side, and he flipped up in the air and came down on the other side of the road, only to be hit head-on by another car."

Death premonitions that occur in a telesomatic or sympathetic bodily form are rare. But my psychologist friend Natalie had a premonition of her mother's death that arrived that way.

Mom Is Dead

Natalie's mother was hospitalized with cancer and fading fast. The day she died, Natalie woke up that morning with a terribly stiff neck. "I really couldn't move my head at all," she recalls. "It was painful to drive, to walk or even sit. And it stayed that way all day during work. I kept wondering if I were going to get a phone call that she had died, but I didn't all day.

"I drove home that evening across a river near my house—it was in the fall and it was foggy and misty. Just as I crossed over the bridge, I got the impression that she had died. I started to cry, and my stiff neck went away immediately. I looked to see what time it was, expecting that as soon as I got home I would hear that she had died. When I got home, I telephoned my father's house, but nobody was home. Several hours later, my father called and said she had died at the hospital. I asked what time, and he said 7:20 P.M. That was the time I had crossed over the bridge."

As Natalie explained to me, "I don't know where my ESP messages come from, and I don't necessarily know how to explain them, but in my mind they are much more than mere coincidence or luck. No question about it."

Natalie's psychic gift for knowing when people have died may have a genetic basis. "Some years before my mother died, we were sitting in the den of her house one day, and she just looked up at me and said, 'Aunt Hazel died.' It turned out Aunt Hazel had indeed died then. My mom just had those psychic moments from time to time. That's why I actually didn't find it strange when I somehow knew the moment when she herself died."

Skeptics do not bother Natalie. "The only bad grade I got in college, a B-minus, was a paper I wrote in psychology class on the topic of parapsychology. The paper wasn't badly written. I got the grade because my professor said parapsychology wasn't real psychology. I was irritated a bit, but it didn't really bother me. I know many people don't see the world the way I do—maybe because they haven't had the psychic experiences I've had. It doesn't embarrass me, or cause me problems. I just view it as ignorance on their part."

Once in a great while, we get a report of more than one person in a family receiving a warning of an impending death in the family. In Nova Scotia, Canada, a woman I will call Donna had a premonition when she was nine years old of her grandfather's death. Her premonition came in a precognitive dream. It was not until twenty years later that she discovered she was not the only one who had foreseen his death.

Shared Death Premonition

"In my dream, a coffin stood in the corner of our living room," Donna explained. "As I approached, I saw that the face in the coffin was that of my beloved grandmother. I awoke stricken with grief. I couldn't sleep the rest of the night. The next morning, I couldn't bring myself to tell anyone about my dream that haunted me so—particularly my grandmother. After several days passed and nothing happened, my spirits rose again and the dream was almost forgotten.

"But within two weeks, my *grandfather* suddenly died of a heart attack. On the day of the funeral, I was taken into the very same room I had seen in my dream. There was the coffin as I had seen it. The only difference lay in the cold, still face—the face of my grandfather and not, as in my dream, the face of my grandmother. My grief was now mixed with alarm, almost terror. My dream had come true. Still, I told no one about the dream. In my child's mind, I feared that mentioning the dream would simply add to the sorrow of our already stricken family."

Twenty years later, Donna was talking with her mother one day, and they got to reminiscing about her grandfather. To her surprise, "My mother confessed that on the day my grandfather died, he had said to her that morning, 'Last night I dreamed that everybody in town was dead—I was the only person alive.' She told me that he looked at her keenly as if to ask whether she understood what he was thinking. Then he went out, waving his hand in his usual lighthearted manner. Within an hour he was dead." It was only at this point that Donna finally informed her mother about her own frightening premonition twenty years earlier.

"For years it has had an icy grip on my life," Donna wrote us, "and as I write, the retelling of it opens old griefs as if they were yesterday's wounds."

If this young girl had been able to discuss her premonition openly and honestly with her parents when she was a child, much of the mystery and pain would have disappeared, and she would have understood it for what it was—a normal precognitive experience. Again and again I hear this type of refrain from people who were unable to discuss their ESP experiences with understanding adults during childhood, or even in later life. This is one of the reasons I am writing this book, to help people understand that ESP is a natural and normal human ability, even though we do not yet have all the answers.

There is another aspect of Donna's dream that is worth mentioning, namely her substitution or displacement of one person for another. She dreamed about a *grandmother*, when it was actually her *grandfather's* death that was to occur. This phenomenon is reported infrequently but persistently in ESP stories, and parapsychologists are working to develop a hypothesis to explain it, including possible subconscious, emotional reasons for making such switches.

Deadly Collision" involved a man who had a life-saving intuition about his brother-in-law. Here are two further reports relating to brothers-in-law for whom the ending was more tragic. In this precognitive dream, a teenage girl foresaw the death of her sister's husband in a hunting accident.

Death Of A Brother-In-Law (I)

"When I was seventeen, my sister Frances got married to a wonderful, talented musician. They were very much in love and happy together. One night, I had a dream that was so real I remembered every single detail of it. I dreamed that my brother-in-law, Ed, was out hunting with a young boy who was faceless in my dream.

"All of a sudden, Ed collapsed from a discharge from the boy's shotgun. The boy had climbed through a fence and didn't have the safety on his shotgun. The pellets hit Ed in the hip, and he bled to death before they could get him to a doctor."

Frightened by her dream, she phoned her sister to warn her. Her sister and Ed laughed it off. That was on Saturday. Two days later, Ed and his friend set out on a hunting trip. "On Monday morning Ed was killed, just as in my dream."

The girl's precognitive dream of the hunting accident was typical in that the dream did not provide a date when the event would occur, although parapsychologists generally find only a small time gap between the premonition and the subsequent event. Perhaps this can be explained partly by the natural tendency of human beings to lose interest in—or even simply forget—a premonition that does not come true for a long time. Here is another premonition involving a brother-in-law, sent in by a woman from Virginia. Again, the foreseen event happens within a day or two.

Death Of A Brother-In-Law (II)

"On the night of February 21, I had a dream that actually came true just twenty-four hours later. I dreamed that my brother-in-law had died, and his wife called me long-distance to tell me about it. In my dream, she was crying and screaming, and I woke up from the dream terribly upset. I told my husband, and later in the day I told a neighbor. They both just laughed at me, and said dreaming of death meant a birth.

"The next day, we got the dreaded phone call. I answered it. It was my sister-in-law and she was crying and screaming exactly as in my dream. She said her husband had been killed that morning. He had been cutting a tree and fell from the tree.

"I don't believe all this is just a coincidence. My husband has four brothers, so why should I have dreamt about that particular brother? It is so mystifying. I wish I knew what caused it."

Without knowing more about her family, we can only speculate why this particular woman dreamed about this particular brother-in-law. Possibly she is more psychic than others in her family, or perhaps she was in a more ESP-conducive state at this particular time. In lab research, it is common to find a "differential effect" by which a subject seems to zone in or show a preference for one type of target more than another. Did she have a subconscious preference for that brother-in-law as a target of her ESP?

The time gap between the experience and the event is so rarely detailed in an ESP experience that I sometimes joke, "Time means nothing to a parapsychologist." Occasionally, a premonition will include a specific date for the predicted occurrence, as happened in this woman's ESP experience.

The Shadow Of Death

A young woman in Brooklyn we'll call Mary, married and living some distance from her parents' home, was unable to see her mother very often. Her young brother came one Saturday to visit her. When she asked him about their mother, he said that she was, as usual, feeling fine.

"We went to sleep," Mary recalls, "but just in that twilight time between sleep and wakefulness I got a sudden, inexplicable feeling. It was not a dream, nor was it a voice telling me something. I can hardly explain it, except to call it sudden knowledge. It was not a ghostly warning of any kind. It didn't come in a frightening manner. But what the feeling foretold, if I had believed it at the time, would have been something to frighten me and make me very apprehensive indeed!

"I called to my brother and awoke him. Angrily, he asked

me why. I told him I'd had a sudden feeling that our mother would be taken to the hospital exactly one week from the following morning; that is, on the eighth day from that night, and that she would be seriously sick—very, very sick.

"He just got angrier than ever and told me to stop talking absolute nonsense and go to sleep. There was nothing wrong with Mom and nothing bad was going to happen either! He wondered what was wrong with me to say such a stupid thing.

"Well, to be honest, I thought it was pretty weird myself. This sort of thing had never happened to me before. My brother convinced me I was talking nonsense. I fell asleep and gave it no further thought.

"On Sunday morning one week later, I was awakened out of a sound sleep by the ringing of the front doorbell. There stood my mother. While in my house, she became dreadfully sick, and I had to call the ambulance and watch them take her away to the hospital. It was her last illness."

Mary's ESP experience involved information about the exact day of the event soon to occur. By contrast, in the next instance the exact time of day appears to be the relevant bit of precognitive information, even though it would not occur for three more years! Marilyn, a forty-two-year-old nurse who immigrated to the U.S. from Romania in 1997, e-mailed me the following report on a possibly precognitive experience she had involving the death of her father. She reports having had several ESP experiences in the last ten years, but this one frightened her the most.

Death At 5:15 A.M.

"It was the most disturbing event in my life," she wrote. "It was 1992, and I was alone at home, sleeping. My dead grandfather appeared in my dream and told me he had come to get my father, but he had to go back to sleep, so I should wake him (my grandfather) up at 5:15 A.M.

"When I woke up from the dream, it was 5:15 in the morning! I had such an uneasy feeling, being sure that it was not just a normal dream. In panic, I called my father, who was in another town at the time. He answered the phone and I was relieved to hear his voice. He assured me he was okay.

"Three years later, in October 1995, I found out the meaning of the visit and the '5:15' message. After being in a coma for three days, my father passed away at exactly 5:15 in the morning."

An unanswered question for parapsychologists is whether her deceased grandfather actually came to Marilyn in this dream state with the forewarning, or whether it was Marilyn's own mind that somehow dramatized her precognitive awareness of her father's death in this way. This issue will be considered later.

Apparitions or visual hallucinations of deceased loved ones that occur at the hour of death, and often seem to be welcoming people to the "other side," have been reported throughout history. Sometimes the figure that appears is an important religious figure. Not surprisingly, the Christian lady involved in this death premonition interpreted her visual hallucination as a vision of Christ.

"I Have Come For Him"

In a Minnesota hospital, a woman had undergone a major operation. As she regained consciousness, she was aware of someone in another room groaning and crying constantly. The nurse said everything possible was being done for the patient across the hall, and that he would be all right. The woman was very concerned and prayed that his pain would be relieved. "Long after midnight," she wrote us, "the nurse finally went to get a sedative so that I could sleep. She went out the door, closing it quietly behind her." Certainly the distinction that a weak or ill person in bed may make between sleep and waking cannot be considered very reliable, but in this instance the patient was not aware of going to sleep.

She was facing the door a few minutes later, when it happened. She noticed the door opening. She first thought it was the nurse returning, but she says, "As I watched, I saw the figure of Christ. He was dressed in flowing, white robes as I have seen him in pictures. He walked slowly and quietly to my bedside. I thought He had come for me but, laying His hand on my pillow, He smiled and said, 'I have come for him. Everything is all right.' Then as quietly as he came, He went out, closing the door behind Him. Somehow it didn't seem at all queer. I turned my head and saw by the clock it was 2:40 A.M."

The next morning, she said to the nurse, "The man across the hall died last night, didn't he?"

"Yes, but how did you know?" replied the nurse.

She told her of the night's experience and finally, after overcoming the nurse's objection to giving out information about another patient, learned that he had died at 2:40 A.M.

From pop culture we all know who the Grim Reaper is, and what he is supposed to look like. He's the symbol of Death—a tall, dark, faceless figure shrouded in a black cloak holding a scythe, come to harvest the living. When the Grim Reaper appears in a psychic experience, most of us would be very upset and suspect a death was involved. But whose death?

Grim Reaper In Suburbia

In Cincinnati, Ohio, one afternoon, a young woman was washing the luncheon dishes. Her husband was out of town on a business trip. Suddenly, looking out the window she saw, as if in a daze, a "vision of the Grim Reaper" running madly across her lawn. It was gone in a flash but left her cold, shaken, and terror-stricken. She knew something terrible had happened.

She expected her husband to be back by 3:00 P.M., but he did not come. By seven, she was pacing the floor when the phone rang. It was a call from the hospital to say her husband was hurt and unconscious. It turned out that, about the time she had her unusual vision of the Grim Reaper, his car had been struck by another car traveling very fast, and he was crushed against the windshield.

As we learned earlier, essential information in a symbolic dream comes clothed in a disguised form, possibly for psychological protection or defense against painful underlying facts. Fortunately in this case, her husband was badly injured but survived.

Like the Grim Reaper, somber figures dressed all in black also symbolize death in Western culture. A lady from Tennessee had an unusual psychic experience involving a black-clad relative whose presence foretold a death. It also contained a substitution similar to the one found in "Shared Death Premonition" above.

Dressed In Black

"In my dream, I was walking along the street. No one was around, but at a distance I saw a figure clothed all in black approaching me, and I finally recognized her as a favorite aunt of mine. She had on long, flowing black robes and a black hat with a heavy black veil that covered her face. In the dream, I laughed when I saw her, because she's always such a stylish, well-dressed person, and I couldn't imagine her in such unstylish clothes. I remember I continued to laugh as she came nearer and nearer, but when I saw her face she didn't smile. She just looked at me and then passed me without saying a word. This, too, was shocking to me because she and I were quite close, more like mother and daughter. As she passed, someone in reality knocked on my door and woke me up from the dream. It was my landlady telling me someone wanted me on the phone. The person calling me was the aunt that had appeared in my dream. She was very much alive—but her mother had just passed away."

While the figure of Christ, the Grim Reaper, and people dressed in black are fairly universal symbols of death in our culture, some ESP experiencers may develop their own bank of personalized symbols that often appear at critical and significant times in their lives. A woman in South Carolina, whom I will call Wanda, reported a terrible series of four death premonitions, always announced by an avenue of trees, that brought her forewarnings about a mother, brother, husband, and, finally, her daughter's friend. The last premonition also involved her daughter but fortunately the daughter was spared in the end.

A Beautiful Avenue Of Trees

One hot, July afternoon when she was twelve years old, Wanda's mother was very ill, and the girl was sent outside to play. She went out in the yard and fell asleep in the swing. "I dreamed I saw my mother," Wanda wrote us. "She was walking down a beautiful avenue of trees, going away from me. I ran as fast as I could and realized that I could never catch up with her. I called her. She turned and put up her hand and said to me, 'Go back. Your father needs you.'

"I immediately woke up and went into the house. My father met me in the hall and took me in his arms and said, 'I need you. Your mother just left us.' When I told him that I had seen my mother, walking fast down this avenue of trees I had never seen before, he said, 'She must have given you her last farewell.' "

On three subsequent occasions in her life, Wanda, no longer a girl, had psychic dreams involving the same avenue of trees and subsequent deaths. "In the first of these, my younger brother was ill in a hospital in another state. I was ill and couldn't be with him, but my father and brothers were by his bedside when he passed away. The night he passed away, I dreamed that he, too, was walking down this same avenue of trees that I had seen in my dream some twelve or thirteen years before, and I tried to catch up to him, and he told me not to come on and just go back.

"When my father brought my brother's body home for burial, I told him about the dream and the hour. He said that my brother had passed away a few minutes before the hour I had awakened."

A few years later, Wanda had a second dream. "My husband and I had had friends over for a game of cards. Afterward, we retired and both went to sleep. That night, I had the same dream—this time it was my husband who was walking so fast. I ran and ran and called and called for him to stop. He, too, as in the other dreams put up his hand and said, 'Our children need you—go back.'

"I was frightened and, turning in my sleep, put my arms around him, awakening him. The first thing he said was, 'I'm so sick. Please call the doctor.' He died in a few minutes."

The third time the avenue of trees showed up in her dreams, Wanda was especially concerned because her daughters and their girlfriend were in the dream. "My daughters and a friend of theirs went to a dance. Before their return, I dreamed that my oldest daughter and this girlfriend of hers both suffered fatal accidents in front of my home, and the same avenue of trees came into the dream.

"When my daughters returned home around one o'clock in the morning, I told them about my frightening dream and expressed my relief that they had returned safely. But the next evening, the day before Easter, my daughters held a party at my home. The girlfriend was killed within a block of our house on her way back to her home, and the accident happened just as I had dreamed it."

We do not hear from many people with multiple premonitions like Wanda's. These accounts are of particular interest because they may indicate above-average ESP ability. Often upon questioning, we discover the experiencers are creative or imaginative people with a history of ESP in the family, something we also see in lab research. The following woman had two death premonitions in the form of precognitive dreams. Both were almost photographic in their detail.

Two Deaths Foreseen

"I dreamed I was in a large building, standing on the staircase talking with three men: my husband, my father-in-law, and one other man who was hazy. We were having a serious conversation, quite concerned over something. I awoke from the dream crying, and whimpered to my husband before I was fully awake that his sister needed blood and must be given a blood transfusion." Neither of them at the time could figure out why she had blurted that out.

"About a year afterward, I was in a hospital, standing on a staircase talking with my husband, my father-in-law, and brother-in-law about the very serious illness of my sister-in-law. I suddenly realized we were standing in the place and positions I had 'seen.' My husband had been called to the hospital to give his sister a transfusion. She died a few days later.

Thirteen months later, she had a second death premonition. "I dreamed of the death of our good neighbor and close friend, a young man thirty-four years old and father to four young kids. In my dream, I saw him lying in the coffin in the living room of his home. His children were running in and out, and I asked his wife if she wanted me to take them home with me for a while. The dream ended.

"When I awoke from this dream, I told my husband, because he knew of my previous dream, and this one frightened me. He advised me to try to put it out of my mind and not talk about it to the man.

"Three weeks later, the man was fatally stricken with a heart attack. I brought his four children over to stay with me."

A woman from New Jersey, whom I will call Alice, seems to live under a rain cloud. She has had a half-dozen ESP experiences bringing her bad news at different times in her

life, including several death premonitions. All of them occurred when she was wide awake. Parapsychologists have
found that some people consistently receive their ESP messages in the form of dreams, while others get ESP messages
only when they are awake. Incidentally, dream researchers
are now finding that regular dreamlike cycles occur during
waking hours as well, with brain activity very similar to the
dreaming brain at night, so there may not actually be that
much difference in these two conditions. Each individual
seems to express his ESP in a form easiest or most appropriate for him, putting the stamp of his own personality on the
ESP process.

In the first ESP experience Alice remembers, she "just
knew" she would get hurt on a winter sledding expedition. It
ended with a broken leg. Chance could easily explain such
an accident, but some of her later experiences seem further
removed from the to-be-expected.

Nothing But Bad News

One time, Alice saw a woman walking on the sidewalk. "An
inner voice told me she would be hit by a car," she said. A
few blocks later, she found the woman lying on the side of
the road, writhing in pain from a broken leg. She had been
hit by a passing car after she stepped off the sidewalk.

Some years later came a different form of ESP experience. As Alice told us, "I was walking to work one morning
when, to my utmost horror, I was stepping right into a room
in a hospital. A figure lay on the bed, his head bandaged. I
gazed at the face of my boyfriend. Then, as suddenly as it
happened, I was again back on the sidewalk.

"A few blocks farther on, I saw him alive and well, and I
laughed to myself about my ridiculous vision." The next
day, her boyfriend was severely injured at his work and died
soon after of multiple skull fractures.

This precognitive hallucination type of ESP experience
did not become an exclusive pattern, and a few years later

she had another intuitive death premonition. "One day my aunt came up to me as I walked on the street. We chatted a moment and then the same inner voice told me I would never see her alive again. The next day, she died of a heart attack."

That was followed a few years later by another scary precognitive hallucination—this time involving Alice herself. "A year ago in September, as I drove home one balmy evening, I suddenly had a vision of my car wrecked, an ambulance along the side of the road, and myself being put on a stretcher, which stood at a certain angle to the roadway. About four minutes later, a car traveling at high speed and out of control struck mine head on. I was very severely injured. My car was demolished, and the stretcher stood in exactly the angle in the road as I had envisaged it."

An Ohio physician, whom I will call Cassie, described an unusual psychic message that came to her in a dream, but her efforts to pass along this information to a skeptical male acquaintance fell on deaf ears.

A Mother's Last Message

"One night while I was asleep, the mother of my optometrist appeared in my dream and said to me, 'Cassie, take care of my son. Let him know I'm going to be okay, and put your arms around him when you see him.' It woke me up from my dream because it was not a good feeling."

Cassie was not very close to either the optometrist or his mother. She had only met the mother twice, both times very briefly, and saw the optometrist perhaps once every year or two. Though she had a history of accurate ESP experiences, Cassie was unsure of what to do.

That morning, still undecided on how to proceed, she walked out the door from an early 7:00 A.M. meeting at the hospital and bumped into Courtney, her optometrist. "He put his arm around me and started crying, because they'd just taken his mom to the ICU and she was dying." She felt it was not the right place or time to share her death premonition, so she said nothing.

Years later, Cassie saw the movie *The Sixth Sense* and, during her eye checkup that year, found out that Courtney had seen it, too. He described it as "kind of weird." Undaunted, she took the opportunity to tell him about her earlier death premonition involving his mother, and the message his mother had asked Cassie to give him. "He looked at me like, 'Well, you're as weird as that movie.'

"I let it drop. I guess a lot of people just don't want to know. If I was bringing a negative message, then I could understand, but it was a positive message. It's amazing to me that there are still so many closed-minded people who won't open up to the fact that there's communication going on that we pay very little attention to."

The vast majority of death premonitions sent to the Rhine Research Center involve the fate of a single individual, usually someone the ESP experiencer knows personally—a spouse, relative, close friend, or acquaintance. So the question naturally arises as to what triggers those ESP experiences of catastrophes like train wrecks, plane crashes, or terrorist attacks involving the fate of complete strangers.

If someone we love is sharing a seat with those strangers on a doomed plane, then a psychic link to the catastrophe is understandable. Their fates are obviously entwined. We foresee the disaster simply as a side effect of foreseeing the fate of someone we love. Such appears to be the case of Nancy, a teenager living in New York. "I have often had experiences of ESP, such as knowing what someone is going to say before they say it, or knowing a certain song is going to be played on the radio before it is played," she wrote us. The most dramatic precognitive experience Nancy had was a premonition of a plane crash that almost took the life of her sister.

Plane Crash In Virginia

"In my dream, I was in my room sleeping, when I was suddenly awakened by a loud noise. I looked out my back window, and there was my sister, who was studying at the time to be an airline hostess. She was there in her blue airline suit, banging at the window in an effort it seemed either to get in or get out of something. The sky was a mixture of red and orange.

"Then, in my dream, the view instantly shifted and I was looking out the front window of my house. There she lay, all black and charred upon our sidewalk, with bits of the airplane scattered around her. The sky was dark with smoke all around. Then I awoke from my dream.

"About two weeks later, a plane chartered from Washington, D.C., to Roanoke, Virginia, via Charlottesville crashed outside of Charlottesville with only one survivor. My sister was scheduled to ride on that plane, but her connecting plane from New York was late, so she had just missed this doomed plane."

The woman who had the next ESP experience—her first and only one—didn't know anyone on the train in her dream, and the wreck had almost no personal significance or impact on her life. The only emotional tie-in may have been the fact that she had traveled the same train route less than twenty-four hours earlier. Had her trip been delayed a bit, she might have ended up on the doomed train.

Train Wreck In Japan

The wife of an air force lieutenant, who says she rarely has dreams or rarely remembers doing so, had a vivid and terrifying dream of a public catastrophe one night. Her husband had been assigned to the U.S. military liaison office in

Japan. They arrived in Nagasaki and took a train to Tokyo, where they were living at the time of the dream.

In her dream, she was standing high on a hillside, overlooking a bay shaped like a half-moon. A railway track ran along the rocky shore close to the water. As she watched, a long, heavy freight train came into view from the south, traveled around the bay and disappeared to the north. A passenger train followed soon afterward, traveling behind the freight train. In her dream, she somehow seemed to know what would happen next. The heavy freight train had weakened the track bed, which was going to collapse.

When the passenger train was directly below her view, the track gave way, and many passenger cars overturned and fell into the bay. The waters seemed shallow, and she next saw survivors far below crawling like ants out of the train windows, and waves breaking on the wrecked cars. She woke up horrified.

Later that day, she accompanied her husband to a luncheon. She was seated on the left of an undersecretary at the United States embassy. She heard the woman on his right ask him if any Americans were on the wrecked train. At the mention of the train wreck, she asked where it had taken place. It was on the train line she and her husband had traveled to get to Tokyo. Before he could give her details, she told her dream.

The dreamed wreck coincided exactly with the actual wreck. Published newspaper photos of the disaster also agreed in every aspect with her precognitive dream.

In some disaster premonitions, we can not identify any personal or emotional link at all between the ESP experiencer and the catastrophe that happens. A thirty-five year-old mother of four children, whom I will call Claire, sent me an e-mail hoping I could explain to her why she received what appear to be premonitions involving *three* major public disasters—none of which included anyone she knew personally.

Death In The Sky

The first one involved a visual hallucination. In January 1986, a few days before the launch of the ill-fated space shuttle *Challenger,* she was watching a space program on TV with her family. In the program, one of the astronauts handed a red apple to Christa McAuliffe, a teacher selected to ride into space with the shuttle *Challenger.* "At that very moment I saw, as plain as day, a red fireball explosion," recalls Claire. "I started sweating and felt an extreme pain in my heart, and told my husband about my vision.

"The day of the *Challenger* launch, my husband was at work and my children were in school. I sat on the sofa with the TV tuned to the shuttle launch. I felt an overwhelming sadness and fear. When the *Challenger* launched, I just knew something terrible was about to happen. Moments later, the explosion occurred. I don't think I've ever felt so sad."

Claire's second possible disaster premonition—this time a precognitive dream—involved a strange airplane accident over the island of Maui in Hawaii. On April 28, 1988, the captain of an Aloha Airlines Boeing 737 jet flying at 24,000 feet heard a sudden, loud bang followed by a "whooshing" sound. A crack had opened in the fuselage. The roof had peeled right off the plane's passenger cabin, sucking out a flight attendant and injuring eight other passengers.

Two days before the accident, Claire dreamed that she was a passenger sitting in a plane seat. "I was in the airplane seat, looking up, and there was no ceiling to this plane. Only blue sky and clouds above me. The wind was very cold. There were fragments of the roof hanging on to what was left of the top of the plane. At that point the dream ended and I awoke.

"A few days later, the news of the accident came on TV and showed the jet landing with the whole top section of the plane gone, just as I had seen in my dream."

Eight months later, Claire believes she precognitively experienced the famous December 21, 1988, Lockerbie airplane disaster, again in a dream and again from the vantage point of someone on that flight. Libyan terrorists exploded a bomb aboard a Pan Am Boeing 747 over Lockerbie, Scotland, killing 288 people.

"In my dream, I found myself sitting a passenger seat in a plane. All of a sudden I felt a thump, as if someone had just hit me hard. Then I felt cold, icy snow hit the side of my face. All I could see were bodies, and then I awoke from my dream, crying and afraid. Several days later, the Lockerbie plane crashed."

What was she supposed to do about her nerve-wracking precognitions, she asked. "If I had called NASA, would they have stopped the launch—or would the FBI have arrived on my doorstep to arrest me? I have asked the clergy what to do and I'm told to 'pray.' Well, I've prayed, and it didn't help. With these premonitions, I wake up in a puddle of sweat, with my heart ready to jump out of my chest. I hope you can offer me some explanation."

I shared with Claire similar stories received by the Rhine Research Center from persons foreseeing public disasters, and reassured her she was not alone. Before a plane crashes, a space shuttle explodes, or a skyscraper is demolished by terrorists in New York City, chances are someone in America is confronting a frightening premonition.

8

TERROR ATTACK:
PREMONITIONS OF 9/11

The events of September 11, 2001, generated the largest outpouring of disaster premonitions we ever received at the Rhine Research Center related to a public, national catastrophe. In Chapter 2, we described Marie's 9/11 precognitive vision ("A Fire at the Pentagon") of billows of black smoke coming out of the Pentagon. It was quite specific, accurate, and true to subsequent events. Marie did not identify the day, but she picked the right building, and she foresaw the specific result as faithfully captured in news photos several weeks later. Most of the other reports we received about 9/11 were more ambiguous and nowhere near as focused, intense and realistic as Marie's, but they too suggested the experiencers may have somehow psychically tuned into the disaster on some subconscious level before it actually occurred.

The 9/11 premonition of a woman from Canada started with an unusual, strong feeling on September 9 that she absolutely had to watch the news the next day. This progressed to a mental picture of the World Trade Center and bombs, but not one of airplanes actually crashing into the towers.

9/11 In Canada

"When I awoke on Monday morning, September 10, I reminded myself I had to watch the news that day. As my day progressed, I became extremely agitated and felt like I was bouncing off the walls. I was in a constant state of confusion. I would be in the kitchen preparing something and going over to the TV to check the news. Finally, around two o'clock in the afternoon, I just stopped and said aloud, 'Why do I have to watch the news today?'

"The second I said that, I pictured the World Trade Center in my head and in the next instant I was in the basement of the World Trade Center. (I have never actually been there.) I could see a lot of cement and was standing directly in front of the exit stairs. Immediately I said to myself, 'They're not going to bomb the Trade Center again?'" She was referring to the fact that the World Trade Center had been attacked almost a decade earlier, in February 1993, by Islamic terrorists who set off an explosion in the building's public parking garage, killing six persons and injuring more than a thousand people.

"But that thought persisted throughout the rest of the day. After my vision of the World Trade Center, my agitation started to subside. By supper I was better, but still not calm. My boyfriend came home after work, and during dinner I told him about my being 'driven' all day to watch the news. When he asked what I thought it could be, I replied, 'I don't know. I keep thinking of the World Trade Center bombing.'"

An elderly man from South Carolina sent me a handwritten letter detailing his haunting dreams, which apparently mixed symbolism with some specific, accurate details.

9/11 In South Carolina

"On Sunday, September 9, 2001, I had a very vivid dream of a building so tall I couldn't see the top. Then smoke began to billow from the structure about halfway down its side. Then the dream quickly switched to another building where people were looking out windows, which were wide and well-defined. The people were dark-haired and had dark complexions. As I dreamed the events, my sense of reason told me no such tall building, like the one on fire, existed in my town. The second building in my dream most resembled our local hospital, and I reasoned that the men standing in the windows were doctors.

"All the next day, Monday, September 10, I felt an urge to contact someone—but who and how? Then in the early hours of Tuesday, September 11, I had a series of dreams so disturbing that I fell out of my bed. I had difficulty getting back to sleep, and when I awoke I had forgotten the disturbing dream. I got up, and when I turned on the TV the World Trade Center disaster was in progress.

"Two days later, NBC showed the second building in my dream, with people staring from broken windows as I had seen in the dream—their faces were identical to those in my dream."

A Catholic woman physician from Indiana with a history of psychic intuitions had a series of frightening dreams on the morning of 9/11.

9/11 In Indiana

"Beginning at two A.M. on the morning of September 11, I had four consecutive dreams of assassinations by Middle Eastern men on totally innocent victims, myself included. The dreams were vivid and horrifying, causing me to awaken after each one. When I finally crawled out of bed that morning, I was struck with a feeling of horror and dread. I couldn't get into my car to go to work, I was shaking so much from fright. I 'knew' that something dreadful was happening involving a plane crash, although I also knew these feelings were totally irrational. I prayed for fifteen minutes until they passed. I arrived at work a bit late, just in time to see on TV the second hijacked plane fly into the World Trade Center."

Guy Ottaway, a forty-one year old, married, crime-scene examiner with the local police force in Yorkshire, England, also e-mailed me shortly after 9/11. He explained that he had a history of "unnerving premonitions" involving public catastrophes. His premonitions included the *Challenger* space shuttle disaster. Shortly before the 9/11 terrorist attack on the twin skyscrapers of the World Trade Center in New York, he had a frightening dream.

9/11 In England

"I was in a city, looking up. The main image I saw in my dream was two tall plumes of smoke. I saw fire, and I felt as though I was underneath the fallout from a volcano. I was taking cover under some kind of shelter from the rubble and boulders flying through the air and raining down. I saw aircraft, and an image of my brother, a former pilot. I awoke in a cold sweat, feeling emotions of extreme fear and shock.

"Remembering the *Challenger* precognition, I got to work and wrote down the details of my premonition on a sheet of paper. The word I used in my notes to sum up the overall feeling was 'Disaster!' I locked the notes in my drawer, and told two friends what I had dreamed."

When the terrorist attack started to unfold on the TV news the morning of September 11, 2001, and the Twin Towers were twin plumes of smoke and fire with debris raining down from the sky on the heads of fleeing people, Guy took out his notes and looked at them again. "I don't know what to do. I am in shock," he wrote to me.

Guy has since given up his police work. Working daily with death and tragedies, he found that his ESP was repeatedly providing him information from or about deceased victims of crimes and fatal accidents. The emotional strain was too much for him.

Dr. Jim Carpenter, my colleague here at the Rhine Research Center and a fellow clinical psychologist, received his own share of troubled calls and e-mails from people who may have experienced premonitions of the 9/11 terrorist attack on America.

When Nightmares Come True

On the morning of September 10, a twelve-year old boy Jim knows woke from a terrible nightmare. In the dream, the boy and some friends were in a nearby mall when a huge jetliner zoomed down out of the sky right on top of them. There was great destruction, and perhaps he was being killed. His parents came to his bedside and reassured him that such nightmares were harmless, and spoke about the safety of airplanes and the security of malls. But he was very hard to comfort, and missed a morning of school because he was so shaken by the dream. The next day brought the planes and fire and horror. Afterward the boy was having anxiety attacks and trouble knowing what to believe.

Our reason tells us that nightmares happen to many people every night, and hundreds of nightmares never come true. But to those telling them, these out-of-the-ordinary experiences are viewed as different, and deeply meaningful.

Nonstop Nightmare

On the night of September 10, a woman awoke after only an hour or so of sleep after a terrible dream. She was in a large building with many other people when suddenly the whole thing gave way and tumbled into space. Then she was in the dark, crawling among broken pipes and electrical wires. She woke up shaking and crying. Her husband held her until she could breathe. She finally went back to sleep, but shortly woke again with the same dream. This happened a third and fourth time, and only stopped when medication helped her salvage a few hours rest. She had never had such a night before in her life.

If you speak with these people, you know they are not attention-seekers and fakers," says Jim. "They are good citizens with broken hearts. If parapsychologists can help us to understand this psychic faculty better, perhaps we can hopefully use it to protect ourselves from future tragedies."

Jim received several stories of bizarre behavior preceding the 9/11 attack, which made some sense viewed in the light of subsequent events.

"I'm Afraid Of The News!"

"On September 15, I got a call from a woman who wanted to talk a bit about the terrible week. She mentioned that she was struck by a strange occurrence with her elderly mother, disoriented from strokes, whom she visited in the nursing home, as she often did, on the evening of September 10.

"Her mother was unusually agitated that night, and could not be calmed when the television was turned to the news. She cried out, 'I'm afraid of the news! The news is bad! The news is bad! The news is bad!' She could only be calmed down when it was turned off. Nothing upsetting was being shown on the news at the time, she usually enjoyed the news, and liked to have it on most evenings. As far as her daughter could determine, nothing upsetting had been on the television earlier that evening, and the daughter wrote it off as an inexplicable piece of ranting by her confused mother."

A pet dog featured in another story shared with Jim of unusual behavior connected to the 9/11 attack.

The Barking Dog

A friend of Jim's had personally lost no one in the tragedy, but his uncle, working in the World Trade Center's South Tower, barely got out alive after fleeing down sixty floors with hundreds of other terrified office workers. According to his aunt, at the precise time the first hijacked jet slammed into the North Tower eighteen minutes earlier, their little dog began barking and whining inconsolably in their apartment for no apparent reason. Neither could recall the dog ever acting this way before, and the apartment was nowhere near the World Trade Center.

The 9/11 events produced understandably strong emotional responses and reactions in the people who foresaw them. The horrific event drove one distraught woman to write me, "I can honestly say that this experience unnerved me. It was far stronger than any others I've had before, and I've had quite a few. It was as if my 'psychic self' took over my body and mind. There was no mistaking the message, and I should have known. But like many Americans before the event happened, I thought it was impossible. I've spent a good part of this week forgiving myself for not trusting my vision and picking up the phone to warn someone."

I reassured this distraught woman, and others who wrote me, that there really is nothing they can do to warn the authorities in events like these. We can only hope that, far in the future, our scientific understanding of these psychic phe-

nomena will be developed to the point that we can reliably
distinguish true disaster premonitions from false ones. Only
then will we be in a position to alert authorities to such
events—and be believed.

Until then, we can listen, and sometimes that is enough.
As one person with a vivid 9/11 premonition explained to
me, "I'm so very grateful for your listening ear. That alone
has allowed me to cope with my experience and move on."

The most puzzling 9/11 report I received in the weeks following the attack came from a woman I'll call Becky Carter.

Becky's Story

Before September 11, 2001, Becky had never heard of
Michael Horrocks. Horrocks was copilot of United Flight
175, commandeered that morning by Islamic terrorists
shortly after it lifted off from Boston's Logan Airport on its
way to Los Angeles. According to television reports, at 8:42
A.M. flight 175's transponder was suddenly shut off and the
jet made an unexpected U-turn over New Jersey back toward
the north, heading for New York City and the South Tower of
the World Trade Center. Horrocks's plane had been hijacked.

On that same day, thirty thousand feet below and several
hundred miles south, Becky told me she had just finished
making breakfast for her husband John, a district attorney,
and their nine-year-old son Matthew, in her kitchen in North
Carolina. Becky did not know Michael Horrocks, or the desperate situation he was in. She had her own worries—how to
get out of a promised trip to Disneyland in Florida without
making her son, brother Steve, and his son Scotty very angry
at her. She had already upset her husband John with her
bizarre behavior.

She had planned the Florida trip three months earlier,
back in June, and had paid for the airline tickets in July. They
were booked to depart September 11, 2001. The bargain fare
even included a free seat for one of the kids. Everyone was

excited and looking forward to the trip, Becky included. It was a family joke: Becky was always the first to pack her bags. She loved to travel and had no fear of flying. She and Matthew had just returned from a trip to New York City.

But as the departure date moved closer and closer, Becky had become unusually anxious about the trip, to John's growing annoyance. The crazy feelings had begun two months earlier, in July.

"She started becoming very disturbed, distressed, disrupted," John later told me. "She showed a strange anxiety that I didn't understand, and she couldn't explain to me."

As the trip got closer, Becky started fishing around for excuses not to go. "She would talk about maybe Matthew not feeling well enough, he had a cold, things like that. I found her behavior very unusual since she had been so excited back in June when she first planned the trip."

Becky remembers that the trip, for some reason, "kept laying heavy on me. The sensation almost smothered me. It got heavier and heavier. It increased in August. I would tell John, 'I don't know about this trip—something is not right,' and he would say, 'You're just probably tired, you've been very busy this summer, you'll be all right when the time comes.' I wanted to scream and say, 'John, I'm not tired! I'm not tired! And I'm not crazy!' By the end of August, I felt like I was literally about to suffocate, I was so anxious."

As her unexplainable anxiety increased, so did John's understandable irritation.

John Carter, in his early forties, is a rational, no-nonsense person, something you would expect from someone schooled in law, working as an assistant district attorney.

"I'm the classic example of your old-fashioned, concrete thinker," admits John. "My whole life, professionally and personally, I've been in tune only with what I can see, hear, touch." Becky, part Cherokee Indian, balanced John's rationality with her own strange intuitions and spirituality, something John tolerated with difficulty throughout their ten years of marriage. Whatever was bothering her didn't make sense to John, and it certainly didn't make sense to her son Matthew.

When Becky finally screwed up the courage to suggest to her son that they delay the trip, Matthew reacted angrily.

"He was very unhappy, he was crying and saying, 'Please, Momma, don't do this to me. You know how bad I want to go. And Scotty's gonna be so disappointed.'" Feeling terribly guilty, she reassured him they could go later. If they couldn't go now, he demanded, when would they go? "I said, I don't know, but not now." But she still hadn't canceled the trip.

On September 4, one week before Michael Horrocks's 767 taxied down the runway at Logan into the morning sky, Becky suddenly awoke at three A.M. from a deep sleep, in great distress from a bizarre dream. In her dream she saw nothing, only felt spinning blackness, but heard a man's voice urgently repeat the same number—"2830, 2830, 2830"—over and over. "It started in a normal voice, but got progressively faster and louder. The number was very clear."

The man's voice then started repeating a name over and over again, but not as clearly as the number. "I couldn't quite make it out," Becky later explained to me.

"It sounded like 'Rooks' or 'Horooks.' But the demanding voice was very insistent. It's like it was saying to me, 'Get up! Write this down! You're not paying me enough attention!'—like a little child does to his mother. The voice was so anxious, it made me feel very anxious, too. It got to the point that it woke me up."

Struggling awake, she switched on the light, found a pen and scribbled down the name and number, even as the voice continued in her head. She knew better than to wake John up. The next morning, Becky told John about her scary dream and the insistent man's voice. "John, something's going to happen," Becky declared.

It was always the same man's voice. Becky had a long history of psychic intuitions, as John learned when they first started going together. She had more than once correctly foreseen the death of relatives and friends, including her father, her mother, and her cousin Michael in Baltimore. In the summer of 1982, the year she graduated from high school,

Becky heard the man's voice on several occasions say to her, "What would you do if your dad died?" Later that year, a week before Christmas, she received a call at college. Her father had been admitted to the hospital at Asheville.

"At that moment, I knew my dad was dead," she told me. When she arrived home, her mom, brother Steve, and sister were packing her dad's things for his stay in the hospital. On the way to the hospital, Steve hurriedly tanked up the car at a Gulf gas station before jumping back in. Becky looked at him and said, "I don't know why everyone is in such a hurry. Dad has already died." Steve was incensed. "How can you say such a thing?" he berated her. When they got there, she remembers her mom holding her dad's overnight bag and thinking how heartbroken her mom was going to be. As they made their way down the hall, they were intercepted by a doctor who ushered them into a room to tell them that he had already died.

Becky occasionally got premonitions of death for complete strangers. In a courthouse in Raleigh, John and Becky were listening to two lawyers trying a case. As one was making his statement to the judge, she heard the same, familiar man's voice in her head say, "You know, he's going to die." A few months later, the lawyer died suddenly and unexpectedly of a heart attack. As a child, Becky had seen the ghost of her grandfather after he died. When she told her mother, her mother warned her, "Okay, Becky, we believe you, but don't tell anyone else because we don't want people to think you're crazy." She also had several clairvoyant dreams that came true, including one involving a fire in a Morganton house occupied by an acquaintance of their close friend.

Most of the time, John had remained skeptical, doubtful. "I spent a great deal of time wondering how much of this was just her overactive imagination or histrionics," John says. "I didn't want to call it bizarre, but it was all very alien to my way of thinking."

Neither John nor Becky had a clue as to what the number 2830 referred to, but John felt he knew where Becky's subconscious had probably picked up the mystery name. A classmate of Matthew's in school was named Rooks, and her father was a friend and colleague of John's. It stood to reason that Rooks was the name Becky had heard in her dream. The number, John guessed, might even be the last four digits of the Rookses' phone number. For John, case closed. But Becky had already checked out the Rookses' home and business phone numbers. Neither had a 2830. John finally told her to ignore the dream. It was nothing to be concerned about. Trying to keep peace in the family, Becky joked that perhaps the number was their lucky lottery number.

But as she later told me, deep in her heart she knew that was not the explanation for the scary, insistent voice that haunted her sleep. Whatever it was, the message was something important. She continued to feel that way as she prepared to leave for work on September 11.

That morning, at 9:03 A.M., UAL Flight 175 slammed into the South Tower of the World Trade Center, snuffing out the life of Michael Horrocks and his fifty-six terrified passengers.

Like the rest of us, Becky and John Carter sat glued to their TV set as the horrific tragedy unfolded, wondering what was going to happen next.

When the TV announcer read the names of the flight crew of UAL 175, and came to copilot Michael Horrocks, a stunned Becky immediately turned to John and gasped, "John, *that's* the name I heard in my dream!" Becky now felt she understood her strange, overwhelming need to cancel the dreaded trip to Disneyland. An airplane was not a safe place to be that day. Not that it mattered—with America's airspace shut down completely, and F-14s patrolling the skies, no one was going anywhere. (After the plane crash, a Web site was created honoring Michael Horrocks. Becky subsequently visited the site to learn more about Michael, and discovered to her surprise that their family and the Horrocks family from Pennsylvania had both vacationed in the same North Carolina coast town on Father's Day earlier that year.

Becky was convinced her mind had somehow tapped into the tragic events of September 11 before they happened.

John was no longer skeptical. They both immediately began to wonder whether the mysterious number 2830 Becky heard in her dream was also connected in some way to the inconceivable disaster that had rocked America.

But nothing computed. "The airline flight numbers came out very quickly—Flight 93, Flight 175—and Becky's number obviously didn't match either of them," recalls John. The casualty count was another obvious possibility. But the first casualty predictions from New York police officials topped ten thousand dead. Failing to find a match between 2830 and the flight numbers, or the casualty count from the twin skyscrapers—indeed, with anything connected to the September 11 tragedy—they finally quit trying.

On September 13, John told Becky to write down the number she had heard in her scary dream a week before the attack on the World Trade Center, put it in a sealed envelope, address it to herself, take it to the post office so it could be postmarked, and mail it back to herself. It was an action befitting a district attorney used to dealing with evidence.

"I told Becky I still thought the number was going to eventually have something to do with what had happened on 9/11, and that she should preserve it in a way that it could be used as documented proof if the need ever arose," says John.

Nine months later, in June 2002, District Attorney John Carter left a voice mail on my phone. He was seeking a meeting for himself and his wife Becky, following a referral from a local mental health psychologist who knew I was a trained parapsychologist as well as psychologist.

The scary dream, the possibility that Becky had somehow foreseen 9/11, and had even received a warning about or from Michael Horrocks was very difficult to handle. Admits John, "The situation had become so troubling to Becky and myself that we decided to get some counseling." But something else had also happened in intervening months. They believed they now knew how the mystery number 2830 fit into the whole puzzle.

When I got John's message coming from a district attorney's office, however, my immediate reaction was mild fear that I might be getting called to court, or would have to scramble through my back files dealing with some clinical forensic evaluations that I had handled dealing with child custody or possible child abuse. But when I finally reached John, he explained that his wife was having psychic experiences that were bothering her, with the 9/11 premonition being the final straw. Their drive to see me would be a long one since they lived more than two hours away, but they needed some answers. I agreed to see them the following week.

On July 12, John, Becky, and their son Matthew knocked on the door of my office at the Rhine Research Center. I found them to be an attractive, upper-class, Southern couple. All three were tanned and nicely dressed in casual clothes. Becky wore a pale green pants suit that suited her blond hair, and John wore a short-sleeved pink shirt. John looked somewhat older than Becky, with a ruddy complexion. Both would have looked perfectly at home in a typical Southern country club.

I remember John began right away to do the talking, and it was apparent that he was the one in charge, even while talking about her issues. If they had engaged me for marriage counseling, I would have intervened at the start. But I didn't sense any real tension between them, so I let him continue with his account.

I soon realized that John was speaking out of his own guilt and true concern for his wife. Essentially, he was saying, "I was wrong. I have hurt her by my attitude in the past, and now I know differently. Help us figure out how to make this right." At several points, he appeared almost tearful.

John had been shaken by the events. His comfortable, rational world had taken a body blow. "Given my background," John told me, "it's been very hard for me to understand the kind of intuitive things my wife experiences and has tried to explain to me throughout our marriage. It's caused a lot of tension in our relationship. But her 9/11 premonition really opened my eyes. It forced me to consider possibilities I wouldn't have considered before that."

As I listened, John proceeded to lay out for me a possible connection between the number 2830 from Becky's dream and the 9/11 terrorist attack on the World Trade Center.

After September 13, when Becky sealed the number in the envelope, posted it to herself, and received it back, they put it away and moved on with their lives, John explained. But a strange thing happened. The casualty count for the World Trade Center soon began to fall rapidly. After two weeks of confusion, frantic digging, and recovering bodies; of patiently contacting companies, families, and embassies reporting people in the Twin Towers at the time of the strike; of cross-checking multiple, separate casualty lists to eliminate duplicate names, the official projected casualty count had dropped to 6,789. By late October, it had fallen to 4,864. A month later, as Americans sat down to their Thanksgiving dinners, the number had dipped below 3,900. John and Becky had also noticed the trend. Where would the casualty count stop?

"Sometime in October or November, we started to seriously consider the possibility that the final number would be 2830," says John.

The freefall gradually stopped. Three more months passed as the number slowly inched lower. By February 2002, most of the missing or dead had clearly been accounted for. On Valentine's Day, the number reached 2838, only eight more than Becky's 2830.

On May 15, 2002, nine months and four days after Michael Horrocks's plane slammed into the World Trade Center, two professors from George Washington University published a study on the attack. The title of the paper was *Federal Emergency Management in the United States: Implications of the Terrorist Attacks of September 11, 2001*. In it, they announced that 2,830 people had perished in the World Trade Center inferno.

We will never know the final death toll. Three years have now passed since the Twin Towers were destroyed, and still only 1,538 of the confirmed victims have been matched to bodily remains. More than 1,200 others are listed as dead simply on the basis of court-issued death certificates provided to families that could prove they had loved ones working or visiting the World Trade Center that day. We don't know how many homeless people were inhabiting the area and killed, because many vagrants lose contact with family and loved ones, dying without anyone claiming their bodies. The number will always remain an estimate.

For John, however, the days of disbelief were over. He felt he owed his wife an apology.

When Becky got her chance to talk, I found her quite verbal, though initially she appeared a bit passive and uncertain. There were a lot of "yes, ma'ams" sprinkled through her speech, as many good Southern ladies do, but I could sense a person at a crossroads in her life.

Their coming as a couple was a turning point in their marriage. Becky felt she had been stifled, unable to fully develop herself since so much of her life had involved psychic impressions she couldn't really talk to her husband about.

Now the dam had finally been broken, and everything came rushing out. Becky brought to the meeting a long, written list of psychic experiences that had occurred throughout her thirty-seven years of life, starting as a child. With John finally in her corner, supporting her, she could lay it all out. She wanted my help. Was she crazy? If not, what did it all mean?

Despite my parents' well-known research, I am quite cautious in my interpretation of psychic claims. My training in psychology and my many years working as a therapist have taught me to look first for more mundane, psychological explanations.

While it was not a professional evaluation, I did not pick up any significant emotional problems or delusional thinking on the part of either of them. Their obvious sincerity came through loud and clear. John is professional, quietly religious, a big hunter, and an avid outdoorsman, married for ten years—nothing that would suggest a loner, an oddball, a social misfit. John also mentioned at the time that he was a candidate for district court judge (he went on to win that race).

Becky was also your average American. She had a North Carolina public school education, had earned her business administration degree from a small, Baptist-affiliated university, and was at that time working in the office of an ear, nose, and throat physician in their home town. She was into gardening, photography, and pets (she had lots, including two prairie dogs!). She was part Cherokee, but didn't seem overly concerned with her Indian roots. I wondered if she would perhaps explain her lifelong history of psychic intuitions by making some glib New Age claim to be the descendent of a Native American shaman. She did not, although the Cherokees do have a long tradition of prophecy and foretelling events, including receiving warnings of future dangers in dreams.

She and John were normal as could be. They had simply had an unusual, troubling experience that bewildered them, and they could not ignore it.

John and Becky clearly welcomed the opportunity to share their experience with someone else. Like Saint Paul on the road to Damascus, John had been knocked off his horse by the Light. I sensed his conversion was both honest and heartfelt. The unopened envelope with the number 2830 remained an object of wonder to them.

"It means something, maybe it's proof of something, I don't know what," declared John. "I mean, what should she do with this?" It was a sincere question, a plea for help. "If you can give us any guidance on this, it would be a true blessing," he concluded.

What does someone do with an envelope with a number in it and a story that stretches our belief, our definition of reality? I believe you simply share it, and let people make up their own minds.

The tragic events of 9/11 changed the lives of millions of people, mostly for the worse. Becky was lucky. In the end, her frightening 9/11 premonition turned out to be a personal breakthrough for both herself and her marriage. She has finally come to accept her experiences. She no longer feels the need to hide them or apologize for them. A great weight has been lifted off her shoulders. More important, her husband no longer looks at her strangely and disapprovingly when she talks about her intuitions. She can be herself and still be accepted by those she loves most.

9

IS FATE INEVITABLE?

One of the most compelling questions to arise from our precognition research is the age-old question of free will versus fate. If someone can accurately know the future beforehand, does that mean that it is already determined? If such is the case, the idea of volitional freedom could just be an illusion.

In "Judgment Day at Butler's Crossing" (Chapter 3), the seventy-eight year-old man in North Carolina dreamed that he would be hit and killed by a car in the town of Butler's Crossing. Three days later, he was run down by an automobile in Butler's Crossing. Could he have done something to avoid it? Are fate's decrees changeable—or was he doomed to die?

The ancient Greeks believed Nyx, the goddess of night, had three daughters—the Fates—who controlled human destinies and determined the length of our mortal life before we were even born. With our allotted time on earth represented by a thin thread, the first daughter spun the thread of life, the second measured out its length according to the decree of the gods, and the third cut it at the appointed time.

Humans could do nothing to change it. In the Middle Ages, Shakespeare populated his plays with doomed lords like Macbeth, and "star-crossed" lovers like Romeo and Juliet who could not escape their predetermined fates. It remains a powerful, persistent belief today. Millions of newspaper readers around the world check the astrology column daily to see what fate has in store for them.

Are such human events—from assassinations and accidents to work promotions and winning lotteries—predetermined by the gods or the movement of stars, and thus fixed and foreseeable? Or is our future simply a matter of chance and thus ultimately unforeseeable?

I have spent some heated moments discussing the pros and cons of this issue with professional colleagues as well as friends. My Dutch parapsychologist colleague Dick Bierman argues that if you can make a successful intervention and change the future, then by definition it is not precognition. You never saw the future, because what you saw never happened.

Other parapsychologists differ on this question, offering arguments relating to the nature and definition of time, the meaning of freedom, and the extent and characteristics of precognition. One theory is that we see possible futures or a maybe even a probable future but the "final" future is not yet determined. My father J.B. Rhine suggested that the critical question seemed to be the efficiency of precognition. Precognition rarely shows us the future in full, complete detail. With the paucity of specific details about the future typically generated during laboratory experiments in precognition and reported by people experiencing spontaneous precognition, there often is some "wiggle room" for a future that can change.

Testing someone's ability to *see* the future is fairly simple to do. In the early days of parapsychology, we used a deck of ESP cards in the experiment. The test subject tried to predict the order of the deck in advance of what it would be after it was shuffled. This "run" through the deck was done many times, and then the hits and misses were tallied. The results were analyzed using statistics to determine if the subject seemed to show some real precognitive ability or not. Today, computers generate random numbers for targets, and automatically tally scores when the testing is done.

But testing whether someone can *change* the future is another task altogether. Because of the "Bierman paradox" described above—if you can change a foreseen future, you did not see the future, because what you saw never happened—it is virtually impossible to design a laboratory experiment to answer this question conclusively.

Given such experimental difficulties, parapsychologists have to turn to spontaneous ESP experiences for whatever answers they might suggest about the inevitability of fate. If we cannot prove people can change a foreseen future, perhaps we can determine that people can act in such a way as to to avoid a foreseen future.

In the most important study to date, we selected out and analyzed 433 precognition reports from our Rhine ESP case collection in which there was enough threat of danger that intervention would be desirable. We ignored experiences that suggested pleasant or neutral outcomes.

To our surprise, we discovered that in two-thirds of these 433 cases the ESP experiencer—for a variety of reasons—never took any action at all, allowing the catastrophe to occur.

Before you can attempt to change the future, for example, you first have to recognize that you have actually been given a glimpse of it.

Mugged On A Street

A man from Charlotte, North Carolina, recently sent me an e-mail relating some of his many precognitive dreams over the years. In the beginning, he did not recognize them as such. It took a tragedy to awaken him to the possibility that he could see the future. He dreamed that he met his cousin Rick, a pharmacist, on a street in Massachusetts. As he reached out to shake his hand, his cousin was attacked from behind and fell to the ground at his feet. He dismissed the dream as a bad nightmare.

Not long afterward, Rick was viciously attacked by a mentally deranged person as he walked along the street on his lunch break. He died a few days later. "It was the first time I recognized the phenomenon of precognition," he noted ruefully.

As we mentioned earlier, ESP comes to us in the same form and manner as our ordinary mental processes, like dreams and intuitions. This makes it very hard, at times, to recognize the difference between an ordinary nightmare and a true, precognitive warning. No special markers distinguish one from the other. We learn the difference only when one or more precognitive experiences come true in a dramatic enough way to make us consider the possibility.

Even more difficult than recognizing and acting on dreams that may be precognitive is the willingness to accept that a vision we may receive while wide awake could foretell the future. For most of us, seeing is not believing when it comes to psychic hallucinations. We automatically assume our eyes are playing tricks on us. Kristin, an eighteen-year-old girl in Colorado, had a precognitive vision she failed to act upon, because she could not recognize its validity quickly enough.

Fall From A Slide

"I was at a fire safety event, and there was this large, air-filled slide that the children were playing on. In my vision, I saw a child fall off, hitting his head on the ground. Then I was looking at the location where he had fallen . . . and he wasn't there. Soon after the vision, I saw the same child go up the slide, then fall off—just as I thought I had seen moments earlier."

Kristin has had several ESP experiences in her short life, but this experience bothered her the most. "I feel I could have stopped it, knowing it was going to happen," she says.

Indeed, it is difficult for most of us to take ESP warnings seriously. Though the majority of Americans believe in ESP, our dominant scientific culture is still skeptical of ESP, leaving us confused about the possibility and a bit embarrassed to entertain the idea. It is easier to ignore our dreams or premonitions than to act on them. A middle-aged woman in Kentucky named Jacquie sent me the following ESP experience she ignored, despite earlier precognitive experiences that had come true.

Don't Take The Bus

"I dreamed that I had taken the bus to visit my sister after work, something I have never done in real life. When I got off at her bus stop, it was raining. Two men appeared and started chasing me. I could identify them and the clothes they were wearing. I was afraid they would catch me and steal my purse, but as I was running down the middle of the block I suddenly awoke from the dream."

The dream bothered Jacquie so much that she told her girlfriend Jean at work about it. Later that day, for a number of reasons, she ended up taking the bus home and getting off at her sister's house, just as in her dream. "Two men starting chasing me, and I suddenly remembered the dream. I wondered what was going to happen to me since my sister had to buzz me into her apartment, and there was no way I could reach there before they caught me. But to my luck, my sister's husband was working on his car out on the street, and he started to chase my pursuers, although he eventually lost their trail."

Why did Jacquie not accept and act on her ESP warning? Jacquie herself finds it hard to explain. "The experiences always have to do with danger to myself or family. They are very vivid and exact, as in the dream. I cannot understand why I do not go with my gut feeling."

Sometimes, action is prevented by the absence of any information at all as to where or when the disaster will occur. That was the case with a mother from Utah, whose story follows. She was left with no choice but to pray that her son's dream was nothing but a child's passing nightmare.

"A Car Ran Me Down"

One morning, her ten-year-old son told her, as she was getting him and her other two children ready for school, "Mom, I had a terrible dream last night. A car ran me down. It was so awful."

She explained to us, "My first thought was to keep him home. But I realized I had to be calm, although my heart was racing with fear. I told him that we couldn't live our life ruled by dreams or we would live a life of fear. When they left, I uttered a silent prayer and told my kids to stay on the sidewalk, which they did, since they're very obedient children.

"Some three minutes later, someone came running to me. A truck had run up on the sidewalk and hit him. He died seventy minutes later, never regaining consciousness."

I have great sympathy for this mother and her dilemma. With my own background in the paranormal, I would probably have hesitated to let my child go out that day, although I might have let him go out the next day. Like this mother, I do not let dreams rule my decisions or my life, but sometimes there are exceptions. Thankfully, I have never been faced with her decision.

In a number of cases, intervention is impossible because the identity of the "target person" is disguised, incorrect, or another person is substituted for the proper one. This is not uncommon in our normal dreams in which we prevent ourselves from knowing what we may not want to know. We may dream of an angry stranger rather than consciously see that someone we love is actually hostile to us. This built-in, psychological defense mechanism protects us against pain. In the following case, this common trick of the psyche seems to have prevented any attempt at an intervention.

"She Was My Best Friend"

"It happened five years ago when I was eighteen years old," writes a woman from Minnesota named Nancy. "I woke up one morning after a restless night with a very vivid dream imprinted on my mind. I often wake remembering my dreams, but this one bothered me particularly. My mother at that time slept on a sofa bed in the living room, I in an adjoining bedroom. My dream started with my mother and me standing in a certain spot in the living room, looking down at the body of one of our best lady friends lying dead on the sofa bed. Everything was exact. I was standing a certain way, my mother the same. My mother sobbed five words, 'She was my best friend.' Then the dream ended, and I woke up.

"I simply couldn't get this dream out of my mind, but I shrugged it off more or less, because it seemed very unlikely that this friend would be dying anywhere, but particularly unlikely that it would be on our sofa bed. She was in perfect health at the time and still is today. Then exactly one month from the day of the dream, it all happened—but the situation was reversed. My mother died in her sleep of a heart attack. I awoke to hear her gasping, called the doctor and this lady friend immediately. The doctor arrived first and pronounced my mother dead. My friend came in, and we both assumed the exact positions as in my dream, and she said the very words, in the same tone of voice—'She was my best friend.' "

In this case, it would appear that the information was psychically received below the conscious level, and the creative and protective dream process reversed and substituted the figures in the dream so as to obscure the truth. The unfortunate result in this case was that Nancy was prevented from warning her mom.

Although I have spent many years studying other people's ESP experiences, I myself have had very few—and even those might be explainable by chance. When I was young, I did once experience a similar, memorable mix-up involving people.

Whose Mother Will Die?

I woke up one morning with a vivid dream that my own mother had died. It was the only time in my life I ever had such a dream, and knowing what I did about psychic experiences from my parents' research, I was understandably quite worried. At the time, I was working very closely with a young colleague at the Parapsychology Laboratory at Duke University, a good friend of mine from another country. We learned later that same morning that her mother had died suddenly, far away in her home country.

Why did my extrasensory perception substitute my mother for her mother? I have always supposed it was a sympathetic type of response for the sorrow that I knew she would feel.

Here is another ESP experience involving subconscious substitution sent us by a woman in New York. This one involved switched places instead of people, but the end result was the same—intervention was thwarted.

Water Damage

"One November, I dreamed that my summer home on Long Island was a veritable shambles from water coming down the ceiling and walls," she wrote in her letter to us. "Night after night, for fourteen consecutive nights, I had the same dream: ceiling plaster down, walls wet and bulging, furniture ruined, etc. I tried going to bed late in the hope that, being tired, I wouldn't have the dream. One night, I even drank a glass of wine. I never touch the stuff because it paralyzes me. I felt dizzy and numb, but that didn't stop my dream.

"I mentioned the dream to my daughter, to my brother, to a friend living in the Bronx. I even called up the caretaker at my summer home, and after telling her of my dream, asked her to have her husband check my place and see if everything was all right. She reported that her husband found my place in perfect condition. She expressed amazement at my superstitious nature.

"I still felt uneasy and called my insurance man, related the dream to him, and made sure I was covered. He laughed, and said he could not believe I was so foolish to give credence to a dream.

"On the last day of December that year, I left the office at five and arrived home at six to find my dining room in my New York apartment a veritable wreck. Water was coming down my ceiling, down my walls; carpets, floors, and furniture were wet and ruined. I discovered that the tenant above me had installed a washing machine without the benefit of a plumber. The husband did the work himself and the pipes weren't properly connected."

The above woman's place transposition experience reminds me of one of my own which might have been an ESP warning.

Where's The Fire?

While in a doctor's office, I began to smell smoke so strongly that I asked him, "Is there something burning in here?" It was not at all the kind of comment I would normally make, being fairly reticent in my younger days. He replied, "No, no, nothing burning in here." When I got home soon afterward I was greeted by fire engines surrounding my house, and firemen in my kitchen. My child and a neighbor child had been playing with matches.

These experiences underline the fact that ESP operates in and through our normal psychological processes, which include continuous conscious and subconscious filtering, making psychic messages more difficult to recognize immediately and act upon.

In other cases of failure to intervene, the reason seems to be simple failure of memory. Sometimes, like Jacquie who ended up taking the bus to her sister's house, the ESP experiencer gets caught up in other things and forgets the warning. That is what happened to this guilt-ridden father in the following case.

The Drowning

A Maine man had a fourteen-year-old son named Walter, who was spending the summer hanging out with a friend who lived about a mile from the father's store. Walter was a good swimmer, and often went swimming in the stream with the other neighborhood boys. One night, his father had a dream. Walter had gone swimming below a certain big tree above the dam and had been drowned. He dreamed when he got there the body had not been found, but a man he knew named John was diving for it. He awoke in great fright, crying, and scarcely able to control himself. His wife tried to calm him, saying that dreams don't necessarily come true but that, just to be safe, he should tell their son not to go swimming when he came in the next day. The next morning, the father went to his store and was busy and preoccupied when his son hurried in and said he was going swimming. At the moment, the father didn't think of the dream. Soon after, someone came running up and yelled, "Come quick! Walter was diving and hasn't come up."

The dream then came back with full force. He raced to the swimming hole. The body had not been found but John was diving for it. It was at exactly the same place as the dream, with exactly the same results. The father's tortured afterthought was, "If I had heeded the dream, my son would be alive today."

The worker in the following case initially remembered his precognitive dream and acted decisively on it—avoiding the predicted scenario all morning. But a few hours later, he simply forgot the warning, and then paid for his forgetfulness by ending up in a hospital bed.

Stay Off The Ladder

In a Western state after a tornado had destroyed some buildings, the company asked everyone to help rebuild them. One of the employees, not a carpenter, was helping with the carpentry. "Early one morning," he wrote us, "about two weeks after I started, I climbed up the ladder, and as I stepped onto the scaffolding there came into my mind a clear picture that puzzled me for several minutes. Every detail was so clear that I was dumbfounded. It seemed to me that I had stood at that exact spot before. Even the design of the wall, and the pattern of the paneling, was an exact duplication. I was puzzled for several minutes, because I'd never been up there before. In fact, I had never even done that kind of carpentry work before.

"Suddenly it came to me. I had dreamed it—six months before. Naturally, I remembered the dream in detail from there on. In that dream, I had fallen, was hurt, and was taken to the hospital in an ambulance. I immediately climbed back down the ladder, found the foreman and told him I didn't feel like working up there, so he gave me a job working on a large sliding door on the ground floor of the building.

"About eleven o'clock, having forgotten about my dream, I climbed back up to the first floor staging to nail in some blocks. As I crossed the staging, a plank suddenly snapped into three pieces, and I fell about seven feet, landing on my back on the concrete below. The blow temporarily paralyzed me from the hips down. I was taken away by an ambulance and ended up in the hospital for fifteen days."

Thousands of navy pilots have trained at the Naval Air Station in Pensacola, Florida, during the ninety years since it was established in 1914 as the first naval air station in the

U.S. Many Americans have seen a flying exhibit by the
navy's world-famous Blue Angels air acrobatics team that is
based there. In the following experience that occurred at
Pensacola, personal animosity kept a warning from being
delivered, leaving a young man dead and a survivor consumed with shame and regret.

Decapitated Pilot

A young naval aviation cadet, whom we will call Adam, was
in preflight school there, probably with a dream of becoming
a *Top Gun* fighter pilot one day. Instead, he had a very bad
dream about another young air cadet. At the time, the cadet
in the dream was a total stranger to Adam. In the dream, the
cadet was flying in a navy training plane when he crashed on
a strange, flat, open field unlike any found around the Pensacola base. The cadet was killed, and to make it worse, decapitated. Adam understandably awoke disturbed and upset
by the horrible dream.

Five months later, Adam was transferred to a different
naval air station for special training. The first day there, he
met the fellow cadet who had died in his dream. Unfortunately, Adam developed a dislike for the cadet from the start,
and a cool relationship evolved between them. Almost a year
later, the cadet was killed—decapitated in a diving crash on
a flat plain of mud just like the one in Adam's dream.

As Adam admits, "It is very difficult to describe the emotional feeling I went through, and I sometimes shudder today
when I wonder if it might have ended differently if I had just
swallowed my pride and given a warning before it was too
late."

Adam's disappointment with himself is understandable,
but if I were counseling him I would have assured him there
was probably little chance the cadet would have taken his
warning, even if it had been delivered. It is difficult to imagine the cadet walking into his commander's office and an-

nouncing he was giving up his flying career because of a dream—particularly since the cadet did not even trust or like Adam. The cadet would have risked becoming the laughing-stock of the base, or being discharged from the service for mental problems. Even if he did take the psychic warning seriously, how could he have effectively intervened unless Adam could give him more specifics on when and where the accident was expected to occur.

An interesting question is why Adam dreamed of a complete stranger in the first place, or of an acquaintance whom he admittedly did not like. We know from our research that only one out of seven cases involve complete strangers. Could the tragedy that was to come, which Adam somehow sensed, have been selected by him from the timeless world of precognition just because he was already sensitized in some way to an emotional conflict that this tragedy evoked? A theory about this has been suggested by the late Dr. Theo de Graaf, a Dutch psychiatrist, who calls it the "Personal Sensitization Factor." According to de Graaf's thinking, Adam may have been already troubled about feeling responsible, say, for a younger brother whom he did not like. In an attempt to resolve such a conflict, he is especially sensitive on a psychic level to situations that repeat that same set of issues. Unfortunately in this case, the animosity just decreased the likelihood of any intervention on Adam's part and probably would have just added to Adam's feelings of guilt.

There are many reasons for the failure of the majority of ESP experiencers to act on their precognition. Of the original study of 433 precognitive warnings of danger, a total of 271 cases, nearly two-thirds, saw no attempt at intervention. And what happened in the remaining 162 cases when people did try to intervene? Unfortunately, a third of those deliberate intervention attempts still failed.

One of the most frequent explanations why interventions were unsuccessful had to do with incomplete or insufficient information. Here is a particularly frustrating example that demonstrates conviction and the will to intervene, and yet ultimately proves unsuccessful.

No Safe Place

On a July evening, a woman I will call Jane was relaxing in a darkened room. As she sat there, half asleep and half awake, she had what she explained was a "vision." In this vision, she saw an awful accident. A child had been killed and was lying covered on the ground. She could not tell if it was a girl or a boy, but by the size of the body, she thought it was a child about five or six years old. Since the child was covered up, she had no idea who it was. She could not forget the vision.

Still fearful in the morning, she described her experience to her next-door neighbor and urged her to keep an eye on her five-year-old child, then she called her son who lived in the heart of town. She told him to watch his two children. She had another son who lived in the country, but she did not call him, because his yard was fenced in. His little girl, Kathy, seemed safe. But that day, Kathy was playing in the driveway when a township truck backed into her and killed her.

Although she actively tried to intervene, Jane failed to save her granddaughter from being struck by the truck because her vision did not convey the identity of the child involved or the location of the accident. Incomplete information is particularly common in ESP experiences that come to a person in a waking state. Waking hunches, intuitions, or visions like Jane's often are experienced simply as strong convictions of danger without enough information on which to act.

Sometimes, the ESP experiencer does all she can do to intervene, but the person foreseen to be at risk does not cooperate. The following mother tried her best, but her son eluded her plan to protect him.

Dog Bite

Susan from New York State dreamed she saw her four-and-a-half-year-old son all bloody, having been bitten by a dog, which she also visualized. Worried by the dream, she kept the child indoors for the next three days. On the fourth day, he ran out to the store next door.

As she explained to us, "Before I could get to the store, I heard piercing screams. I found that he had run into the store and bumped into a dog with a sore tail. The dog whirled around and bit my son in the eye. The injury was a slit just under the eye. I thought he was blinded, and I fainted. It was the same dog I dreamed of that bit him."

ESP dreams, just like normal dreams, usually provide a feeling of location, but typically unfold in a timeless, dateless, mental world. In Susan's dream, the dog bit her child, but there was no information about the date or the hour the bite occurred. No calendar was visible in her dream showing a date four days from then. If so, she could have let her little boy roam free until that date, then kept him home on the fourth day. She was in the frustrating position of knowing the future, but not what day the event would arrive.

In a few cases, the very effort to intervene backfired, and the action taken actually made the fatal chain of events come true, as in the following case.

Inescapable Injury

A woman in Oregon awoke one morning with an unaccountable fear for her three-year-old son and with the strong impression that he would be involved in an automobile accident. She guarded him very carefully but she finally decided to run away from her feeling. She took the child and drove some miles to her mother's house. While visiting there, the fear suddenly lifted. The relief she felt was so great that she burst into tears. Just then came a ring on the doorbell. A policeman with an excited crowd behind him was holding her little boy, limp in his arms. The child had been hit by a runaway car. The child had been sitting quietly under a tree in the yard when the car jumped the curb and hit him, injuring him severely. The mother closed her sad letter to us with the comment, "How he got out of the house unnoticed is a mystery to me. But evidently, it was to be."

This mother's fatalistic resignation reminds me of an old Iraqi parable retold and made famous by the English writer Somerset Maugham in his story "Appointment in Samarra." In it, a merchant in Baghdad sends his servant to the bazaar. The servant returns, trembling and frightened. He tells the merchant, "I was jostled in the market, turned around, and saw Death. Death made a threatening gesture, and I fled in terror. May I please borrow your horse? I will leave Baghdad and ride to Samarra, where Death will not find me." The master lends his horse to the servant, who flees to Samarra. Later that day, the merchant goes to the market and sees Death in the crowd. "Why did you threaten my servant" he demands. Death replies, "I did not threaten your servant. I accidentally bumped into him and was surprised to see him here in Baghdad, for I have an appointment with him tonight in Samarra."

Fatalism is defined in the dictionary as the view that all events are "necessitated by the nature of things, or by the fixed and inevitable decree of the arbiters of destiny." This view might be justified if a large number of the ESP experiences in our collection turned out as the one above. Fortunately, most do not. A future foreseen is not a future written in stone.

These examples of failed intervention attempts are greatly outnumbered by successful interventions. The important point we learned from this study was when ESP experiencers did actually try to intervene, they were successful about twice as often as not.

One of the most convincing intervention cases in our Rhine ESP files is the following story sent to my mother by an L.A. trolley conductor. The city of Los Angeles operated a streetcar system up until the 1960s, when the automobile and the freeway finally drove it out of business.

Dream Come True

A streetcar conductor in Los Angeles dreamed one night that, headed south, he pulled into a certain intersection on his ordinary route, near which was an off-ramp for auto traffic. At this intersection, cars sometimes made an illegal left-hand turn.

In his dream, he crossed the intersection just as a northbound trolley, No. 5, passed him. He waved at the trolley motor man, and suddenly just ahead and without warning, a big truck painted solid, bright red cut in front of him coming from the exit. The other trolley car had obstructed his view of the off-ramp, and the truck making the illegal turn couldn't see his trolley for the same reason. There was a terrific crash. People were thrown from their seats, and the truck was overturned. Three people were in the truck, two men and a woman, in his dream. The men were sprawled in the street dead and the woman was screaming in pain. The conductor walked over to the woman and she looked at him with the largest blue eyes he had ever seen and shouted at him, "You could have avoided this!"

He awoke from his dream with a start, soaked with perspiration. It was nearly time to get up, which he did, quite shaken from his dream. He reported for work and by his second trip that day had put the dream out of his mind.

But then, at the intersection of his dream, he became queasy. As he left the intersection when the signal changed, he saw the northbound trolley, No. 5. He felt definitely nauseated, but it was when the motor man on No. 5 waved to him that he remembered the dream. He slammed on the brakes and shut off the power. A truck—not a big truck completely red as in his dream, but a panel truck with space for advertising on the side painted over with bright red—shot directly into his path. Had his trolley been moving at all, he surely would have hit it.

Three people were in the truck, two men and a woman just like in his dream. As the truck passed in front of him, the woman leaned out of the window, looked at him with the same large blue eyes he had seen in the dream, and gave him the A-OK sign with her thumb and forefinger, thanking him for stopping. He was so upset by the near accident that he had to be relieved from work.

My mother Louisa Rhine cited this account as one of the most convincing intervention cases in her collection. It met all of the criteria she felt necessary for any one case: the event as dreamed occurred hours after the dream and so it was clearly precognitive; the advance information was specific in all essential details; and the collision seen in the dream presumably would have occurred if the warning had not been heeded and if the attempt to intervene had not been the proper one. Incidentally, the case is also a good example of how even in realistic precognitive dreams, there are often incorrect details such as the color of the truck.

Here is another dramatic case of intervention from the original Rhine case collection study, sent in by Beth, a seventeen-year-old girl from South Carolina. Beth's case was selected for a special study of children's and adolescents' ESP cases by Dr. Athena Drewes. It happened when Beth was fifteen years old.

Friends In Caskets

"This is the strangest thing ever to happen to me, and I thank God that it did," she wrote. "It all started with a dream I had. In the dream, as I was walking along I saw a cream-colored car drive toward a truck. As it traveled toward the truck, the car stopped then changed very slowly into a recognizable, dark-colored 1957 Oldsmobile. Then it started up again with a jerk and rammed into the truck, which I could see now had the name 'Frady's Transport Service' written on it. When it hit the truck, it went into a shapeless mass of metal. The scene then faded, and in my dream I walked on.

"Eventually, I found myself in a funeral home looking at six caskets. The people in the caskets were my five friends Martha, Ginger, Sonja, Clare, Sandy, and myself. I noticed that Martha and Ginger were in beautiful, silvery-white metal caskets with white lining. Clare was in a bronze casket. I woke up from the dream in a state of great nervous tension. At school the next day, Clare asked me to eat supper with her that night, but it turned out that her mother had scheduled a Cub Scout meeting at her house that evening, so she didn't feel like cooking. She suggested Clare take all of us girls to a local restaurant for supper instead. I was supposed to be at a talent show rehearsal at 7:30 that night at school, but she promised we would be done in time. I agreed to go. When Clare came by for me in her father's car, she had already picked up Martha and Ginger. Sonja had a date, and Sandy was sick, so they couldn't make it. But another girl, Melinda, took their place.

"When I saw the car Clare was driving, I simply froze. It was a dark-colored 1957 Oldsmobile. I don't remember what I said, but I made some excuse to get out of going, and another friend of mine drove me to the show instead. Once there, for some unknown reason, at exactly four minutes before eight that night, I almost fainted. But I managed to go ahead and sing anyway, leaning on the piano for support. As I was going off the stage a burning, indescribable feeling went through my body. I had to sit down.

"A few minutes after I left the stage, officials came into the teachers' lounge where I was resting, still feeling weak. They told us that there had been a car wreck at five minutes before eight that night. Clare had braked at a stop sign, then had started up again and had driven straight into a truck owned by 'Frady's Transport Service.' Of the four in the car, Ginger and Martha were killed instantly, and Clare died the next afternoon."

Just as she had foreseen in her dream, Ginger and Martha were buried in identical silvery-white caskets with white lining, in a double funeral. Clare had her funeral the next day and was buried in a bronze casket. Melinda, the only one who had not appeared in her precognitive dream, was the only survivor.

As young as she was, Beth had enough confidence to trust in her ESP dream and act upon it, although she regrettably did not have enough conviction and courage to share her dream with her friends. Had she done so, three lives might have been saved.

Keeping a diary of our dreams can help us recognize the difference between an ordinary nightmare and a true precognitive warning we need to act on. A good friend of mine on the Rhine Research Center Advisory Board, Dale E. Graff, has been keeping a dream journal for more than twenty years. Dale served as manager of the U.S. government's secret Star Gate psychic spying program where Joe McMoneagle worked. Not too long ago, he had the following dream. Taking it seriously may have saved his life.

Exploding Car

"In my dream, I am standing on the porch at the entrance to our house. My attention is drawn toward our white station wagon in the driveway. As I observe the car, I notice a small cylindrical object on the floor of the backseat area of the car. One end of this cylinder begins to glow bright red. Suddenly, the car explodes, and the car becomes totally enveloped in flames. I woke up, startled.

"I have been keeping a dream journal since 1970, and am quite familiar with the various types of dreams that I routinely experience, including those that have suspected psi content. This 'car explosion' dream was clearly not typical of day residue or review dreams. Due to its brevity and highly destructive imagery, I suspected that it was either a significant, personal, symbolic dream or a precognitive warning dream. Since I could not associate it as being a personal dream representing anger or approaching physical illness, I felt certain that it was very likely precognitive of an approaching event.

"The central image of the dream was clearly our white station wagon and I thought it best to examine the car as soon as possible. This car was the one my wife Barbara drove. I rarely used it. That morning, I examined the backseat area, suspecting that a leaking can of flammable material might be there.

"However, there was nothing at the rear seat or the open back area behind the seat that could be a potential fire hazard. I checked the underside of the car and the engine area but found no gasoline leaks. When I test drove the car, I could detect nothing unusual. I began to suspect that the dream might not have been a warning dream. However, the explosion imagery was too compelling to ignore, and I took the car to an auto repair garage as soon as convenient for a routine tune-up and safety check. I did not expect anything unusual to be found—maybe a change of spark plugs or some other minor work. A few days later, the garage owner called to tell me the car was ready for pickup. As I chatted with him at the garage, he said, 'I have something interesting to show you.' He picked up a small cylindrical object and remarked, 'Do you realize that you were driving a time bomb? Look at the fuel pump. One end is charred and the insulation on the connecting wires is burned off. You had an electrical short that could have led to a gas tank explosion. It's good you brought it in when you did. On this model car, the fuel pump is inside the gas tank.'

"I gazed at the damaged fuel pump, almost disbelieving what I saw. The thin, long fuel pump resembled the cylinder I had seen in the dream. I did not know that the fuel pump was mounted inside the gas tank. All cars I had ever owned had fuel pumps in the engine area."

He drove home slowly, reviewing the dream and its implications. In time, the failing fuel pump may have simply ceased to function or it may have shorted sufficiently to create an explosion. The potential for a catastrophic explosion did exist. That was all he needed to know, and it appears that is what the dream provided in dramatic style. It got his attention, and he made sure the potential explosion did not occur, even though he was uncertain about the true significance of the dream.

Far beyond the power of any human to deter, of course, are nature's rampages—hurricanes, earthquakes, and floods. Although a natural cataclysm will happen regardless of the wishes of the human beings concerned, a psychically fore-warned person can still take some effective action to avoid or reduce the negative impact of that disaster.

Tornado Coming

A Georgia man bought a building for an auto dealership, putting in a large plate-glass window and hanging a big electric sign in front. One night, his wife dreamed a tornado came and blew the sign into the plate-glass window, shattering it. Concerned by his wife's dream, and lacking any tornado insurance on his premises, he went out that day and bought some. Not long after, a tornado came through and blew the sign into the plate-glass window just as his wife had dreamed.

The salesman could not move his auto showroom out of the path of the tornado, but many other successful interventions involve deliberately getting out of the way—for example taking the baby out of the crib as a precaution as the mother did in the falling chandelier case described in Chapter 1, or changing travel plans to avoid a predicted plane crash. These interventions might not prevent the disaster itself from happening, but they can save the person from getting hurt by it, as may have happened in the following case.

Town House Robber

A young woman, spending the summer with her parents at their country home, decided to return to the city for a day, spend the night in the family's unoccupied town house, and return the following day to the country. The night before the trip, she dreamed she was sleeping in the house in town and was awakened by a man bending over her who put his hands on her throat and started to choke her. She awoke, terrified.

Nevertheless, the next morning she started out for town, determined to stick to her plan. Halfway to her destination she thought the better of it, turned around, and returned to the country. The following day, the family received a call from the police saying that their town home had been robbed the night before.

Would the girl have encountered the robber if she had returned to the city and spent the night there? We will never know, but she avoided a probable dangerous situation by acting on the warning delivered in her dream.

Of course, there are die-hard skeptics who believe that such warnings are utter nonsense, and they might go ahead and take the chance. I think there are a large number of people, even somewhat skeptical about the paranormal, who keep open the possibility that they might have received a psychic warning. They are likely to adopt the sensible philosophy of "It's better to be safe than sorry." If they can avoid the situation with minimal disruption to their lives and schedules, as the young woman could by simply staying in the country house, they will take no chances. This may be particularly true with mothers getting premonitions about their children, as seen in the following case.

Stay Away From Boy Scouts

A woman in Maryland, whom I will call Pam, dreamed one night that her little son followed two Boy Scouts to a nearby creek popular as a fishing and swimming spot where, to her horror, the toddler fell in and drowned. In her dream, Pam could clearly see the faces of the two Boy Scouts, whom she did not know and had never met before. She awoke frightened by the terrible dream.

Later that morning, she looked out the window and saw the very same two Boy Scouts she recognized from her dream sitting on the curb of her front lawn. Pam's response was very simple. "My son did not get out of the house that day," she wrote us.

Was Pam's dream psychic or was it simply a run-of-the-mill nightmare? Given that she did not go outside and look at the boys up close, were the two Boy Scouts on the curb really the same ones she saw in her dream? If so, were they actually heading for the creek? If so, would her toddler really have managed to get out and follow them down there? And if he managed to do it, would he really have fallen in and been drowned without anyone being able to save him? That is an awful lot of ifs, a skeptic might argue. But this mother was not about to take the chance with her precious child. She intervened to eliminate any chance of her son following the Boy Scouts—wherever they were headed.

In other cases, as with the trolley conductor in "Dream Come True" and the mother in "Falling from a Windowsill," no sustained attempt is made to avoid the situation and the foreseen accident starts to unfold as predicted. The event is cut short, because the person has been forewarned and is prepared that something might happen. In such cases, we can argue the foreseen calamity probably would have happened if action had not been taken.

Beware The Antenna

A California woman dreamed that her husband was lying jerking on the ground. He had been electrocuted when the TV antenna fell as he and a friend, who wore a green work suit, had been taking it down. In her dream, the antenna had fallen over the electric wires in front of the house. People had gathered around and a bright red fire truck was there.

As a result of the dream, she begged her husband not to take the antenna down. He said she was being silly, and two weeks later he started to take it down. His friend, wearing green work clothes as in the dream, came to help. A wind came up and blew the antenna down, but, because of her warning from the dream, they managed to push the falling antenna in the opposite direction, away from the electric wires.

I have often heard skeptics say, "Real scientists do not have ESP." My good friend, psychologist and professor Dr. Charles Tart, helped to debunk that myth by creating TASTE (The Archives of Scientists' Transcendent Experiences), an on-line journal offering accounts of transcendent experiences voluntarily reported by scientists. The goals of this unique database are to give scientists a safe place to report these experiences without embarrassment, to debunk the stereotype that real scientists do not have psychic or mystic experiences, and to build a database to help scientists further understand the powers of the mind.

The Rhine Research Center also receives ESP stories from scientists. A retired defense industry scientist recently sent me two striking examples of successful interventions. John Alexander gives me permission to quote him by his full name, adding "I find it very annoying in the books I have read that people require the use of only their initials, which really negates a significant measure of their credibility." After checking his notes to refresh his memory, John writes about two experiences in his earlier years that involved a type of waking, precognitive "vision" similar to what Kristin experienced when she foresaw the accident on the school slide ("Fall from a Slide"). In Kristin's case, she failed to act on the psychic warning, leaving her sad that she had not taken heed. Fortunately, John took action.

Tumble At The Museum

"One year, we were visiting the Natural History Museum in Los Angeles. We had a very dear friend with us who was much older than my wife and me. At the museum I separated from the rest to see a particular exhibit of interest to me, which the others declined to see. We agreed to meet in about fifteen minutes to have lunch together in the basement restaurant of the museum. As I observed the exhibit, I suddenly had a clear vision superimposed on the exhibit, without blocking it, in which I was going down the stairway that led to the basement with my stepson immediately to my right and my wife, my stepdaughter and Elizabeth, the older lady, coming along behind on the stairs. I heard a scream from behind me and to my left. I immediately turned and saw Elizabeth, who had fallen on the slick marble stairs and was rolling toward me. I very quickly bent over and caught her and prevented her from rolling all the way to the bottom, which was about thirty steps and could have caused her serious, if not fatal, injuries."

Taken aback by this sudden, unexpected vision, John sat down to think about it and try to make some sense out of it. "But I soon realized it was time to meet the others and put it out of my mind as some kind of aberrant experience. A little while later, we decided to go down to the basement restaurant and have lunch.

"As we started down the stairs, the exact series of foreseen events unfolded and, if I had not been prepared by my 'vision' for what had happened, I could very well not have been ready to take the quick, successful action I did. Although Elizabeth was somewhat shaken up, she refused any treatment by the museum staff, and after a while we proceeded to have lunch. I didn't tell anyone about this experience for a long time afterward, as it was sufficiently strange that I felt few, if any, would believe me."

John was so puzzled by this experience that he decided to do an experiment. He selected a dozen top scientists of the day and wrote a kind of form letter describing this precognitive experience, asking for their opinion. "I got only three responses," he writes. One suggested psychiatry and therapy as a solution to his problem. The other two were more helpful.

One came from the late Dr. David Bohm, an eminent

physics professor who was a coworker of Einstein's at Princeton and author of *Quantum Theory* (the standard college textbook on quantum physics for several decades). Some parapsychologists are aware that Bohm felt that there was room in quantum mechanics—perhaps even a necessity—for psychic phenomena and was not shy about saying so. Bohm earned his PhD from the University of California, Berkeley, and was the last student to study under atom bomb pioneer Dr. J. Robert Oppenheimer. From 1961, he served as professor of theoretical physics at Birkbeck College, University of London. Confident in his professional reputation and always willing to think outside the box, Bohm was one of several distinguished scientists to test spoon-bender Uri Geller's psychokinetic abilities in controlled laboratory experiments in the 1970s. He sent John a copy of a monograph on his theories, which John found very informative and interesting, but unfortunately the materials did not offer John any relevant conjectures or suggestions as to the how and why of his psychic experiences.

The other response was the most satisfactory—a phone call from Nobel laureate physicist Dr. Richard Feynman, a world-famous scientist, teacher, raconteur, and musician who assisted in the development of the atomic bomb, expanded the understanding of quantum electrodynamics, and translated Mayan hieroglyphics, among other achievements.

"He actually called me at the company where I worked at the time, and where he had many friends. He told me he had checked me out through other scientists he knew at the company and found that I had the reputation of being a 'solid citizen,' as he put it, and thus accepted at face value what I said about my experiences. He told me he had previously heard of such experiences but never from someone who had some scientific credibility.

"After some extended discussion, he suggested a course of action I might take if such an event should ever happen again. The instant I had such an experience, I should stop and make a note of it so there was proof that the psychic premonition had preceded the actual event. If another psychic event did happen and I followed those instructions, he invited me to contact him and discuss where to go from there. He was outspokenly skeptical that such a thing would happen, but was willing to keep an open mind. He gave me his personal phone number."

Several years later, John finally got the opportunity to put into action the plan Feynman had suggested, although the great physicist was no longer alive to learn the results of his suggested psychic experiment.

Speeding Sports Car

"After retiring in 1988, I was called back to do some consulting work on one of the key projects I had been managing. Over the twenty-four years I worked at this company, I had developed some very roundabout ways to travel the twelve miles between my office and my home. One of these was an almost rural, little side street named Newman. It was a short, two-lane road with no sidewalks that meandered through an old area of the town. On the day of the event, I had made no plan for going this route, but as I was driving down the main traffic artery, I again had a visual experience identical to the museum experience. Suddenly superimposed on the view I had of the street I was driving down was an image of Newman Street, the little side street I told you about. Somehow, neither image masked the other. I could see both at the same time.

"In this vision I had of Newman Street, there was a large truck stopped to pick up trash. It was parked on the opposite side of the road facing me, and blocking its lane on that side of the road. As I approached it in my vision, a little red sports car without a top suddenly swerved around the truck and directly into my path. At that point the vision ceased." John now had the scenario he and Dr. Feynman had discussed twenty years earlier. Here was a chance to try Dr. Feynman's suggested experiment. "I made a note of the vision with the only material I had at hand, which was a pencil stub and the back of my checkbook. Between where I was and Newman Street was about a mile. Since the two roads crossed each other at that place, when I arrived at that intersection I deliberately turned off the main road and onto Newman.

"I was about halfway down Newman when, right there on the other side of the road, was the stopped trash truck, exactly as in my vision. I immediately pulled off onto the shoulder and managed to avoid a head-on collision with a little red convertible sports car—driven by a redheaded girl who had also appeared in my precognitive vision a few minutes earlier. My car was much larger than the sports car, so I might not have been injured. But certainly, at the speed she was driving, she would have been seriously injured or killed and my car severely damaged.

"From my subjective viewpoint, both the museum 'vision' and the sports car 'vision' saved someone from injury, and I feel they indicate something beyond chance or coincidence."

John's ESP manifests itself primarily in the form of a type of visualization that he himself calls a "quasivisual anomaly," although we have been lumping these together under the term "visual hallucinations" as opposed to dreams or intuitions. John reports that he has an exceptionally strong talent at visualization, a talent that proved extremely valuable to him in his forty-two years as an engineer and scientist. "It took a long time for me to realize this was not a common ability among my coworkers. Even in those cases where physical objects were not involved, I was frequently able to visualize the problem in such a way as to be very helpful in solving the problem at hand. I did a lot of work in the field of microwaves and optics, and was able to 'see' and mentally manipulate the various elements to find the solution." It makes sense, then, that ESP might most easily break through to his conscious mind in the form of a vision.

A similar successful intervention experience involving a "vision" comes from Marie, the woman who had the terrifying precognitive vision of the 9/11 attack on the Pentagon.

Marie's ESP experiences are frequent enough that she has learned to take them seriously. In this experience, a few key elements were mixed up, but specific details were plentiful enough to help her make an appropriate intervention and prevent a likely tragedy.

The Car That Wasn't There

Marie was driving down this steep hill, and "saw" a car backing out of a driveway. It was so real that she slammed on the brakes, then she realized there was nobody there. As Marie explained, "I thought, well, how could that be? I mean, everything was very realistic, very specific, right down to the fact that I noticed it was a Taurus sedan, white or tannish-white in color. How come there's nothing there? Then I told myself, okay, that may have been a precognitive vision of some sort. I need to keep my eye out for a car backing out of a driveway."

About a mile down the road, Marie saw a truck—not a car—but it was, in fact, backing out of a driveway. And running toward that driveway on the sidewalk was a little boy, running ahead of his mother who was walking a dog and a baby. The mother wasn't paying attention to the child up ahead, who had gotten three houses ahead of her. Neither the little boy nor his mother could see the truck backing out of the driveway because there was a big wall in front of the property, hiding the driveway. "As I drove past the truck, I looked in the rearview mirror and realized the truck and the boy were on a direct collision course. So I slammed on my brakes and started reversing backward as fast as I could, beeping my horn like a crazy person. And the truck stops, and the child stops, and then the mother realizes what's going on. My apparent 'prevision' had made me alert to watch out for some danger coming ahead."

Intervention was successful in this instance, because Marie has learned over a period of years how to be more sensitive to her own ESP messages. Unlike Kristin, the teenager from Colorado who ignored her vision of the school slide accident, Marie has developed some ability to sort out the nonessential information from what is essential in a psychic message.

Although rare, some people report that a certain, special feeling usually accompanies their precognition experiences. If that feeling is present, they take the premonition seriously. Such is the case with a thirty-seven year-old Jewish-American man I'll call Hershel who gets a feeling of "walking through molasses" when he senses a precognitive warning. Hershel was originally from New York State, but after visiting Israel, he decided to move there permanently in 1991. Of course, Israel is locked in a bitter dispute with its Palestinian and Arab neighbors and is a country where suicide bombings can occur anywhere at any time. Hershel now lives in Jerusalem, a divided city that has been the site of several suicide bombings. Hershel has had an interest in psychic phenomena ever since he can remember, starting with "ESP games" played with friends during childhood. When he moved to Israel, his ESP ability ceased being a game and became a matter of life and death. When Hershel starts "walking through molasses," he takes notice.

Bomb In The Market

"One day, as soon as I got off the bus and started my shopping at my local market, I got what has become, for me, an all-too-familiar feeling—like I'm walking through molasses. I've learned to identify this specific feeling with impending, though not immediate, trouble. I just knew that a bombing attack would happen there soon. I remained anxious the entire time I was there shopping. Later that day, while standing at a bus stop near the market, I felt the most anxious I had ever felt since the troubles began here in Israel. The very next day, six people were killed at the market in a bombing."

• • •

The successful intervention cases we've described indicate that precognized dangers can be avoided if the proper preventive action is taken. We might wish for a larger number of successful intervention cases, but the ones we have certainly suggest that a foreseen fate is not inevitable. We can change the future to some extent. A person needs to receive enough details by precognition to know when, where, and how to intervene and he needs to be in a situation where action is possible. Beth had both the information and the ability to act when she refused to get into Clare's Oldsmobile, and thus was able to save her life ("Friends in Caskets"). The Los Angeles streetcar conductor also had the knowledge, necessary ability, and authority to intervene ("A Dream Come True").

Intervention can be difficult or impossible in some cases, despite knowing what will happen, when the experiencer has neither the authority nor credibility to intervene—as is usually the case with strangers or public catastrophes. This helplessness can lead to strong guilt feelings. The person is left wondering what he could have done to change it.

"That's The Plane!"

"I was a wreck for weeks wondering how I could have prevented it," wrote a young woman after describing the sequel to a terrifying dream that had awakened her one morning. "In my dream, I had clearly seen a plane crash on the shore of a nearby lake, and the roof of the third cabin on that dirt track was in flames as a result. There was only one man involved, and he was burned up. I found myself telling my friends about my dream, and also the fact that the fire engine would go in by the Canal Road and be unable to get to the plane until it was too late.

"The dream was so clear that I was conscious of every plane that flew overhead that day. Late in the afternoon, I was at the stove, fixing something for dinner when I said to my husband, 'That's the plane! The one that's going to crash! Robert, stop the firemen before they try the Canal Road. They have to take the Basin Road, and they don't know it.'

"My husband went outdoors to listen, and stuck his head back in to say, 'That plane's all right,' only to have me shriek back, 'It is NOT!'

"Within seconds, the plane crashed. The firemen took the Canal Road instead of the Basin Road, and the pilot was burned to a crisp. I was a wreck for weeks wondering how I could have prevented it."

This terrible guilt is echoed repeatedly in the letters I receive from people describing apparently accurate premonitions involving catastrophes like plane crashes and terrorist bombings. These people desperately want to do something, to stop the tragedy, yet they cannot. They do not have the credibility or authority to act. They are never 100 percent sure their premonitions are accurate since their premonitions often lack certain details necessary to act. Authorities will rarely listen.

My friend Marie continued to have other terrible premonitions in the months following the September 2001 terrorist strike on America. Since she had been correct with her earlier information, she took her intuitions and dreams seriously, and even courageously attempted to share these later ones with the FBI.

For example, a month after 9/11, Marie had a very vivid dream of a nuclear power plant getting blown up. "It scared me really badly, because I wondered if it was another accurate premonition, and if it was, who would listen to me?" she explained to me.

In her dream, Marie was at the beach with her two older sisters, her mother, and their husbands and kids. "We were all looking out toward the ocean, and off to the left, in an inlet, a huge nuclear bomb went off, like a big mushroom, and it was so vivid in the dream it scared the hell out of me. Everybody starting packing up and running, and I got left behind. I was very frightened."

Embarrassed, but trusting her psychic gift, Marie actually called the FBI. "The receptionist took the call," Marie told me, "but in truth, what was she supposed to do? What could she do?" The lady dutifully wrote down what Marie told her, but nobody ever called her back. Marie did not really expect them to. She was intelligent enough to understand their dilemma. "I couldn't tell her it's going to happen here, at this one place, at this particular time, though I felt it might be the Fourth of July at a South Carolina beach since my sisters had a trip planned then. All I could tell her is, I'm just a regular person, but I had all these accurate premonitions in the past, like the attack on the Pentagon, and now I've had this dream. . . ."

Still, as she talked, her frustration was evident. "If someone were able to predict September 11, would anyone have listened? It is my hope that the government will at least be open to collecting this type of information in the future. We should be open to the idea that some people can indeed pick up this kind of information as a warning. It's not a warning if nobody will listen."

Marie's dream may not have been precognitive, and may never come true. A prior track record of success does not guarantee the next dream will automatically be precognitive as well. Many an extremely vivid dream, filled with specific details and accompanied by an absolute certainty on the part of the dreamer that it is precognitive, subsequently turns out to be a fantasy spun by the subconscious. It will take many more years of ESP research before we are able to learn how to separate the true premonitions from the false alarms and provide public authorities with enough confidence to ground an airliner or shut down a power plant. Until then, we live with a catch-22. We do not know if our dreams are truly precognitive until they happen. And if they happen, it is too late to act.

For now, controlling our own fate will have to suffice.

10

ESP IN WAR

In the 1998 Academy Award–winning film *Saving Private Ryan,* director Steven Spielberg creates a horrific, emotionally draining reenactment of the bloody U.S. invasion of Normandy, France, in 1944 during World War II. As the first wave of tense, silent American soldiers crammed in the landing craft head for the beach and their unknown fate, you can see the anxiety and fear in their eyes. In a few minutes, they will find out if they will live or die.

More than 425,000 young American men (and women) have died in combat between World War I (1917–1918) and the First Gulf War (1990–1991). Another 1.2 million were wounded in combat. War generates intense emotions of fear and anxiety for soldiers. "Will I be killed?" "Will I be injured?" "Will I ever make it home again to see the people I love?" Meanwhile, the same emotional worries and fears haunt loved ones back home. Both share a desperate desire to communicate with each other in times of danger, to exchange news, solace, and support, but military censorship and secrecy routinely limits, delays, or even denies communication.

Given this intense emotional need to contact a loved one,

we shouldn't be surprised to find that ESP sometimes fills that gap when normal communication channels are slow or unavailable. Our Rhine collection of spontaneous ESP experiences contains a large number of remarkable stories of psychic dreams, intuitions, and visions shuttling important messages between soldiers, sailors, and airmen and their worried parents, spouses, relatives, and friends back home.

The most important information a parent or spouse of a soldier needs to know as soon as possible is the fate of their child or loved one—is he dead or alive? Victoria in Fayetteville, North Carolina, recently sent me an e-mail describing her mother's fascinating wartime ESP experiences spanning three different wars. Each time, her psychic gift brought her the answer to that burning question concerning three different important men in her life.

Three Wars, Three Messages

Only a child during World War I, Victoria's mother had no experience dealing with military matters. One day she dreamed that her own mother received a Western Union telegram from the government stating, "War Department regrets to inform you that your son Walter has been wounded in action." Prior to her precognitive dream, she had never seen nor heard of such a message. A day after her dream, the family received a telegram that announced Walter had been severely wounded in France on November 11, 1918, the last day of the war. Fortunately, Victoria's uncle Walter later recovered, became a successful businessman, and lived to be ninety-five years old.

Her mother's second war-related ESP experience actually started before World War II began. Victoria's father, Ted, at that time was a career military officer who had served in France in World War I like Walter, but remained in the army after the war ended. "My mother had a series of nightmares in which she saw my father in gray clothes and gray flesh standing on the other side of barbed wire, unable to speak to her and looking very sad. She would wake up from these dreams calling 'Ted, Ted' and tell him about the dream."

Her mother's precognitive dreams came true shortly after Japan attacked Pearl Harbor. When World War II began, Ted was commanding officer of the U.S. 57th Infantry in the Philippines (Philippine Scouts), and was forced to surrender to the Japanese on April 9, 1942. He survived the infamous Bataan Death March and spent more than three years in different POW camps in Singapore, Japan, and Taiwan before being shipped to Japanese-occupied China, where he was liberated in September 1945. During that eternal stretch of waiting and hoping he was still alive, her mother received little news from the army. Her mother's continuing ESP about her husband brought comforting messages. "Sometimes Mother would 'see' him standing silently by her bed, and she would tell us that she had seen him. She felt he was letting her know that he was alive and okay. After the war was over, she found that the dates of his psychic manifestations in her bedroom corresponded to dates when he had been transferred to another prison camp." Victoria's father survived the ordeal and remained a soldier on active duty until he retired in 1953. He died in 1978 at the ripe old age of eighty-four.

Her mother's third wartime ESP experience involved the Korean War. Victoria's brother was in uniform when the war broke out on June 25, 1950. He had just graduated from West Point three weeks earlier and was shipped immediately to Korea.

As Victoria explained, "On Sunday September 3, my mother, who never 'ailed,' stayed home from church with what she later told us were severe stomach pains. She didn't tell us because she didn't want to worry us and keep us from church, but she later told us she 'knew' it had something to do with my brother. On September 22, we received the terrible news that he had been killed on September 3. He was only twenty-two—and her only son."

Victoria's mother's ESP awareness came in the form of

precognitive dreams about her uncle and husband, and the information about her West Point son's death in Korea came in the form of a telesomatic hallucination—a psychic message delivered in the form of a sympathetic pain directly to her body. This form of ESP occurs below the level of consciousness, and is not uncommon in wartime ESP experiences.

In the following Korean War case, news of a serious injury came in the form of a psychic intuition received not by the soldier's mother or father but by an aunt.

Purple Heart In Korea

A well-to-do, young California woman named Elizabeth was preparing to set out on a round-the-world tour. Shortly before she left, she was awakened in the middle of the night by a brilliant light and an accompanying psychic message that her sister's son fighting in Korea at the time was in very serious danger. Though the intuition did not provide a lot of details, she somehow "knew" that it involved his death or possible death. The message was so vivid and convincing that she got out of bed and wrote down what had happened and her prediction. She then sealed her statement in an envelope and gave it to a relative to deliver to her sister after a sufficient time had elapsed for the sister to receive official notice from the army in the event the son had actually been killed or injured as predicted. Then she left on her trip. Shortly afterward, Elizabeth received word from her sister that her nephew had indeed been severely wounded at the exact hour she had been jolted from her sleep. Today, the boy's Purple Heart medal given to soldiers wounded in combat and her prediction letter sent to her sister sit in a box of honor in her sister's house.

Without more information, we do not know if there was some particularly strong emotional bond between this aunt and her nephew, or whether she was just a better receiver of ESP information than the parents. We do know that some people are naturally more psychic than others, even in the same family.

The Korean War was tragic, but the carnage, destruction, and death caused by World War II (1941–1945)—which had ended just five years earlier—was measurably greater. Combat deaths were eight times higher (292,000) than in Korea and the wounded count was six times higher (670,000). With more soldiers overseas and their anxious families back home facing emotional crises, the Rhine Research Center received a flood of letters describing ESP experiences from the World War II era.

Relatively common among the World War II cases in our ESP case collection are accounts of "visions" of dead or dying soldiers appearing to their loved ones that seem to inform them of their passing on or deliver a good-bye. Here is one visual hallucination report.

Son's Last Good-Bye

A farmer in California had a son in the army who was wounded in Italy in 1943. After three months in the hospital, he was sent back to the front again to fight in France. One night, the father went outside to lock up the chicken coop for the night, something he did every night when dusk fell. He was just closing the door when, to his great astonishment, he saw his son, fully dressed in his army uniform, standing in some nearby bushes.

"Dad," the boy said to him, "I'm very sorry. I always wanted to be a good boy."

The surprised farmer could only stammer out, "Alfred, what are you doing here?"

As he reached for his flashlight, his son simply disappeared. He looked all over but could not find a trace of his son. One week later, the army notified him that his son had been killed by shrapnel from an artillery shell.

This type of psychic hallucination has been called a "crisis apparition," because it occurs within a short period of time following a major crisis, for example, an actual or impending death. In parapsychological literature, crisis apparitions are the most frequently reported type of "ghost." In this case, the son appeared to want to apologize to his dad about something before he departed this world. Since the father both saw and heard his son, thus involving two of his senses, he was convinced that this was not just his imagination or a daydream, and that his son had actually visited him. We will have more to say about apparitions in the next chapter.

Alfred's father was unprepared for his son's death and surprised by his psychic appearance. A very young girl named Olivia was equally unprepared for a midnight visit from her father, who was at the time fighting in the jungles of Vietnam. The Vietnam War claimed the lives of 58,000 American soldiers and left another 153,000 wounded. The bitterness and divisive nature of the war left many soldiers and their families reluctant to talk about their wartime experiences. But our Rhine ESP case collection does include some dramatic Vietnam war ESP stories like Olivia's.

Shot In The Shoulder

"In 1965, I was five years old and living in Italy with my mother and baby sister. My mother is Italian, and my dad was in the army. We were stationed in Texas, but my mom didn't drive and spoke little English, so when my Dad got orders for Vietnam we packed up and moved back to Italy.

"What happened to me that night I will never forget, and the images are as sharp in my mind today as when they happened all those years ago. Funny, that I don't remember much else about being a five-year-old! Anyway, I woke up one night to see my dad standing in the doorway of my room in full army gear. I remember being soooo excited about him being home and wanted to hug him!

"He said, 'No honey, tell your mother I'm shot in the

shoulder and waiting for help. Don't be scared, tell your mother." I started crying, and then he was gone.

"I was so upset I went to wake my mom, and, of course, the rest of the family awoke—my grandparents and my aunt. I told my mother what happened and she became very upset. Back then, there was really no family support for army spouses. The Red Cross was the only means of communication. We all stayed up the rest of the night, too upset to sleep.

My mom contacted the Red Cross the next morning. While they were trying to find my dad, a telegram came saying that my dad was missing in action. Three days later, the Red Cross found my dad in an army hospital. He had been shot in the shoulder but was alive."

No wonder Olivia remembered this remarkable experience after all these years! As in the last case, she both saw and heard her father. Since two of her senses were involved, the likelihood of its being just a dream is reduced. Second, the apparitional father figure gave her detailed information about his injury that she could not have inferred or dreamed up and later was confirmed. Third, the family knew the details of her experience before knowing the outcome, adding veracity to her report, as well as helping in recall of the details. It is a tribute to her family that they took her experience seriously and did not just send her back to bed as if it was nothing more than a bad dream.

Olivia's father was a career military soldier, having served in World War II, in Korea, and three tours in Vietnam. He recovered from this wartime injury and lived many more years. On the day he died in 1994, Olivia's usually quiet black Labrador dog kept pawing and nipping at her all morning. She read it as a sign that she should go see her father at the VA hospital. He died that afternoon, shortly after her visit.

Sometimes the knowledge that someone has been wounded or killed on the battlefield comes in the form of a symbolic dream. Just as truths can be conveyed through fiction as well as factual description, ESP messages can be expressed through un-realism rather than realism. Symbolic dreams are much harder to recognize and interpret, but in retrospect the information can be right there staring us in the face. Take the case of this symbolic dream experienced by a San Francisco mother just before the end of World War II, described in a poignant letter to my mother.

The Drowned Sailor

"In January 1945, I dreamed that my young son, and only child, who was overseas in combat duty in the Southwest Pacific theater, came to me while I was busy in the kitchen and handed me his uniform, which was soaked and dripping wet. He had a most distressed expression on his young face. Feeling disturbed and confused but saying nothing, I mechanically began to wring the water from the uniform, the navy-blue dye clouding the water in the process and increasing my disturbed and bewildered feeling.

"Willie, standing next to me, took the uniform from my hands and, dropping it into the laundry tub, turned me around and took me in his arms, saying 'Isn't this terrible! Oh Mom, it's all so terrible!'

"Although he had never given me any cause for concern when it came to getting into any mischief of any major degree in the growing up process of his nineteen years, I thought—in the dream—that he might have gotten into some sort of difficulty that he thought would be distressing to me.

"He said, 'This is the one thing, Mom, that I had hoped you would never have to hear!' So in my dream I said to him as I had at times when he was growing up, 'Willie, remember? There is nothing so terrible that we can't sit down together and talk it out.'

"In the dream, we went into the living room and when I sat down in the chair he sat down in my lap, put his arms around my neck and his head on my shoulder, sobbing quietly. I held him in my arms and suddenly he was a little infant again, and I was rocking him as I had in his babyhood! As his sobbing ceased, I awakened abruptly from my dream, but the dream remained with me most vividly.

"That was on a Monday night. The following Sunday afternoon a chaplain from the 13th Naval Base in Long Beach, California, came to me with the message that something had happened to Willie's ship. There was a long list of those missing, and his name was among them. It was later established that all those listed as missing—250 boys—were killed, having been blown into shattered, unidentifiable bits when the ship, laden with tons of ammunition, depth charges, and bombs, was torpedoed by the enemy at Guadalcanal, on the very night of January 20 when I had dreamed so vividly of Willie."

Did the dream tell the truth? Scarcely a detail was real, from the first scene of wringing out the soaked uniform to the boy's transformation in his mother's arm to the infant he used to be. Yet the symbolic dream was quite true in its deeper meaning and message.

At other times, the message is delivered by a sudden, strong, emotional intuition with no vision, voice, or imagery. Bill Olive, a highly respected attorney and long-time friend of mine from Durham, North Carolina, shared with me an ESP experience his mother had when he was overseas fighting with the 95th Infantry Division in World War II.

"Billy Needs Me"

One night in mid-December 1944, Bill's mother, Virginia, got out of bed and began to pace the room, wringing her hands with worry for Bill. "Billy needs me," she kept saying over and over. "Oh, I know Billy needs me." It was uncharacteristic of his mother, who had never acted that way during the time Billy was in the service.

Two weeks later, the family received a cable from the

army announcing that Billy had been wounded in action near the Saar River in Germany.

According to Billy's sister Betsy Ann, when they later pieced together the chronology, "the hours that Mom was so distressed were the same hours that Billy was lying on the battlefield, wounded and in freezing weather." The nurse who took care of Billy at a field hospital that night later told Billy that he kept calling out "Mother! Mother!" as he lay on the stretcher.

Psychic intuition during wartime is experienced by mothers around the world, as in the following case of a German woman in World War II. This report was sent by my Dutch parapsychologist friend Dr. Joop Houtkooper who works in Giessen, Germany. A thirty-five year-old German business-man related the story to him.

Sad Christmas

"In my family, the story is told that during the second World War, the following happened: It was Christmas and the fam-ily was all together at the house of my grandparents. Sud-denly, my grandmother stood up, opened the window although it was freezing cold outside, and threw the Christ-mas tree out the window, saying: 'For me, no Christmas. My son is dead.'

"Two weeks later, the message came that on that same day her son had died on the eastern front. I have asked all people who were still alive about this story, and everyone agrees this is how it happened."

Earlier in this chapter, we reported how severe stomach pains were the modality by which Victoria's mother became sym-pathetically aware of her son's death in Korea ("Three Wars, Three Messages"). Here is the report of another, equally mov-ing telesomatic hallucination, this one affecting the mother of a soldier serving in occupied Germany after World War II.

Gunshot To The Head

"On Thursday morning February 10, about four A.M., I jumped out of bed, feeling like I was dying. I felt as if blood or something was pouring down from my head, choking me, and I was trying desperately to catch my breath. My husband got up to help me. He tried to get me to the bathroom for some water to stop my terrible choking spasms. They soon diminished and I grew very weak. I thought I must be really dying.

"My husband laid me down on my bed to rest but I felt so 'all gone.' Then I thought I heard my son call out, saying 'Oh Momma, help me!' in such anguish.

"Later that day, I went to the doctor to get an X-ray of my chest. I thought given the acute pain I had felt that something must be wrong. But the doctor couldn't find anything wrong with me.

"On February 12, we received a telegram from the army saying our son was killed by a gunshot to the head at one o'clock on February 10. There is a nine-hour difference in time zones. So I feel he called me as it happened, and that I heard his groan and felt his dying moments."

Parental anxiety starts long before a child goes into combat; it starts the day the child enlists or is drafted. The die is cast, and fathers as well as mothers are usually helpless spectators until the child finally is discharged from the service. This may explain the following father's ability to foresee his son's fate. In June 1943, while his son was still safe in the U.S., far from combat, his father had a precognitive dream that revealed, in realistic, detailed images, the looming death of his oldest son George. The boy died in August 1943, just before graduating from advanced pilot training in the air force.

The Field Of Death

"In this dream, I was standing on the edge of a shallow, dry irrigation ditch, looking toward a high ridge of mountains, which appeared to be no more than a mile away, and approximately six thousand feet high. The field seemed to be dark and black on the surface, as if it had just recently been plowed for planting. Scattered around the field were a few large trees with dark green foliage. I had never seen the area before in my life.

"In my dream, I saw four men in uniform walk off the field carrying a stretcher with a body on it. They crossed over the irrigation ditch just a few feet in front of me. They didn't seem to notice me standing there, and I didn't speak to them. I heard a disembodied voice say they were carrying the dead body of my son, but I didn't know which one—my younger son, in the army, had just been shipped out of San Francisco to an unknown destination.

"At this point I awoke and tried to shake off the dream, but it persisted in clear-cut detail. However, I didn't tell my wife or anyone else about my frightening dream."

Two weeks later, he received a letter from his younger son in the army. The boy was in the Aleutian Islands off Alaska, and no fighting was expected in his area in the near future. This quieted the father's fears somewhat, though the frightening dream remained clear in his mind. His reprieve proved to be cruelly premature.

"Two months later, on August 23, I received a call from my daughter-in-law, George's wife. She told me George had been killed in a plane crash that afternoon. I told her we would come as quickly as possible, and we got there just after midnight.

"The next day we went out to the air force base and made arrangements to have his body returned home. Later, after the funeral, I again pondered my dream and its possible association with George's accident. I decided to go back to the base and see if I could get permission and an escort to go out to the scene of the accident.

"When we did, I discovered that the topography of the area was exactly as I had seen it in the dream two months earlier. I went and stood on the bank of the dry irrigation ditch just as I had seen myself do in the dream. To my right was the blackened field, with dark green foliage on live oaks scattered over the area. The blackened surface of the field had been caused by fire spreading from the wrecked plane and not from plowing as it had seemed to be in the dream. The lieutenant who had driven me out there from the base had been there with the rescue crew at the time of the accident. I had not told anything about my strange dream. We stood there where the stretcher bearers had brought out the body and where the ambulance had waited. He said they had brought the body from the field and crossed over the dry irrigation ditch just a few feet in front of where we were standing. This was exactly as I had seen it in my dream."

Occasionally a telepathic experience comes through in such a strong and encompassing way that it convinces a parent that she is actually with her child in his crisis. One mother from Georgia, whom I will call Helen, had a son in basic training camp in Mississippi. After having him home too briefly on a short furlough, Helen drove him back to the station for a tearful departure after which he caught a train back to his camp.

Lost On Maneuvers

"Two nights later, I was sound asleep when I thought I heard a loud knock on the kitchen door. I got up and turned on the kitchen light, then opened the door. There stood my son. He had bandages on his legs and tears in his eyes. I told him to come on in.

" 'I got lost from the other boys tonight,' he explained. 'I was in a swamp. I just wanted to come home and see you once more. Now I have to go back and see if I can find them.' He turned and went down the steps toward the garage. It was raining a little and foggy, and he just disappeared into the fog. I shut the door—and woke up!

"Sitting up in bed, I knew my experience was a warning or a vision. I prayed for my son's safety and finally went back to sleep.

"Several days later, I received a letter from him. He said, 'The first night after I got back, we went out on night maneuvers. I was sent back to the camp for something we forgot, and I took a shortcut and got lost. I was really lost for hours, and I didn't think I would ever see you again. I prayed I would find my way out of there. I followed a light, like a star, and finally made it back to the road.' "

Helen ended her letter with a question. "Was this a dream I had, or a vision, and did my prayers help him?"

Since most days most soldiers are not engaged in combat, psychic messages between a parent and child during wartime do not always deal with life and death issues.

Sunburned Son

"During World War II, my mother's cousin John was sent to the North African war theater. One night his mother had a dream about him where she saw him unloading cargo from a ship in the hot sun. He wasn't wearing a shirt, and in her dream she scolded him for not being more careful. He was Irish and fair-skinned. A few weeks later, she received a letter from him saying that he had been hospitalized for sunburn while unloading a ship."

Among the millions of Americans who served in some branch of the armed services in World War II were thousands of men who sailed into harm's way crewing the freighters, troop ships, tankers, and other vessels that fed men and material from the U.S. to battlefields around the globe. This merchant marine fleet was constantly harried by German submarines and airplanes, and many U.S. sailors died in attacks that never got reported in the newspapers. All the censorship and secrecy in the world could not stop the mother in the following story from receiving a hallucinatory "call" from her son, warning her that he was in great danger.

Torpedo Attack: World War II

A young man named Joe, serving in the merchant marines during World War II, was escorting a ship convoy from Cuba to New York along Eastern seacoast waters populated by German U-boats hungry to sink slow targets. On August 15, a hot and humid night, Joe decided to leave his cabin and try to sleep outside on the deck where it was a lot cooler. To avoid detection, all the merchant ships were blacked out, and there was no moon, making it even darker. He had hardly fallen asleep when a tremendous jolt brought him back to full alertness. Flames shot up in the sky. Joe realized that the convoy was under attack and ships were being torpedoed.

He ran wildly to higher ground on the ship's bridge and stayed there as the convoy desperately fought off the attackers. Though the torpedoed ship was sunk, the rest of the convoy finally limped into New York.

Not long afterward, Joe made it out to California on furlough. The first thing his mother demanded to know was what had happened the night of August 15—despite the fact that all mail was censored and the news of the ship's sinking was never mentioned in the media.

"You could have knocked me over with a feather," Joe wrote in his letter to us. "I said 'Nothing' and tried to let it go at that." His mother persisted. She said she had awakened from a sound sleep that night, and heard him call "Mom! Mom!" several times. She answered so loudly she could have been heard a block away, and found herself out of bed and covered with perspiration. Her voice had awakened his grandmother, who slept in the same room, and the grandmother verified her story.

When my mother began her case collection in the late 1940s, the memory of World War I was still alive in the minds of many people of that day. One of these reports involved a merchant marine sailor whose life was saved as the direct result of his wife's taking action on the basis of her vivid precognitive dream.

Torpedo Attack: World War I

During World War I, a woman whose husband served as chief engineer on a supply ship and had been at sea for three months, got a message to go to Philadelphia to meet him at Pier 101 at four A.M. when his ship would dock.

"I had a bath, shampooed my hair, and went to bed about 9:30 P.M.," the woman wrote my mother. After falling asleep, she had a strange dream. In the dream, her husband's ship docked, quickly unloaded, and then loaded up again, immediately departing for India. On its way back to the fighting, a "tin fish" torpedo hit the ship and sank it, killing her husband. Jolted awake at 3:40 A.M. by the frightening dream, she hurriedly dressed, hailed a cab, and raced to the dock where her husband's ship was just finishing tying up. "I handed the taxi driver a ten dollar bill, ordered him to wait, ran by the surprised guard at the base gate and up onto the ship, hysterical and crying, with the guard chasing behind me.

"My husband was waiting on deck, and I ran into his arms crying, 'Don't go, don't go! The ship is going down!'" She was so determined to get him off the ship that he asked the shipping company's permission to skip that sailing and take the next run instead. The company granted his request. The ship, which was indeed bound for India as in her dream, was torpedoed and sunk by a German sub. All the crew on-board spent sixteen days in a life raft until they were eventually rescued.

In Chapter 9, we learned that people can sometimes avoid a foreseen fate, as the merchant marine engineer above did by acting on his wife's premonition. Superstitious soldiers faced with poor odds of survival might find it difficult not to believe in premonitions of disaster. Soldiers throughout history have swapped stories of buddies who somehow "knew" they were going to get hit before a certain battle, and then were killed or wounded that day.

A U.S. Marine fighting in France in World War I had seen horrendous trench warfare in 1918, the last year of the war, as a desperate Germany made one last attempt to force the Allies to sue for a negotiated peace instead of an unconditional surrender. He had seen the worst kind of bloody battles during June, July, and August, with nonstop shelling and poison gas attacks and had heard many men tell of a hunch that their "number was up." In many cases he had found his comrades to be right in their psychic predictions, so he was very prone to take such intuitions seriously— including his own.

A Bullet With His Name

"By September 12, 1918, I was one of the few men left in my company from the original group that went into battle. I was completely exhausted and feverish. I had gotten gassed earlier, but was determined to stick it out. Still, in this physical state I was of little use to anyone, and to make things worse I 'just knew' that unless our unit was relieved the next morning, I was in for a 'hit.' I tried hard to shrug off the feeling, but it just wouldn't go away."

Finally, unable to shake the premonition, he focused on where he would accept getting hit. "In my mind, I rejected wounds to various parts of my body until, at last, I settled for a flesh wound in back of my left shoulder."

On September 14, his company was moved during the night to a salient on the battlefield offering almost no cover. "We were practically face-to-face with the Germans, except they were dug in. I commanded a 'suicide section' and was ordered to move it into position on a small knoll. When I looked at the spot, I 'knew' this was the place where I would be wounded.

"A German machine gun was spraying my position, and I could hear the whizzing from the bullets inside my helmet. While I was hugging the earth, a shell flew over my body, barely missing me, bursting just beyond my feet. I felt a hot, searing pain. I wriggled off the knoll and found that I had a flesh wound in the rear of the left shoulder! I am convinced that wound was 'in the cards' and that it could not have been avoided."

Soldiers often learn to do things a certain way all the time in order to execute an action safely and efficiently despite the inherent chaos and confusion of battle. That is why the World War II veteran who recently sent me the following story was surprised but ultimately thankful that his psychic intuition allowed him to ignore his usual iron-clad habit before one bombing raid.

The Parachute

"During World War II, I was a bombardier flying out of England in a B-17 bomber. During every mission, Dick, the navigator, and I always placed our respective parachutes leaning up against our oxygen tank. They would always be put in the exact same place so that we would instinctively know where they were in case we needed them in an emergency. We never varied as to where we placed them.

"On our seventh mission (which happened to be the first air raid on Berlin), as we took off, I turned as usual to give my thumbs-up to Dick, but instead of returning my thumbs up he reached across and threw my parachute underneath his navigator table. Not only was it contrary to everything we had always done, it was from my standpoint the worst place he could have put my 'chute. It was now unreachable in case I needed it in an emergency. His moving the 'chute was the first 'strange' thing, but the second 'strange' thing was that I saw him do it and did not react to it. Instead, I gave it no thought.

"About twenty miles south of Berlin, we were attacked by a group of German fighters. As soon as we were attacked, I gave no thought to my parachute, but got on my nose gun and began firing. Suddenly a twenty-millimeter shell exploded against my oxygen tank, setting the oxygen on fire and causing the whole nose section of the plane to be an inferno of flames.

"My first thought was, 'Well, I'm going to die,' and then I said, 'but I don't want to die.' My face was completely in flames and my only thought was to jump out of the plane to get away from the fire. I was aware that I didn't have a 'chute, but there is nothing that compares to flame on your skin.

"As I started to make my way back to the escape hatch, my right hand happened to rest against my 'chute where Dick had thrown it under his navigator table. I said to myself, 'I'll be damned,' and I put it on and dove out of the plane."

The bombardier survived the jump, ended up in a POW camp and finally made it back home to the States. When he called Dick, who had also survived the crash, he said, "Dick, I've got a question to ask you." And Dick laughingly interrupted him to say, "I know what you're going to ask—why did I throw your chute under the table? And the answer is, 'I don't know.' "

In reply to our request on the Rhine Research Center Web site for wartime ESP experiences, a young American soldier named George sent us the following account of an interesting auditory hallucination during a surprise Vietcong attack on his airbase during the Vietnam War.

"This Is Not The Place Where
You Will Die"

"People were yelling at me to take cover, but I decided I was going to stand there and look my killer in the eye. As the bullets whizzed by, I began to mentally prepare myself to die. But then something strange happened. All of a sudden I felt very protected and at peace. The scene around me seemed to be in slow motion, like I was watching a movie in a theater, and not actually involved. I was totally removed emotionally and physically, just an observer.

"I could hear the bullets whizzing by and hitting the ground. I could see others running, looking for a place to hide and some just diving to the sandy dirt. I could hear the continued shouts of a couple of guys urging me to take cover. I was totally unaffected by it all, because I was standing there surrounded in this envelope of total peace and serenity.

"And then came the 'voice.' It was the calm, soothing, and peaceful voice of a woman. The voice was unknown and familiar to me at the same time. I felt that the voice knew me immensely and had come to comfort me and assure me. The voice spoke only three short sentences: 'This is not the place where you will die. There are still things that you are to do. This will all be over in a moment.'"

Seconds later, a Cobra attack helicopter flew over his head, unloaded its rockets on the attackers and drove them back. George survived without a scratch. He tried to tell his buddies about the mysterious voice, but they decided he was just crazy. "I walked back to my barracks alone, wondering about what I had just experienced."

George's experience has no easy explanation and leaves me wondering almost as much as he himself did back then in Vietnam. In his memory of this strange experience, it sounds as if George had a guardian angel or some other spiritual figure who protected him in the face of almost certain death. If stretched to find a more mundane explanation from what we suspect is possible, we might suppose that George somehow knew by precognition that he would survive despite his conscious fear to the contrary, and then his unconscious mind produced a hallucinatory voice or presence to calm him and help with his emotional survival. In either case, George's experience sounds quite similar to a near-death experience, where the mind or spirit seems eerily detached from the actual physical body.

Besides getting killed or injured, soldiers in combat also get captured and taken to prisoner of war (POW) camps. Escape attempts are dangerous, but the desire to get back home to loved ones is powerful. During World War I, a corporal in the Canadian expeditionary force was captured in Germany after a mine explosion and taken to a POW camp. Dick escaped and made his way two hundred miles through Germany all the way to the Dutch border. Without the help of an unusual crisis apparition, this might have been as far as he got.

POW Escape: World War I

It was a hazardous, exhausting trek of many days. He had little to eat, and he reached the border completely exhausted. To make matters worse, it was night and snowing hard. He came to a crossroads. He knew if he chose the right way he would end up in friendly Dutch hands; if he took the wrong way, he would almost certainly encounter a German checkpoint or patrol. He didn't know which road was correct and he was much too exhausted to try both options, trudging over plowed fields in the dark and in the midst of a snowstorm. He hesitated, then started up one of the roads. Just then, his brother who was also serving in the same war, stepped out of the snowstorm right in front of him and said, "No, Dick, not that way. Take the other road, you damn fool!"

To Dick, his brother appeared as real as anything he had ever experienced in his life—except at that moment his brother was warm and snug, asleep in an officer's barracks in the south of England. Dick took the other road and ended up safe in Allied hands.

When Dick finally made it back to England a few days later, he thanked his brother for saving his life. The astonished brother didn't know what to say. "He had never been in Holland or Germany, and he couldn't recall any dream about the event at all."

Although rare, there are additional reports in our collection in which a vision or apparition saves a person's life. Since the brother had no recollection of trying to help his brother, we can surmise that Dick himself was the agent of his own salvation in this case. In his desperation, he may have projected the figure of his brother as the carrier of the extrasensory information he needed to save his life.

Thirty years later, as World War II was finally winding down, the army could not tell a worried wife in New York whether her POW husband was alive or dead, but her sixth sense came to the rescue. As is typical of psychic intuitions, her experience came unannounced, brought no details, but carried tremendous conviction.

POW Escape: World War II

"It was the end of World War II, and I knew my husband was in a prisoner of war camp in Germany. We had had no letter from him during the last few months of his imprisonment. As the war in Europe came to an end, news came almost every day of POW camps being liberated. My husband's camp was never mentioned, and I became more and more worried about his safety. Everyone noticed how blue I was, and I felt really depressed from this constant worry.

"On the evening of April 18, I suddenly had the feeling that my husband was safe. Some mention was made on the radio about prisoners, but not about my husband's camp. I think the radio announcement was what started me thinking about it. At any rate, I was sure that my husband was safe. I wrote the date in the scrapbook I was keeping, and after it I wrote, 'The day I knew Hank was liberated.'

"The next day, my employer and friends asked if I had had good news, because I looked so happy. I replied that I had had no word, but that I was sure my husband was safe.

"On April 30, a cable came from my husband in England. When he got home, he told the story of how he and a buddy had escaped from a group of prisoners being moved. They hid in the woods for several days until, on April 18, they saw British tanks coming down the road. They came out of the woods, and the soldiers fed them and saw they were returned to England."

In an earlier case in this chapter, "Purple Heart in Korea," an aunt received the psychic premonition of her nephew's injury instead of the boy's mother. In the following World War II experience, a friend's remarkable psychic gifts came to the rescue of another mother distraught with worry over the fate of her son in the European theater of action. In laboratory research, we find fairly consistent differences among people's ESP ability, so we should certainly expect that to be the case in real life. Certain individuals seem to be naturally better able to pick up ESP messages than others, or perhaps they are in a more receptive state of mind at that time. Whatever the reason, this mother was glad to have a friend who could be such psychic help.

Finding A Lost Soldier

"My friend was crying almost day and night. It had been six months and she hadn't heard a word. We would tell her, 'No news is good news. Don't carry on until you hear from the government one way or another,' but she couldn't stop worrying. Then on three successive nights in February 1945, I dreamed the same dream, but a little different.

"On the first night, I was looking for my friend's son among the dead and the wounded. I was directed to a hospital and woke up. The second night, I was in the hospital going from bed to bed, looking for him. There were so many I couldn't finish, and woke up again. The third night, I found him, his eyes closed, uncommunicative. I was told he was all right but had had a great shock and some nervous disorder.

"I related my dreams to my friend and said, 'Don't worry, no limbs or organs are missing. Only he is very sick and unable to identify himself.'

"Four months after my dream, he was brought to the hospital in Staten Island. His mother learned that for a long time they had been unable to identify him. His identification tags had been lost and he was without clothes or memory. Months later, he began to remember. They found out he was an officer, but was hospitalized with enlisted GIs, so his hospital was changed, and because of this change he was at last found."

Over 16 million American soldiers served in the military between 1941–1945. Keeping track of each and every one was a clerical nightmare made even harder by the fact that armies must keep moving forward as quickly as possible. The dead left behind on the battlefield are hastily identified and buried. Supporting paperwork is shuffled through an overloaded system. Mistakes and errors are expected. Without the help of her psychic neighbor, it is doubtful the mother in the story that follows would have ever discovered the ultimate fate and final resting place of her missing son.

Finding A Grave

"Shortly after February 17, 1944, my neighbor had been notified that her son, James, was missing in action. She received no further word whatsoever, but she knew he was missing in Italy. She wrote several places for information with no success.

"A year later, a few days after Memorial Day 1945, I picked up a paper containing a news picture of services held in a small cemetery near the Anzio beachhead battleground just south of Rome. I gazed intently at the picture of the hundreds of rows of crosses and suddenly began to cry. The certain sure feeling came to me: 'Jimmy is buried here.'

"Against my husband's wishes, because it was so preposterous, I wrote the lieutenant commander at Anzio, asking if he would try to find out if Jimmy could have been buried there. On July 10, 1945, I received a reply, a letter that I gave to my neighbor, the dead boy's mother.

"The commander had made a search, James was found to be buried in that place, and snapshots of the cross bearing his name would follow." Further inquiry revealed the bureaucratic errors that explained why the boy's death and final burial place had somehow never reached the mother.

The Rhine Research Center recently launched a modest PR effort to contact veterans in the Durham, North Carolina, area to see what new ESP experiences we can add to our database. We hope to receive some ESP experiences from soldiers involved in Desert Storm, Afghanistan, and the current Iraq war. We do not expect many. The total number of U.S. soldiers involved in these conflicts is a small fraction of the number who fought in World War II, Korea, or Vietnam. American troops total less than twenty thousand in Afghanistan, and 135,000 in Iraq. More than five hundred thousand U.S. troops served during the first Gulf War, but just 147 soldiers lost their lives because Saddam folded in four short days of battle. In Afghanistan, an estimated one hundred American soldiers have been killed there since the start of conflict in 2001, and in the current Iraq war 1,100 American soldiers had lost their lives as of November 2004. Fewer soldiers in combat means fewer life-threatening situations conducive to ESP. E-mail, cell and satellite phone, Web cams, and video conferencing are also available to American troops today, allowing them to contact loved ones faster and more frequently than past wars, perhaps reducing the need for ESP as a channel of communication between a soldier and loved ones back home.

One interesting e-mail involving the Middle East conflict I did receive came from a military wife I will call Charlene. Charlene apparently had a premonition of the terrorist attack on the U.S. Navy guided missile destroyer *Cole* the day before it happened. On the morning of October 12, 2000, the *Cole* was refueling in Aden harbor in the Middle Eastern country of Yemen, when suicide terrorists drove a small boat laden with five-hundred pounds of explosives up to the warship and detonated it, blasting a forty-foot hole in its hull. Seventeen American sailors were killed and another thirty-nine seamen were injured in the attack. The night before, Charlene had a dream.

Attack On The USS Cole

"I had just recently moved to Atlanta, Georgia, to get married," she wrote me. "I was staying in the barracks with my husband Keith at the time. I woke up in the middle of the night following a horrible nightmare. I sat up with a start. In my dream, there was a large military ship in a harbor. Four or five men were sitting in a small boat, all dressed in dark clothing with black masks on their faces, whispering in a foreign language I could not understand. They went into the water with things in their hands. They swam under and around the bigger boat, setting things up there—I was not sure exactly what or where. They then climbed back into the small boat and departed quickly but quietly.

"All of a sudden, there was a large explosion. There were bodies flying through the air—some were slammed against the hull and landed in the water. Men were blown apart, their bodies being torn like they were just pieces of paper. Blood was everywhere, men yelling, screaming in pain, moaning.

"I remember watching the expression on one young man, probably in his late twenties or so, dark hair, whose eyes had a look in them of total terror, lying there while he died. I swear he stared into my eyes that night, begging for help, for relief from the pain in the seconds before his death. I wanted to reach out and hold his hand while he died, to comfort him in his last seconds of life, but I couldn't. I felt so helpless.

"I felt the terror, pain, and chaos of the men on that ship that night. I saw the fire and actually felt it upon my face. After the young man died, I sat up in bed terrified because of the nightmare I had just had. I couldn't even talk about it for a while, and had a difficult time falling asleep afterward.

"The next day, Keith and I looked at the front page of the newspaper, and there were the photos showing the damaged *Cole* and the destruction I saw in my dreams. I thought I was going to pass out from shock. I am convinced I was somehow there with those men when they died. That one young man who sought comfort in my face . . . Did I help him find peace? I pray I did.

"I don't ever want to experience that again. It was one of the worse experiences I have ever had."

Imagine how helpful it would be if America could harness such premonitions to thwart terrorists, or use ESP to spy on hostile enemies. Believe it or not, we already have begun.

In 1995, the United States military finally revealed that it had secretly tested ESP in the laboratory, confirmed its existence, and had applied it to the Cold War battlefield. The United States government had quietly launched this particular ESP research program in 1972. Successful laboratory experiments quickly spawned a secret, classified program to employ psychics with ESP in the service of their country. This intelligence gathering part of the research program was not publicly confirmed until 1995, when the government admitted that for almost twenty years the CIA and many other government agencies had used specially trained clairvoyants—described as "remote viewers" by the program—in a variety of operational missions to penetrate secret Soviet military installations, hunt down Libyan leader Moammar Gadhafi, locate a downed Soviet Tupolev-22 bomber lost in the jungles of Zaire, look for an American general kidnapped by Italian terrorists, and other still-classified missions. The list of government agencies using the services of psychic spies included the

CIA, the Pentagon, the U.S. Army, the U.S. Air Force, and the National Security Council.

Twenty million dollars were spent on the remote-viewing ESP program eventually dubbed "Star Gate" before it was reportedly terminated in 1995. The Star Gate program's non-classified research experiments provide us with some of the best scientific evidence for the reality of ESP. An excellent scientific summary of Star Gate's early ESP experiments, written by the scientists who actually ran the program can be found in the spring 1996 issue of the *Journal of Scientific Exploration*, a publication of the national Society for Scientific Exploration. Joseph McMoneagle, introduced in Chapter 3, was one of the most respected and well-known remote viewers employed by this secret military program. A much-decorated retired army officer, Joe went on to become the founder and owner of the Intuitive Intelligence Applications company in Nellysford, Virginia. Joe has written several books describing his long and extensive experience as a remote viewer with the now declassified Star Gate program.

The remote-viewing research was funded at the height of the Cold War by the United States government, fearful that the Russians had developed and were using psychic weapons against us. Many of the actual spying activities conducted under this secret ESP program remain classified to this day, but some of the successful scientific experiments conducted at Stanford Research Institute (now SRI International), and at Science Applications International Corporation that spawned Star Gate have now been made public. The remote-viewing clairvoyant technique was based on earlier parapsychology research into ESP, but various researchers added new twists during the twenty-year period the program operated. One of its most unusual, and successful, approaches was to use geographical coordinates—latitude and longitude expressed in degrees, minutes, and seconds—to identify the target to be viewed clairvoyantly. The first research experiments achieved some remarkable successes, which soon caught the eye of the CIA.

Psychic Spies

In one now-unclassified, double-blind test in mid-1973, two remote viewers in California were asked to direct their clairvoyant vision to a specific latitude and longitude in West Virginia three thousand miles away and to describe what they saw there. The two remote viewers, a New York artist named Ingo Swann and a California former police commissioner named Pat Price, did more than simply draw a detailed map of the building and grounds seen at the CIA-selected target, which was the National Security Agency's secret electronic eavesdropping post at Sugar Grove, West Virginia. Price was able to enter the supersecure building with his mind and use his clairvoyant vision to read the names of facility personnel from desk placards, read the titles of documents on desks, and labels off folders inside locked cabinets at the site—a feat that understandably set alarm bells ringing at the government agency responsible for the security of the site. The information Price produced was later verified as substantially accurate.

In another early test, Price turned his remote-viewing to the other side of the globe for a target that later turned out to be a Communist radio listening post in the Ural Mountains of the Soviet Union. He located the target and, as often happened, described it in surprising detail.

"Elevation 6200 ft. Scrubby brush, tundra-type ground hummocks, rocky outcroppings, mountains with very steep slopes . . . Area site underground, reinforced concrete, doorways steel of the roll-up type. Unusually high ratio of women to men, at least at night. I see some helipads, concrete. Light rail tracks run from pads to another set of rails that parallel the doors into the mountain. Thirty miles north (5 degrees west of north) of the site is a radar installation with one large (165 foot) dish and two small, fast-track dishes."

His description of the Urals mountain site was substantially correct, as verified by other sources.

In July 1974, Price performed yet another amazing feat of remote viewing ESP. After being given a set of geographical coordinates, Price was told that the site was a Communist research and development facility.

Seeking Soviet Secrets

Price sent his mind to what turned out to be a very secret Soviet atomic bomb laboratory in Semipalatinsk in the Soviet Union. Once there, he described and drew a picture of an unusual multistory, industrial crane, among other things. His drawing almost exactly matched the crane seen in a classified satellite photo of the site taken by the U.S. military.

Impressed by Price's ability, the CIA let him continue his spy effort at Semipalatinsk. Price managed to view the inside of a closed building at the site, which U.S. satellite photography obviously couldn't penetrate. He described a large room in which people were assembling a giant metal sphere of some sort, which he drew. Price reported his impression that the people in the building were having trouble welding the object together. After the session, the CIA left Price without any feedback on how he had done, and returned to Washington.

Three years later, *Aviation Week* magazine essentially confirmed Price's mental observations inside the building. It carried a story on operations at Semipalatinsk, describing how Russian scientists there were trying to build a giant metal sphere that could be used for nuclear weapons testing. It also mentioned that American physicists doubted whether the Russians could create a strong enough weld to make it work.

Once again these laboratory experiments found that distance did not affect the results. A superstar remote viewer like Price could see a target ten thousand miles away as easily as he could view a target a mile away.

Like the young teacher in "The Stranger in the Photograph," remote viewers sometimes sense the past at a target site as well as the present. Price did just that in one unusual remote-viewing experiment. He accurately described a swimming pool complex in Palo Alto, but included two water tanks that were not there. Twenty years later, the scientist who conducted the experiment, Russell Targ, received a centennial annual report for Palo Alto. It included a picture of the swimming pool site Price had viewed remotely, but as it looked back in 1913. The photo included two water tanks, just as Price had drawn. The site had once hosted the municipal waterworks.

Information received by remote viewers, including Price, was not 100 percent accurate. Observations often had inaccurate details and information mixed in with the accurate. But occasionally remote viewers could achieve "blueprint accuracy" and reliability as high as 80 percent.

Remote viewers, once selected, seemed to improve with training—something that has not been demonstrated with any reliability other than in this military setting. Even so, remote-viewing is not a common, natural skill. Only one out of a hundred persons who volunteered to attempt remote-viewing proved consistently successful.

From the beginning of remote-viewing research, the abilities of Ingo Swann and Pat Price were special compared to most other remote viewers recruited during the life of the program. In 1977, CIA chief Admiral Stanfield Turner described a person believed to be Pat Price in a *Chicago Tribune* interview. Turner declared that the agency had found someone who could use his psychic powers to "see" what was going on anywhere in the world.

Joe McMoneagle was another extraordinarily gifted remote viewer, earning a National Legion of Merit Award for his ESP skills employed on more than two hundred missions, including the following declassified operation.

Find The Kidnapped General

U.S. Army Brig. Gen. James Dozier was kidnapped in Italy in 1981 by the Red Brigades terrorist organization, and the army turned to Joe for help in pinpointing his location.

Joe described the hideout as the second floor of a house in Padua, Italy, and drew a picture of the distinctive storefront of the shop below the house. He also drew a street map.

In the end, the Italian police did not use McMoneagle's information. They had learned Dozier's whereabouts from confessions made by other terrorists they had caught. When they finally stormed the house, it matched the location and description produced by Joe.

On November 28, 1995, the Central Intelligence Agency released an official report on the U.S. Department of Defense's remote-viewing program and its achievements. The report was entitled *The American Institutes for Research Review of the Department of Defense's Star Gate Program*. The report evaluated both the laboratory research experiments in remote-viewing as well as intelligence operations employing the remote-viewing techniques. Two university professors were recruited to help the American Institutes for Research in-house staff evaluate the project: Dr. Jessica Utts of the University of California, Davis, and Dr. Ray Hyman of the University of Oregon, the well-known skeptic of paranormal phenomena, who challenged Honorton's groundbreaking Ganzfeld ESP research.

The American Institutes for Research final report concluded that the laboratory experiments testing remote-viewing showed statistically significant results. As program reviewer Dr. Jessica Utts noted, their success was not due to chance, methodological flaws in the experiments, or fraud. From there on, she recommended, researchers should focus on how the phenomenon worked, not on proving whether it existed "since there is little more to be offered to anyone who does not accept the current collection of data." Her counterpart, Dr. Ray Hyman, focused his attention on the later experiments conducted at Science Applications International Corporation. He agreed that those experiments were well-designed and the results were not dismissable as statistical flukes. He didn't conclude that the experiments proved the reality of psychic functioning. He admitted that "the case for psychic functioning seems better than it ever has been," and that "I do not have a ready explanation for these observed effects."

In contrast to the laboratory experiments conducted on remote-viewing, most of the actual psychic spying operations remain classified to this day. In a speech in September 1995, President Jimmy Carter confirmed that the CIA successfully used a remote viewer to find a downed plane that had crashed in the jungle in Zaire that American spy satellites couldn't find.

Find The Downed Soviet Bomber

According to one account, the plane was a Soviet Tupolev-22 bomber that the Americans wanted to find before the Soviets did in order to examine the Russian plane's communications technology. The Pentagon turned to their remote viewers. Gary Langford "saw" a river running through the jungle, and the tail of the aircraft sticking out of the water, and described the roads and topography of the area in detail. A second remote viewer, a woman named Frances Bryan, subsequently produced a sketch that closely matched what Langford had described. Their work was so specific that the CIA was able to locate the site they had described on a terrain map. The CIA eventually found the plane within three miles of the spot Langford and Bryan described. A photo was taken of the site and later circulated around the offices of ESP researchers at the Stanford Research Institute office. "Langford's sketch agreed with the picture so completely that he might have copied it."

During the Iran–Iraq War of 1980–1988, remote viewers were employed by the U.S. military to help them find and target Chinese-made Silkworm missiles fired by Iran against Kuwait and at oil tankers passing through the Persian Gulf. During the first Gulf War, in 1991, the U.S. government reportedly used the Star Gate psychics to spy on Saddam's troop locations, weaponry, and the dictator's movements within Iraq. The Star Gate psychic spy program was officially terminated in 1995, but since September 2001, some former remote viewers report receiving calls from various government agencies, including the FBI, anxious to use every tool available to locate and stop future terrorist attacks. Rhine Research Center board member and former remote viewer Joe McMoneagle believes they are smart to do so.

"There's no doubt in my mind that remote-viewing could contribute in a major way. During the Cold War, it was used many times by many agencies to identify and thwart threats to America at home and abroad: everything from tracking kidnap victims to identifying arms and munitions storage depots. It proved its capacity for differentiating between friendly and hostile forces; previously unknown methods of ingress and egress; when and where to point other forms of intelligence collection methods; and in providing accurate descriptions of the emotional and military readiness of the enemy.

"It was almost exclusively used on cold targets, those with virtually no leads that, while critical, had been dormant for long periods of time without solution. The degree of difficulty in these kinds of targets is essentially the same as those we now find associated with terrorism."

The remote-viewing assignments given America's psychic spies are comparable to laboratory ESP experiments in which the test subject is asked to produce ESP on demand. Remote-viewing, like ESP in the lab, remains unpredictable, quirky and difficult to produce at will. Correct details are mixed in with incorrect ones. The fundamental rules under which it operates are still inadequately understood. But Joe believes we need to use every tool in our toolbox if we expect to defeat terrorists. "Some critics speak to the low percentage of accuracy as a reason not to use remote-viewing. In my opinion, any information that might open up a new lead should be utilized when American lives are at stake."

It would not surprise me to learn twenty years from now that the U.S. government did not really shut down its remote-viewing operations, and that it used psychic spies to search for the elusive Osama bin Laden.

11

MESSAGES FROM THE DEAD

Of all the barriers encountered by the human mind, none would seem more difficult to penetrate than death. Humans have long believed that another reality exists beyond this physical world, but this notion has remained in the realm of belief, not fact. The evidence for ESP may have some bearing on this important, age-old question. It strongly suggests that the human mind can transcend the boundaries of space and time. In addition, many spontaneous ESP experiences appear to be direct messages from the dead or dying. Receiving ESP messages from the dead would mean we have transcended the ultimate space–time barrier to communication and made contact with the "other side." It is a complex issue.

Whatever the answer, we do know people continually report visits by those they believe are dead or dying friends and relatives, manifested primarily in the form of visual and auditory hallucinations. The most common information delivered through these psychic experiences are messages of consolation and last good-byes, words of advice, or information needed to complete unfinished business or to right an old wrong.

We have already recounted several of these experiences. In "Daddy's Dead" (Chapter 5), the figure of a dying father appears at the foot of his young daughter's bed, bathed in a beautiful light, delivering a last good-bye to an absent daughter away at camp and unable to be there when he passed on. The silent, visual hallucination effectively delivered the message. As the experiencer explained, "I was a child that knew nothing of death. Yet I knew he was gone."

Final good-byes are among the most commonly reported messages delivered through such hallucinations, as the following story illustrates.

"Going On A Wee Trip"

When Mary was a thirteen-year-old girl living in Canada, she knew that her grandmother, a strict and proper Scotswoman, had had a stroke and was very ill. One night, as Mary and her sister prepared for bed, their mother told them that she and their father were going to drive over to Grandma's house to she how she was doing.

Later that night, while she was still awake in her room, Mary suddenly saw her grandmother standing in the doorway. She had on her suit and the mink she always wore. She had her handbag in one hand and her suitcase in the other. She looked at Mary, smiled, and said in her familiar Scots accent, "Don't worry, pet. I'm just going on a wee trip." Then she was gone.

Mary wasn't frightened, but she was puzzled. She thought Grandma was home sick in bed, so how could she be here, too? When her parents returned some time later, Mary ran to them excitedly. "Mommy, Grandma came to see me while you were away!" Her mother looked at her queerly. "You must have been dreaming. Grandma died tonight. She's gone, dear."

The following realistic visual hallucination of the dead is rare. It involves two people sharing the same hallucination.

Father In The Doorway

A woman and her fifteen-year-old daughter had recently moved to California from their previous home in Washington, D.C., where they had left the woman's father very ill. One day not long after moving, they entered the dining room, and to the woman's great surprise, there stood her father. "Why Dad, when did you get here?" she exclaimed.

At that point, her daughter turned around to look, and she, too, saw the figure of her grandfather, his hand upraised in a gesture of greeting or perhaps blessing, but he slowly faded away, and they both suddenly realized that he was not really in California in their house. Shortly afterward, they received the news that he had died.

In "A Mother's Last Message" (Chapter 7), a dying mother intrudes into the dream of a friend of her son, as if she were determined to pass on a message of consolation to her son through the friend: "Let him know I'm going to be okay."

A remarkable "I'll be okay" type of experience, involving two of his senses and the strange behavior of two pet dogs, was reported to me by retired aerospace engineer John Alexander, whom we met in Chapter 9. John is a hard-nosed scientist, who tends to approach his psychic experiences with a high degree of scientific curiosity, analyze them logically and systematically, and produce provocative hypotheses to help explain them. John sent us this account from detailed notes that he had made many years ago.

Saying Good-Bye

His "message from the dead" goes back to when he returned home from the service after World War II to live with his mother and grandmother, who were both were very ill. His parents had divorced a decade earlier, and his grandmother had kept his mother's illness from John while he was in the army so as not to worry him. It was this grandmother who figured prominently in the experience. It was the first ESP experience John ever had.

"I was the only person able to help them," he recalls of his mother and grandmother, "so I essentially undertook the full-time job of caring for them. I had been raised by them, loved them both very much, so I didn't view this as a burden." John's grandmother was by far the sickest of the two. She was fully bedridden, taking oxygen and painkillers. His mother, though ill, was still ambulatory and able to do most of the cooking. John's mother, a poet and artist who taught in the Santa Monica school system, was a very sensitive and emotional person. His grandmother, on the other hand, was much less emotional. She had been a journalist and talented pianist as well as a teacher, and John was very close to her. One major conflict between his mother and grandmother were two Chihuahua dogs that his mother loved dearly and his grandmother could not stand—and the dogs knew it. They figure in the story.

At the time of her death, his grandmother was in the living room, lying on a hospital bed under an oxygen tent, where she had been sleeping from the effect of a morphine shot he had administered to her. John usually slept in the same room to be available if she needed him.

"Because my grandmother usually slept for a couple of hours after the shot, my mother and I went way out in the back of the house and sat in a garden swing in a semienclosed patio. Due to the intervening structures and the distance to my grandmother, she could have screamed her head off and I would not have heard her—even if she had been in good health. We had the two dogs with us. As we sat there chatting, I heard my grandmother quietly call my name. It wasn't a shout. It was in her usual conversational tone. I looked around and saw nothing. My mother didn't respond so she must not have heard anything. But the dogs, who had been running around and playing as usual, suddenly ran to my mother's feet and stood there staring at the back of the house. Nothing was there. I turned to my mother and saw no response. While I was looking at my mother, I again heard my grandmother call my name.

"I turned to look toward the back of the house where the call seemed to emanate from. This time I saw my grandmother standing there in her favorite dress, which she had made herself and always wore for special occasions. I was startled and speechless for a moment. In that moment, she put her fingers to her lips as if to shush me. She seemed perfectly solid, and her body visually blocked a trellis of dark wood on the white wall of the house.

"At that point, the two dogs began whining and distracted my gaze to them. They were agitated, trembling, and clearly frightened. They initially started to move toward the image, then stopped, turned, and jumped onto my mother's lap, and proceeded to wet all over her. My mother was shocked by their behavior and later told me they had never done such a thing before. As she tried to sooth them, I turned back to the vision of my grandmother. Smiling at me and still holding her finger to her lips, she slowly faded away.

"All of this probably lasted less than a minute and was very disturbing to me. It was clear that my mother had not seen the image and that's probably a good thing. With her illness and nature, it probably would have devastated her, and my grandmother apparently knew that. Using some excuse, I rushed into the house and found that my grandmother had just died, as there was a faint 'death rattle' coming from her throat and her false teeth had fallen out."

Being of a logical, scientific bent, John explained that he would have probably attributed his vision to fatigue, as he had become tired from the continuous demands of caring for his grandmother, "but the fact that the dogs saw something, too, and reacted as they did convinced me that I had experienced something unique—that it did actually happen and was not a fantasy. According to my mother, the dogs never acted that way before or after." John never told his mother what had transpired that day.

This report has several features that give it credibility:

two senses were involved in the ESP experience: the dogs' unusual behavior suggested they were seeing something very frightening, and John was a critical, careful observer who kept detailed notes after the occurrence of this event.

John provides more interesting detail. "My grandmother was a very cool and solid person, not given to emotional responses. Her behavior in the apparitional form, brief though it was, was typical of her. As a journalist, her approach to things was very factual, and her favorite subjects were politics, history, and science." John went on to report an earlier incident involving her.

"She had been very ill and had had a hysterectomy as a young woman while married to my step-grandfather, a doctor. She had nearly died on the operating table. When I was much younger, she told me of an experience during that operation that we would today call an 'NDE,' a near-death experience. During the operation, she floated to the top of the operating room and looked down to see her husband—who had attended the operation—break into tears and collapse. She said she was attached to her body on the operating table by a 'silver cord' that she initially tried to break. When she saw how unhappy her husband was, she tried to move down and comfort him and the cord pulled her back into her body. She only mentioned it that one time, and we never speculated about it."

The message from John's dying grandmother seemed to be: "I don't want to scare your mother, but it's time. I'm going away. But as you can see by my smile and my pretty dress I'm not afraid or unhappy about it. Neither should you be."

In John Alexander's case, the psychic message was delivered by his grandmother at or near the very moment of her death. As we learned earlier, parapsychologists call these hallucinations "crisis apparitions" because they occur within twelve hours of death, either as the end approaches or shortly thereafter. The hallucinations in both "Daddy's Dead" and "A Mother's Last Message" also fall into this category. Statistically speaking, crisis apparitions make up the majority of hallucinations of the dead. Hallucinations of persons who have been deceased for longer than that—a day, a week, or several centuries—are called "postmortem apparitions." They are the classic "ghost" stories.

People who buy or rent existing homes sometimes experience hallucinations of the deceased previous owners or renters, as if they are annoyed at the newcomers' presence in a house. This visual hallucination is typical of many in our files.

Get Out Of My House

"I once lived in a three-room apartment on the ground floor. One night, all the doors were locked, so I was sure that nobody could come in, and I was all alone. It was evening, and I was just getting around to making my bed, when all of a sudden, I had the strange feeling that someone was in the room with me.

"Looking up, I saw a young man standing in my room, looking at me as if he wanted to say, 'This is my house. What are you doing in here?' He was dressed in a brown suit, a red necktie, and black shoes.

"Before I had a chance to come to my senses, he was gone. I was in the habit of visiting my landlady each evening, so I told her about my odd experience. No sooner did I finish than she turned almost green in her face. She told me that, not long before, the same well-dressed man once lived in my apartment and had taken great pride in fixing it up. He had died in my apartment, leaving a young wife and baby."

In "Son's Last Good-bye" (Chapter 10), the farmer had a combined visual and auditory crisis apparition, but the farmer's soldier son delivered more than a simple message of good-bye. He also sought forgiveness, apologizing for not having been a good child. It is best to make peace with loved ones before we die since taking regrets to the grave can be painful for both parties in a fight. In the following case, emotional bonds within a family may have played an important role in the apparition seen.

Forgive Me

"I was sitting in my home in the living room, reading a book I had just borrowed from a library. I glanced up at the door to my room and saw my mother's uncle, dressed in a dark suit. He didn't speak."

When the hallucination disappeared, the woman rushed to the kitchen where her mother and the rest of the family were. They feared something was wrong with the uncle.

"My mother had a severe grievance against that uncle and had sworn that she wouldn't forgive him until his dying day, but she had no knowledge he was ill. Nevertheless, she and my father went to see him. His wife and children said that he kept repeating my parents' names in the end. He was unconscious when she got there. Mom asked, 'Why didn't you send for me?' She could have forgiven him. We have always believed that was what he sought."

In the next experience, shared with me by Dr. Jim McClenon, the unfinished business involved a bitter child custody battle. A woman named Priscilla had requested, before her death, that her husband not be allowed to raise her children. Shortly after her death, Priscilla's spirit appeared to her sister-in-law in the form of a combined visual-auditory hallucination as the sister-in-law describes.

Protect My Children

"One night I was awakened by a very soft and light voice calling out my name. When I opened my eyes, Priscilla was at the foot of my bed. All I could see was her face and the long pink gown she was buried in. She was floating in the air. She had a very worried look on her face.

"She told me to go to the house where she had lived, look under her bed in a trunk, and get out the letters that were in the trunk. After she told me this, she disappeared. The next morning, I told my husband what had happened. We went to the house and looked in the trunk and, sure enough, the letters were there. Apparently Priscilla was the only one who knew about these letters. The letters contained evidence that helped us win the custody trial."

Priscilla's instructions were very detailed—go to the house, look under the bed, find a trunk, take out the papers, and look at them. Unlike the visual portion of the hallucination, the auditory element was complete, sustained, intelligent, and explicit.

The following apparition sought help for a daughter she left behind, who was being abused by her grandmother. The words spoken by this figure were as extensive and explicit as those delivered by Priscilla in the previous case. This apparition acted like it was fully alive, engaged, and relentless in its determination to right the wrong that had been done.

Save My Child

"My stepbrother told me about five years ago that he was going to work one morning at the auto garage he owned. Just as he was unlocking the door to the shop, he saw his deceased sister-in-law come across the street as natural as life, with the wind blowing her dress. He was frightened and entered the garage as quickly as possible, closing the door after him. He immediately crawled under a truck he was working on, shaking like a leaf. He said he couldn't utter a word.

"From under the truck, he heard his dead sister-in-law speak, as plainly as if she were there in the flesh. 'I want you to go to your mother's house and get Diane, my daughter. Your mother has beaten her unmercifully, and she is sick in bed. I want you to take her to your home and take care of her. She is in danger there.'

"My stepbrother said that his sister-in-law then walked out of the garage. He felt very weak and shaky but crawled out from under the truck, went home, and told his wife. He immediately went to his mother's house in the next town where he found the daughter in bed sick from the beating she had received. He bundled her up and took her home with him.

"He told me 'Sis, you know I wouldn't lie to you. What I have told you is the gospel truth. I saw her just as plain and as lifelike as I see you now.'"

In the following experience, the deceased person appeared in a symbolic form that was seen, heard, and even lightly felt by the daughter who knew that the message was "Mom has passed away."

Visit From An Angel

"My mother lived in California and I lived in Wichita, Kansas. At 9:40 A.M. on February 17, I was sitting in my bedroom at my dressing table, brushing my hair in front of the mirror. Suddenly the room was illuminated with the strangest light, one I can't fully describe. I then felt a rustle of wind across my shoulders, and a faint sound like the brushing of birds' wings. Then I looked in the mirror.

"My mother was standing behind my chair, the most beautiful angel you can imagine. She just stood and smiled at me for a full thirty seconds. I finally said, 'Mom!' and rushed for her, but she disappeared, light and all. I was so upset by this that I shook for an hour. When my husband came home for lunch, I told him about it and got myself ready for a phone call that mother was dead. I was sure she was, and so was my husband. Sure enough, about one P.M. that same day, the call came that my mother was gone. My husband told the men in his office and one of them nearly fainted because of my experience."

• • •

In contrast to this symbolic figure of the mother, the hallucination described below might be called ultrarealistic. Can a hallucination carry a physical object? If a hallucinated apparition is seen carrying a book from one room to another, and a moment later the same, physical book is found on a desk in that new room, how do we explain how it got there? This very uncommon visual hallucination of the dead, sent to my mother, happened in Boston.

The Book-Carrying Apparition

Mr. Anderson and Mr. Barnes worked for the same company, in adjoining offices. One evening, after Anderson had left for the day, Barnes took the elevator down to the main floor and started to exit the building when he was stricken with a heart attack and taken to the hospital where he died.

Later that evening, the night watchman came on duty, unaware that Barnes had died earlier that evening. Making his rounds near midnight, the security guard walked by the two adjacent offices and saw Barnes, dressed in his normal business clothes and carrying a book, walk out of his office and into Anderson's office. He called out a greeting to Barnes and was surprised that the man didn't respond with a hello, as he usually did to the guard when working late.

The guard knew that Barnes had some health problems, so he decided to follow him into Anderson's office and make sure everything was okay. When he entered the room, Barnes was not there, though the room had no other exits. Wondering whether his mind was playing tricks on him, he was alarmed to see on Mr. Anderson's desk what appeared to be the same book he had seen Barnes carry into the room a few seconds earlier.

The night guard called repeatedly for Barnes, and searched the entire building but couldn't find him. Troubled by the whole experience, he related his story to the day watchman, who relieved him the next morning, the first person he had seen since coming on duty the night before. The day watchman told him that Barnes had died around five P.M. the day before.

Auditory-only hallucinations that convey ESP information account for over half of all reported hallucinatory experiences. Sometimes they seem to come from living persons undergoing a crisis at a distant location, and other times they come in the voice of someone deceased. Sometimes it's a single word or two, perhaps the experiencer's name, or a warning like "Look out!" Other times, it is a phrase or complete sentence. Here is a good example taken from a letter in our files.

"Wait Until Friday"

"I feel so strongly about a recent ESP experience of my own that I am going to write and tell you about it. I am an only daughter and, when my father was alive, I could count on him whenever I was in need of help. After my father died last June, I felt really alone and somewhat afraid. My husband had been ill for two years, and though he is out of the hospital now, we are badly in debt. Our car payments were behind three months, and two weeks ago they came to repossess the car. While I was talking to the man at my front door, I heard my deceased father say, just as clear as my own voice, 'Tell him to wait until Friday.' Without hesitation I said to him, 'Wait until Friday, and I'll pay you.' He agreed and left. After he had gone, I wondered how I was ever going to raise $280.

"Thursday afternoon, my dad's lawyer called me and told me to come to his office and pick up a check for $417. The courts had collected from an old account owed my dead father, which I was to receive. When I hung up the phone, I looked up and said silently, 'Thanks again, Dad.'"

A young woman in Boston, Massachusetts, read about my mother's research in *McCall's* magazine and sent her a description of her unique ESP experience. It started with a premonition of her mother's death, followed several months later by a multisensory hallucination of her dead mother that even included the sense of smell.

The Smell Of Perfume

"I am a college student in Boston and will be nineteen very shortly. I, too, have had a strange experience that may fall into the ESP classification. In October, I went out on a date with my boyfriend and another couple. We wound up the evening at the other girl's home, watching TV.

"At midnight, the program was just beginning to get interesting when I had a sudden urge to be at home. My home was about five miles away. Although I heard no voices in my head or any such thing, I still had this urge to be at home. I finally persuaded my boyfriend to take me home and, when we arrived, a doctor was just entering my house. My mother, who hadn't been sick at all, had just had a heart attack. She died at two A.M. that morning. If I hadn't had that urge to go home, I probably wouldn't have been with her when she died."

But that's not the end of the story.

"About three months later, I awoke about five in the morning. My mother was sitting on the edge of my bed. She said she only had a minute. She told me that everything in my life would be fine and that I would marry, have children, and live to be very old. She then disappeared. I thought I had dreamed this, but to make sure, I got out of bed and turned on the light. There was an indentation where she had sat on the bed, and it felt very warm. I could also smell a faint odor of perfume. I had no perfume on at the time."

Mike, the oil industry executive we met in Chapter 3, believes he was twice contacted during his dreams by the deceased. On one occasion, he experienced a spirited conversation.

Dead Man Talking

"My best friend died on February 21, 1977. The night before his funeral, just after I had gone to sleep, he visited me. We had a detailed conversation about how he was doing.

"Ten years later, on April 20, 1987, my brother committed suicide. I saw him in a dream. He did not speak with me, but he was walking with my grandfather who had already passed over. My brother was being comforted."

Mike is absolutely convinced both dreams were more than just ordinary dreams. "I'm a prolific dreamer of regular, old dreams, but there is never any doubt about which dreams are 'the real McCoy,'" he wrote. Actually he wrote "never" seven times, but I got the point. "Like I said, I always know the difference—the psychic dreams always wake me up. Also, they have a sense of the 'real' about them. It's as if I see the event as it happens, and I'm in it, living it."

Mike's mother was an artist and psychic in her own right. "Forty years ago, my mother was living in Lubbock, Texas. She had a dream in which she saw my father on fire. He was on a business trip in Louisiana at the time. Mom called his office, and they told her he had gone to the hotel to take a nap. She directed them to run to his hotel room and check on him.

"When they got there, his room was on fire from a cigarette. He was passed out from smoke inhalation, but they were able to pull him to safety and get the fire out. So I guess I get my ESP from my mother."

What he finds odd is the fact that "I always thought my psychic mother would visit me after she died, but she never has."

Why did Mike receive a visit from his brother and his friend but not his mother? This is just one of the many puzzles that parapsychologists have been pondering for some time. ESP just does not seem to always operate by rules of human logic.

The moment just before a loved one dies is obviously very emotional for the dying person and family members in the room praying and crying. In minutes or seconds, someone loved deeply will be gone forever. This situation may be one that heightens the extrasensory perception abilities of all involved, as could be the case in the following hallucination.

Coming To Take Her
Daughter Home

"My aunt, who helped raise me, was dying of a cerebral hemorrhage. We had all been up for five days and nights with her. The candles were flickering, and she was in a coma. I went to get a cup of tea and my husband remained in the room with her, saying the rosary at her bedside.

"All of a sudden, he ran down the stairs past us, appearing pale and visibly shaken. When we could finally get him to talk, he said that while he was praying, my aunt seemed to come out of the coma and started flailing her arms around in the air, holding them wide open as if she were trying to reach someone, and crying 'Mom! Oh, Mom.'

"My husband felt a breeze, and suddenly a little woman stood next to him, less than five feet tall with a plaid shawl over her head, wringing her hands, and my husband saw tears running down her face. Although he heard nothing from the woman, he did hear the rustle of her dress. She was in black. He said that he prayed hard that he could muster the strength to get out of the room. When able, he rushed out and down the stairs.

"He described the experience to relatives at our house, and another aunt said, 'Well, that was her mother. She has been dead since 1910.' When we went back upstairs, Mom was dead with a peaceful smile on her face."

Hallucinations reported by the dying were a subject of a special study by the late Dr. Karlis Osis. Early in his career, Dr. Osis worked with my father at the Duke Parapsychology Laboratory, the forerunner of the present Rhine Research Center. Just out of college, one of my first jobs was to assist

Dr. Osis in his work on human–animal telepathy, with cats as our test subjects. Dr. Osis went on to work with the American Society for Psychical Research in New York City, and later coauthored *At the Hour of Death,* the classic book describing deathbed visions. He reported that the most frequent message from these hallucinated apparitions is that they have come to help the ESP experiencer make the transition to another world.

Coming To Take His Wife Home

An intelligent, seventy-six-year-old woman had suffered a heart attack. The nurse confirmed to Dr. Osis that the patient at the time of her vision was not under sedation, had no history of hallucinations, and her mind was very clear and sharp. She was also convinced she would make a full recovery and return home to a daughter who needed her.

Suddenly she called her nurse and asked her if she saw what she (the patient) saw—her dead husband Charlie, standing with open arms waiting for her. She continued on, describing the beautiful place she saw, with its flowers and music, and Charlie patiently waiting for her. She died shortly afterward. The nurse concluded the woman had seen her husband.

Dr. Osis and his coauthor Dr. Erlendur Haraldsson analyzed more than 37,000 responses to scientific questionnaires they sent out over a period of two decades to doctors, nurses, and other health personnel who regularly work with dying people. They concluded that the evidence gathered from deathbed observations favors the postmortem survival hypothesis, namely that there is life after death. As Dr. Osis declared, "It doesn't clinch it, but it gives it support."

Can we conclude from all these experiences that there is life after death? Many parapsychologists, including my mother in her day, felt that this conclusion was premature.

She came to this position partly because she received many

reports in which visual or auditory hallucinations of living persons were experienced by people. The persons who were seen in the hallucinations were usually undergoing some crisis at the time of the incident. We reported such a case earlier ("Shot in the Shoulder") in which the young girl "sees" her soldier father wounded in Vietnam. This led my mother to wonder: If our minds seem to be able to create an apparition of a living person, could they not also do that for a deceased person? In some cases that could be checked, the living person in crisis was found not to be even thinking about the person experiencing the ESP at the time, which seems to reduce the likelihood of telepathic connection, and to put more responsibility for the experience on the ESP experiencer himself.

Here is one such report of an apparition of the living that seems to have been extremely helpful in a time of need of the ESP experiencer.

A Friendly Face

A college girl, whom I will call Gayle, was at school when she was called home quite unexpectedly by the tragic death of her younger brother. She was able to catch a train that should have brought her home by midnight, but the train was delayed, and the connecting train had already left when they arrived at the transfer town. Knowing no one in the town, Gayle did not know what to do.

A close friend of her brother emerged out of the crowd. He said to her, "There is no other train tonight, but there's a good hotel across the street. I'll take you over there and tell them to wake you in time for the five o'clock in the morning."

As Gayle reported to us, "He did just that. That night, I sat in that hotel room full of grief and loneliness but grateful that this friend had happened to be there.

"The next afternoon, the friend came to our house and I said, 'In all my life, I was never so grateful to see anyone as I was to see you last night.'

"He replied in surprise, 'But I didn't see you—I was planning to go to meet you, since I knew you'd be coming in on that train and I knew you couldn't make connections, but I never got there. My train was late, too.'"

Gayle concluded, "I knew this young man well. I have not the slightest doubt that it was he who helped me. What I don't know is how?"

If she had reported glimpsing him off in the distance, it could have been explained as a case of mistaken identity or poor eyesight, someone who looked like him but was not. But she carried on a back-and-forth conversation with him, and he apparently spent more than a few seconds, perhaps a minute or more, in her sight as he accompanied her to the hotel across the street. Yet, he claimed he was never there.

In my mother's effort to try to understand the source of the apparitions of the deceased, whether from the mind of the ESP experiencer herself or from that of the deceased, she analyzed the motivation of the people who reported such apparitions. In the majority of the 258 cases that she analyzed, the experiencer had a clear desire and motivation to communicate with the deceased. In those cases, at least, it would be reasonable to suppose that the mind of the living person created the illusion of the deceased out of grief or emotional need. This is an alternative explanation that must be considered as well as actual communication from the dead.

Sometimes those who see apparitions still do not believe them. John Alexander, the aerospace scientist we met in Chapter 9, sent me two visual hallucination cases involving his wife. John's wife, skeptical of life after death, had to have a hysterectomy when quite young. Her postoperative condition was so poor she was not expected to survive.

"While in bed, she saw her father beside her bed, although he appeared to her only from the chest up. He looked at her with great love and sympathy and slowly faded away," explains John.

The second ESP experience she had occurred when she was older. "After her favorite brother died, she grieved for a while and then gradually adjusted to the loss. Some time later, she woke up one morning and saw a figure standing by her bed. At first she did not recognize who it was, but soon realized it was the figure of her brother as a glowingly healthy young man."

To John's surprise, her skepticism was not shaken by either experience. "She is the most interesting and erudite person I have ever known," says John. "Her library consists of over three thousand books, ranging from philosophy and archeology to history, music, and religion. She has a highly critical, logical mind. To top it all off, she is also an atheist. She sees her visions solely as an artifact of her grief from some subconscious level in her mind, and perhaps she is right. To me, however, her experiences are significant, something more than that."

The wish fulfillment hypothesis might help explain some, though certainly not all, of the apparitional cases—particularly those reports in which the apparition is a bother or a burden. In "Get Out of My House," why would the ESP experiencer want to see the angry apparition of the apartment's former tenant? Likewise, in "The Bleeding Lady on the Bike" (Chapter 5), the child had no obvious motivation or desire to have a hallucination of a deceased accident victim who was a stranger to him and his family. Nor was there any motivation for the watchman to hallucinate the dead office worker in "The Book-Carrying Apparition."

One of the most provocative reports of accurate psychic communication between the living and the deceased happened in 1925 in North Carolina.

Last Will And Testament

When farmer James L. Chaffin died from a fall on September 7, 1921, his wife and four sons knew that the farm would go to Chaffin's third son, Marshall. In a signed and witnessed document the whole family knew about, James Chaffin had given Marshall the farm in his will of November 16, 1905. Consequently, no one contested the will.

What no one living apparently knew was that in January 1919, two years before he died, James Chaffin had actually changed his mind and written a new will, giving all four sons a share in the property. He didn't file this amended will in the court, or even inform his wife about it. He simply hid it in the pages of an old family Bible.

For four years, Marshall enjoyed the farm his father had apparently willed to him alone. In June 1925, one of Marshall's brothers, named J.P., began to have very vivid dreams in which his father James appeared at his bedside, wearing his old black overcoat. In the dream, the son heard his father say, "You will find my will in my overcoat pocket."

The son awoke convinced that his father had come back from the dead to explain some mistake dealing with his last will. He discovered that his mother had given his father's coat to his brother John who lived twenty miles away. When he went there and examined the coat, he found sewn in the lining a piece of paper in his father's handwriting that said "Read the twenty-seventh chapter of Genesis in my daddy's old Bible."

Convinced more than ever that something important was about to be revealed, J.P. asked a neighbor to be a witness when they actually opened the Bible. After searching the house, they finally found the Bible and the updated will. The second will was then submitted to the court, and the State of North Carolina ruled it to be valid.

In this case, an apparition appears to have communicated successfully with a living person to inform him of the existence of a document unknown to anyone at that time but the deceased. The Society for Psychical Research in England carefully investigated the Chaffin case, sending a lawyer to North Carolina to review the written court documents and sworn testimony of witnesses, to interview family members and to inspect the second will. Had someone faked the handwriting of James Chaffin? Ten witnesses in the court record recognized the handwriting as Mr. Chaffin's. Did J.P. know about the will all along? Then why did he wait four years to claim his inheritance, instead of submitting it when his father died? And why would he have let the valuable overcoat be sent away, perhaps to be lost or discarded before he could recover it? The investigator for the Society for Psychical Research concluded: "It is hard to suggest a satisfactory explanation of the facts on normal lines."

Such cases do not constitute scientific proof of spirit survival by themselves, but they help keep us open-minded to the possibility that another reality may exist and, if it does, that our minds can reach even there. Meanwhile, we need much more research into such carefully observed and provocative cases.

12

MAKING SENSE OF YOUR ESP

My father raised me to strike a balance between open-mindedness and critical judgment in evaluating various claims of the paranormal. This approach helped him and his colleagues delineate the basic facts about ESP, which essentially confirm what people of all ages, races, cultures, countries, and religions have reported throughout history—human beings can sometimes see the future, read other peoples' minds, or psychically observe events unfold, as they happen, even when they take place hundreds, or even thousands, of miles away. Extrasensory perception is quirky, unpredictable, and only partially understood, but it is real.

Sixty-five million Americans have personally experienced ESP. If you are one of them, let me share with you some final thoughts to help you put your psychic experience in perspective.

Millions of Americans are still reluctant to admit their unusual psychic experiences publicly. Over and over again, people tell me, "You know, I've never told this to anyone before, but . . ." or "Please don't tell anyone, but . . ."

If you think you have had an ESP experience, there is no

reason to be apologetic about it. If you have read this book, you now know that enough good evidence exists to allow any sane, intelligent person to conclude—without apology or fear of embarrassment—that ESP exists.

That said, you might wonder if you can fool yourself into believing you have experienced ESP when you have not. Writing your experiences down in a journal can help you to determine the validity of your experience. Keeping a record allows you to see how many of your dreams, premonitions, and intuitions were accurate, and how many were just plain wrong. Try it. A diary can help you distinguish true ESP from mere wishful thinking or a faulty memory.

I try to steer folks away from an obvious obsession with ESP ability when it does not appear to be healthy, or of any help in their daily life. This appears to be the case for an elderly man living in a Southern state who sent me the following letter, written in all capital letters and addressed to "Dr. Feathers." Some of his unusual experiences do, in fact, sound like the kind of spontaneous ESP experiences we study at the Rhine Research Center, but then he goes on to claim too much, fails to give enough detail, and does not mention any verification.

My name is Lanny [not his real name], and I have experiences that boggle my mind. I shall list them below, only three I can verify.

No. 1. Son of Sam, N.Y. I called a city detective at the time, he then gave me a number to call, which I did. Reporting I was watching TV about the murders in New York and that I saw a picture in my mind of a building where he worked that had the look of a post office or library with large pillars. I was put off with a cold thank you.

No. 2. My sister in 1978 was supposed to fly to Florida for a court case. As I'm talking to her, a picture came to my mind of a plane crash. I told her not to take her

flight, I then told her why. The flight she was supposed
to go on crashed in Georgia.

No. 3. When the woman drowned her children in her
car in a lake, the police couldn't locate the car. I called
the police and told them to look in a lake within five or
six miles. Verifiable.

No. 4. When Frank Sinatra's mother's plane crashed,
police couldn't find it, I called them and told them the
location within one mile, again with that skepticism,
thank you for calling . . .

Lanny's list goes on for another page or two of such
claims, including predicting the crash of a Delta Flight 800,
apparently confusing it with the famous crash of TWA Flight
800 off Long Island in July 1996. He offers questionable
claims for being a medical intuitive, reports odd visions involving gasoline trucks and sewers, and claims the FBI is
bugging his phone. Lanny concludes his letter: "I've forgotten other happenings, maybe for the better. Please do not use
my name. I am seventy-five-years old and need no problems
from any jackass agency of the govt. Thanks for listening. I
am alone and had to tell someone."

Lanny clearly has no one to share his experiences with,
no one to offer an alternative explanation for his experiences, no one to provide a necessary reality check.

One of the most important reality checks we can all apply
to ESP experiencers or to so-called psychics is their ability
to recognize and admit that they can sometime be wrong in
their psychic predictions. Marie, the woman who had the accurate precognitive hallucination involving the 9/11 attack
on the Pentagon, certainly passes that test. She readily admits that not all her many premonitions have been accurate.
In fact, she has been spectacularly wrong at times, something we expect based on our parapsychology research.

Once, she got a feeling that her mom's good friend in
New Jersey was going to die. Her mother was living in

Florida at the time. Marie was afraid the lady's relatives would not be able to reach her mother because they did not have her mother's phone number in Florida. So Marie called her mother and told her to call New Jersey, because Marie thought her friend had passed away. "I told my mom the feeling I had gotten wasn't that strong. It was kind of choppy. But I sensed she had died. My mom didn't want to call, because she did not want to deal with her friend's death. She eventually called, and it turned out her friend had not died at all but was still alive—much to my embarrassment."

Marie came away from these false ESP experiences with a valuable insight. "I realize I can't tell if a dream is psychic or not. The best I can say is this: If they're accompanied by very strong emotions, if they wake me up in a dead sweat, and I'm having heart palpitations, these tend to be true, at least for me. But even then you can't say it's going to be true until it actually happens—only then is it true."

If you have the strong suspicion that you have ESP ability, you may want to test yourself at home. If so, do this on several occasions and under different conditions to get a better estimate of your ability. The Rhine Research Center rarely serves as a place for evaluating individuals in this way. Unfortunately, we do not have the resources and we also have found it is difficult to get a good estimate of someone's ability from just one test performance. Since ESP is quirky, people who show up to "perform" often do not do well when put on the spot. Our regular research participants are local individuals who are tested as part of a larger group, or in some cases are involved in testing over a series of several sessions.

The Rhine Research Center does offer, through our Web site, the opportunity to obtain ESP test cards, record sheets, instructional manuals, and other testing materials that will allow you to test yourself. If you are curious and want to learn more about ESP, you will find a list of helpful books, journals, papers, and Web sites in the Appendix that follows and on our Web site.

If your ESP experiences have frightened you, or led you

to worry about "going crazy," please understand that experiencing ESP by itself is not a sign of mental illness. Again, extrasensory perception is a natural human ability—we probably cannot repeat that phrase too often. How you handle the experience can sometimes cause considerable anxiety, particularly if you are already experiencing personal or marital troubles, a spiritual crisis, or have neurotic tendencies. But the simple reception of verifiable, accurate information about people and events without the help of the traditional sensory system should not make you—or anyone else—question your sanity.

That said, a few people who call or write clearly seem mentally troubled. There is a different quality to their "psychic" visions and voices that is not difficult to detect. If I suspect a person is emotionally disturbed, I simply tell him that what he describes does not sound like the type of experiences we study in parapsychology. I explain as gently as I can that it sounds as if he is dealing with something else, something that really may need attention. If a disturbed person is at all open to the possibility, I will suggest he talk to his local doctor, minister, or counselor about a possible medical or chemical imbalance, or perhaps even see a psychiatrist.

Fortunately, such letters and e-mails are fairly rare. Much more common are the fears that seem to accompany normal paranormal experiences in our Western culture. Several years ago, two staff members here at the Rhine Research Center, Dr. H. Kanthamani and Dr. Jim Kennedy, conducted a study of the effect of paranormal experiences on people's lives. Though most people reported the experiences produced positive changes in their life, almost 45 percent admitted the experience scared them at first. The fear tended to be temporary.

In many cases, this fear stems from the mistaken belief that ESP is supernatural. Nothing could be further from the truth. Vision, hearing, taste, touch, and smell are natural human senses. ESP is simply a natural sixth sense. If you have an ESP experience, do not view yourself as someone chosen by God to bring a message to the world. Conversely, do not view ESP as the work of the devil. If you have had an ESP experience, you are neither blessed nor cursed. You are simply human.

In the end, my goal in sharing these stories with you is to help you accept, understand, and embrace any ESP experiences that you or someone you love may have, to view them as a gift, and to integrate them into your life in a psychologically positive way.

When we humans can do this, then the work of my father and mother will truly be done.

APPENDIXES

INVITATION TO READERS

Spontaneous ESP experiences are extremely important to the study of parapsychology. If you have had an ESP experience you want to share with me, I would love to hear from you. Please send me a written account via e-mail or postal mail at the address below. Your experience will be added to our collection. I will try to send a reply. However, for practical purposes a reply is not always possible. But please accept my thanks for sharing your story!

Dr. Sally Rhine Feather
Rhine Research Center
2741 Campus Walk Avenue
Building 500
Durham, NC 27705
E-mail: sally@rhine.org

SUGGESTED READING

GENERAL INFORMATION

Broughton, Richard S. *Parapsychology: The Controversial Science.* New York: Ballantine Books, 1992.

McMoneagle, Joseph. *The Stargate Chronicles: Memoirs of a Psychic Spy.* Charlottesville, VA: Hampton Roads, 2002.

Radin, Dean. *The Conscious Universe: The Scientific Truth of Psychic Phenomena.* San Francisco: HarperEdge, 1997.

Schmicker, Michael. *Best Evidence: An Investigative Reporter's Three-Year Quest to Uncover the Best Scientific Evidence for ESP, Psychokinesis, Mental Healing, Ghosts and Poltergeists, Dowsing, Mediums, Near Death Experiences, Reincarnation and Other Impossible Phenomena That Refuse to Disappear,* 2nd edition. San Jose: Writers Club Press (iUniverse), 2002. (www.booksbymichael.com)

Sheldrake, Rupert. *The Sense of Being Stared At: And Other Unexplained Powers of the Human Mind.* New York: Three Rivers Press, 2004.

IMPORTANT RESEARCH ARTICLES IN PARAPSYCHOLOGY

Bem, Daryl and Charles Honorton. "Does Psi Exist?: Replicable Evidence for an Anomalous Process of Information Transfer," *Psychological Bulletin,* 115, 1994, pp. 4–18.

Honorton, Charles and Diane Ferrari. "Future Telling: A Meta-Analysis of Forced Choice Precognition Experiments, 1935-1987," *Journal of Parapsychology,* 35, 1989, pp. 281–308.

Hyman, Ray and Charles Honorton. "A Joint Communiqué: The Psi Ganzfeld Controversy," *Journal of Parapsychology,* 50, 1986, pp. 351–364.

Rhine, J.B. and J.G. Pratt. "A Review of the Pearce-Pratt Distance Series of ESP Tests," *Journal of Parapsychology,* 18, 1954, pp. 165–177.

Rhine, Louisa E. "Factors Influencing the Range of Information in ESP Experiences," *Journal of Parapsychology,* 28, 1964, pp. 176–213.

Schouten, Sybo. "A Different Approach for Analyzing Spontaneous Cases: With Particular Reference to the Study of Louisa E. Rhine's Case Collection," *Journal of Parapsychology,* 47, 1983, pp. 323–339.

Weiner, Debra and JoMarie Haight. "Charting Hidden Channels: A Review and Analysis of Louisa E. Rhine's Case Collection Project," *Journal of Parapsychology,* 47, 1983, pp. 303–321.

ESP "CLASSICS"

Pratt, J.G., J.B. Rhine, Charles R. Stuart and Joseph E. Greenwood. *Extra-Sensory Perception After Sixty Years.* Boston: Brandon, 1966.

Rhine, J.B. *Extra-Sensory Perception.* Boston: Brandon, 1973.

Rhine, J.B. *New World of the Mind.* New York: William Sloane, 1953.

Rhine, J.B. and J.G. Pratt. *Parapsychology: Frontier Science of the Mind.* Springfield, IL: Charles C. Thomas, 1974.

Rhine, Louisa E. *ESP in Life and Lab.* New York: Macmillan, 1969.

Rhine, Louisa E. *Hidden Channels of the Mind.* Alexandria, VA: Time-Life Books, 1961.

Rhine, Louisa E. *The Invisible Picture: A Study of Psychic Experiences.* Jefferson, N.C.: McFarland and Co., 1981.

Rhine, Louisa E. *PSI: What Is It?* New York: Harper & Row, 1975.

PROFESSIONAL JOURNALS

Journal of Parapsychology

Journal of Scientific Exploration

Journal of the American Society for Psychical Research

Journal of the Society for Psychical Research

European Journal of Parapsychology

International Journal of Parapsychology

Journal of Consciousness Studies

USEFUL INTERNET SITES

Rhine Research Center—http://www.rhine.org

American Society for Psychical Research—http://www.aspr.com

Cognitive Sciences Laboratory—http://www.lfr.org

Parapsychological Association—http://www.parapsych.org

Parapsychology Foundation—http://www.parapsychology.org

Princeton Engineering Anomalies Research (PEAR)—http://www.princeton.edu/~pear

Society for Scientific Exploration—http://www.scientificexploration.org

The Archives of Scientists' Transcendent Experiences (TASTE)—http://www.issc-taste.org